BOOKS
ARE FRIENDS FOREVER

NO STONE UNTURNED

Related Titles from Potomac Books

Minefields of the Heart: A Mother's Stories of a Son at War
—Sue Diaz

Veterans on Trial: The Coming Court Battles over PTSD
—Barry R. Schaller

NO STONE UNTURNED

A *Father's Memoir of* His *Son's Encounter with* *Traumatic* Brain *Injury*

JOEL GOLDSTEIN

***Foreword by* LEE WOODRUFF**

Potomac Books
Washington, D.C.

Library of Congress Cataloging-in-Publication Data
Goldstein, Joel, 1949–
No stone unturned : a father's memoir of his son's encounter with traumatic brain injury / Joel Goldstein ; foreword by Lee Woodruff. — 1st ed.
p. cm.
Includes bibliographical references.
ISBN 978-1-61234-464-5 (hardcover edition) — ISBN 978-1-61234-465-2 (electronic edition)
1. Goldstein, Bart—Mental health. 2. Brain-damaged children—Rehabilitation—Biography. 3. Brain damage—Patients—Rehabilitation—Biography. 4. Brain damage—Patients—Biography. I. Title.
RC387.5.G644 2012
617.4'8104430092—dc23
[B]
2012000621

Printed in the United States of America on acid-free paper that meets the American National Standards Institute Z39-48 Standard.

Potomac Books
22841 Quicksilver Drive
Dulles, Virginia 20166

First Edition

10 9 8 7 6 5 4 3 2 1

In the struggle with traumatic brain injury there are no victors, only survivors.
This book is dedicated to the survivors and their loved ones.

Also with love and gratitude to Dr. David Harter,
Dr. Guiseppina Feingold, Duffy Violante LMT,
Coach William Defino, and John and Marlene Kennedy

If you are going through hell, keep going.

—Winston Churchill

Contents

Acknowledgments

Without everyday heroes, there would be no book, no comeback to celebrate. Jeff Salt, first on hand, and the rest of the New Paltz Rescue Squad rapidly stabilized Bart, calling for a helicopter to Westchester Med, where Dr. David Harter and his neurosurgery team operated without parental consent, do-or-die. Nurses in the PICU and NICU and chaplains Rosemary Parandelis and Anne Gentile kept Bart alive after all-night surgery. Later at Helen Hayes Hospital, the fourth-floor crew—nurses, aides, and therapists—worked doggedly, lovingly, to bring him through the early stages of coma emergence, teaching him to talk and take those first trembling steps.

Other health professionals deserve special mention: Dr. Scott Groudine, Dr. Michael Compain, Dr. Scott Marsel, Dr. Nicholas Mezitis, Gail and Ricky Kriesberg, Leslie Callis, Mary Ellen Zacharov and Joanie Arbusto, Josephine Todaro, Melinda Pearson, Tim Hickman, Ralph LaCasio, Dr. Ingrid Duerme, and Dr. Louis Calabro.

The love of close friends Marlene and John Kennedy, for all purposes Bart's aunt and uncle, made retuning home more bearable. The good counsel of Jan and Dan Stivers helped ease Bart back into school. Our Mujigae family's prayers and acts of love were godsends. Special thanks to Ashlee Danford, Kaili Stanley, Dr. James Chang and Jane Chang, Paula Nowak, David Quinn, Tamis Groft, and Heather Murphy. Parsons Child & Family Center director and long-time Mujigae booster, Raymond Schimmer, was ever a staunch friend.

My employers at Cambridge Corporate Services, John Dockery and David Blaum, were supportive, patient, and helpful. With bosses like them, the world would suffer far less "quiet desperation." Others did their part—Lou and Lisa Badalato, Arlene Siev, Cheryl Storm, Elias and Elise Zappas, the Koutopoulos family, Joe Vacarro, Marianne Drussano, Jane Derenowski of NBC, Elias Neofytides, my sisters Judi Marsel, Cathy Buckwalter, Candace Groudine, and Gloria Shepherd and brothers Mel Marsel and David Goldstein. Special thanks to Fr. Rick Curry, SJ, for prayers, inspiration, and practical help.

New Paltz High School was the stage upon which much of Bart's struggle played out. Heartfelt gratitude to Coaches Defino, Tegeler, Ciliberto, Matter, Phelps, Acosta, and Veder, as well as Mary Kay Fiore, Allan Podell, and the fine special ed staff, JR Ridgeway, Dave Moore, Pam the bus driver, Patti Matter, Maureen Zadrowski, Nurse Krivda, Serena Wunderlich, and the administration and staff.

Warm thanks to the staff of Maria College, Albany, folks with the courage of their convictions, especially Deb Corrigan, Sister Jean Roche, and Prof. Sandy Jung. Phoenix Hammond, Danielle Uccellini-Roadcap and the crew of University Heights, Rob Korotitsch, Mike Cognetti, Brian Roman and the staff of Living Resources, and Len Travaglione, Joan Gold and Sue Cavallaro of NPRS all took Bart under their wing. Countless others, most forever unknown, who've prayed for Bart's recovery—thank you all.

Without the invaluable contribution of Hilary Claggett, a senior editor at Potomac Books, there would be no book. Dr. Joel Fisher and Bill Kelly both made notable photographic contributions. Finally, a boundless debt of gratitude is owed "the Old Breed," my parents Eva and Morris Goldstein, and Aunt Ethel and Uncle Norman Cohen, whose examples taught me most of what I know about being a parent, and a mensch. Forever first and last in my heart, partner-in-life Dayle, daughter Cassidy, and of course the hero of our family saga, Barty boy—"Love ya, Fam."

Foreword

Lee Woodruff, author (with Bob Woodruff)
of *In an Instant: A Family's Journey of Love and Healing* (2007)
and *Perfectly Imperfect: A Life in Progress* (2009)

On January 29, 2006, my family joined a club no one wants to be a member of: the families who understand and live with traumatic brain injury (TBI). Most brain injuries, as you will read in the pages of this book, happen in seconds, the result of a car accident, stroke, aneurism, fall, violent assault, or sports injury. In my family's case, like in so many cases of the nation's military forces who have served in Iraq and Afghanistan, it was a bomb on a dusty road south of Baghdad.

Our story begins, just like the Goldsteins' story does, with an unexpected event. My husband, Bob Woodruff, an anchor of ABC News, was embedded with the military near Baghdad during the Iraq War in 2006. While traveling in a tank with his cameraman, on assignment, standing with his head and chest exposed, he was hit by a remote-controlled 155mm shell that exploded at close range. The force of the blast blew off Bob's helmet and crushed his left temporal lobe. Hundreds of rocks, packed around the improvised explosive device (IED), penetrated deeply into the side of his face, chin, and neck.

Army medics flew Bob and his cameraman, Doug Vogt, by helicopter to Baghdad and then to Balad, where within the hour, sixteen centimeters of his skull was removed as his brain continued to swell. The rapid response and close attention paid by everyone in Bob's chain of care was certainly one reason for his miraculous recovery and positive outcome. In a severe injury such as his, the earlier the skull can be partially removed, the more brain tissue can be saved, and that golden hour of medicine is critical in so many medical emergencies.

In an instant, my world and life became focused solely on Bob's survival as he lay in a coma for thirty-six days, battling back from the injury and then succumbing to sepsis and pneumonia following numerous surgeries. Like so many before me, I became a full-time caregiver by the bedside, balancing my children's needs against those of my husband and praying, hoping, believing that he would recover, despite the grim prognosis.

Miracles and hope are not things readily found or dispensed in an ICU, especially in a military hospital where the war's most critical head injuries are on display among men who were barely into their twenties. Like the Goldsteins, I would work hard in the hospital halls to keep a flicker of hope alive and to tell myself that love, friends, faith, and the power of sheer human resilience counted as much, or more, than help dispensed in the form of cc's. I would align myself with the nurses and therapists and doctors who, in the absence of percentages and empirical knowledge, could tell me their stories about the patients who had recovered in amazing and unexpected ways. During this time, I became determined to acquire as much information as I could about brain injuries, as painful as it all was to absorb at times.

Once Bob did wake up, in a sudden and unexpected way, the hard work began. After the acute stage of a brain injury, the long, repetitive, and time-consuming journey of rehabilitation begins. Time, energy, commitment, and dedicated professionals supplied the framework to help Bob heal, and the therapists, doctors, and nurses in rehab were some of the finest, most patient, and motivating people I have ever met. The love and encouragement of family and friends was invaluable and it challenged and spurred Bob every day to "get his brain back."

A brain injury is a life-altering experience. For some, the changes are subtle, hidden. For others, the differences can be more dramatic, causing profound changes in personality, thought patterns, and movement that are permanent. And for every one of the brain-injured, there are hopefully dedicated and loving caregivers—be they spouses, parents, siblings, children, or friends—who are advocating, praying, hoping, and believing that there will be a good outcome, despite anyone's ability to really know.

Before Bob was injured, I had never thought much about head injuries at all. I didn't know anyone well who had suffered a TBI, and to be honest I wasn't overly cautious about wearing a helmet while skiing or biking. Like so many younger people, I hadn't contemplated the possibilities of having a loved one permanently impaired. I had considered Bob's risk of dying while reporting in areas of conflict, but I had never once thought about anything happening that might rob me of the essence of the person I'd fallen in love with.

For anyone navigating the journey of brain injury, or their loved ones, it is a frightening, complex, and often discouraging road. There are far too few beacons of information, hope, or realism. And there are far too few books like this one that lay out the journey in an honest, realistic, but palatable and even inspiring way. While many survivors have self-published memoirs, these stories never really seem to receive the wider attention they deserve because this is such a stigmatized injury. "No one wants to read about such a downer," one publisher said to me when I forwarded the story of a friend for his review.

And yet these stories are the very stuff that keep the rest of us going, that bring hope in a world so circumscribed by illness, loss, grief, and uncertainty. It's the very nature of stories like that of the Goldsteins' that pull us back from the brink and show us that good things can come out of bad, that people are survivors, that human beings can be as resilient as corks, that good days can chase bad ones.

No Stone Unturned, the story of Bart Goldstein written lovingly by his father, Joel, is familiar territory for me. And when I first read the book I braced myself, as I often do when reading other survivor accounts, for it to take me back to that dark place my own family experienced. But what I found instead in the pages of this book was a wonderful and compelling story. I found warmth, wisdom, love, fear, pain, and resilience in what you are about to read. It is a story that must be shared and passed to others. These stories about people like Bart and Bob and the more than 360,000 service members who have returned from the wars in Iraq and Afghanistan with some form of a brain injury—these are the stories that must educate, illuminate, and continue to keep the spotlight on prevention, research, and education about this insidious, life-changing injury.

We will never be able to eradicate brain injuries from humanity. There will always be accidents, injuries, violence, and the unpredictability of life. But one thing that can ease the journey is a book like this, which offers some good sense out of what is often, especially initially, a senseless situation.

Introduction

Traumatic brain injury will always be with us. Snuggled safely at home, you may yet trip, fall, and wake up with a concussion, in coma, or worse. Falling in the shower or down stairs is a principal cause of TBI, though not in young adults who are more likely to be involved in a car crash or, if serving their country, blown up by an IED. A stubborn permanence distinguishes brain injury from other conditions such as breast cancer, HIV/AIDS, and even autism, for which we may someday see vaccines or cures.

It is also distinguished by sheer weight of numbers. Far and away the leading cause of death and disability among persons under the age of forty-five, TBI strikes 1.7 million people each year, with 50,000 dying of their injuries. The Centers for Disease Control and Prevention (CDC) estimates that 5.4 million Americans are permanently disabled with TBI—roughly 2 percent of the population! Millions more, whose injuries do not quite meet the rigorous standard of "legal disability," struggle with life-altering deficits. Someone joins their ranks every minute or so. It's been said that "one man's death is a tragedy, a million deaths are a statistic." We hope that Bart's story of tragic loss, grief, endurance, as well as triumphs, helps to put a human face on TBI.

How on earth does such a vast, sprawling epidemic manage to remain invisible? The answer lies partly in the difficulty of identifying an underlying condition such as TBI, since brain injuries present a mind-boggling diversity of symptoms. That diversity reflects the brain's complexity and pervasive influence on every aspect of life. In the public's imagination, brain injury may vaguely suggest coma, amnesia, paralysis, loss of sight or speech, and perhaps weird, erratic behavior. Yet TBI survivors may present none of those symptoms, and may even appear perfectly normal at first blush, all the while suffering debilitating cognitive, perceptual, or emotional deficits.

Though it is sometimes difficult to pin down the root cause of the array of behaviors and symptoms, nearly all survivors of a moderate to severe brain injury share three common traits. Cognition is compromised, especially short-term memory, intellectual acuity, and judgment; emotional stability and self-control are diminished; and motor control is impaired.

Every state has a Brain Injury Association, but the general level of public awareness remains notably low. For their part, most TBI survivors and their families are simply too exhausted by the daily scramble to meet the basic needs of life to become effective public advocates and organizers. Prior to the media campaigns that finally brought them to light, breast cancer, HIV/AIDS, and more recently autism were subjects similarly lost in shadow. With TBI now becoming the signature injury for wounded veterans returning from the wars in Iraq and Afghanistan, there is an urgent need for similar consciousness-raising about traumatic brain injury. We hope our story contributes to an emerging grassroots movement.

Three areas call for urgent attention: prevention, improved treatment for survivors, and research on brain repair. Prevention should concentrate on driver education, improved headgear design and use in winter sports and in high school and college athletics, and mandatory helmet laws for bicyclists and motorcycle riders. Whenever I visit a state without mandatory helmet laws, I fight the urge to drag bikers off their hogs and haul them to the nearest hospital neurosurgical ICU for some authentic consciousness-raising.

A critical shortage of long-term services for survivors has worsened with tens of thousands of wounded veterans returning from the wars. Qualified practitioners do not grow on trees, especially in specialized fields such as cognitive rehabilitation and speech, vision, occupational, and physical therapies, to say nothing of alternative approaches such as craniosacral and hyperbaric oxygen therapies. It will take a national effort over some years to adequately ramp up. Best practices must be painstakingly learned at cutting-edge institutions such as the Kessler Institute, the Rusk Institute, NeuroPsychologic Rehab Services, and the Michael E. DeBakey VA Medical Center (MEDVAMC), and then replicated throughout the land. In most communities there is no satisfactory treatment available to survivors.

Nothing less than a "Manhattan Project" is called for to discover how to repair injuries to the central nervous system. Since other countries have already begun to blaze the way, it should be a multinational effort. Today science is in striking distance of achieving a dream of the ages—the paralyzed may yet walk and the blind may see again.

When Bart was injured, neither my wife, Dayle, nor I had ever even heard of TBI. I began writing to lay to rest some of my own demons, and to leave a fresh, raw record for family and friends before memories faded or were burnished by pride beyond recognition. But then Dayle, my comrade-in-arms in our private war with TBI, insisted that we "go public." After all, our saga might well be any family's story—especially those with a child struggling with TBI, cerebral palsy, autism, mental illness, or other grave affliction, and even families lucky enough to have dodged those bullets. The ancient Greeks counseled, "Count no man lucky until he is dead." Everyone, every family, is but a heartbeat away from tragedy. We offer our story in solidarity and fellowship with all those facing hard fights.

1

Saturday Night, December 29, 2001

Streaking down the New York State Thruway, we bantered nervously about not speeding too fast. It wouldn't do to have an accident tonight. Twenty minutes earlier we had spoken by phone with a police lieutenant. Dayle and I comforted each other with the thought that our son, Bart, was uniquely qualified to survive a head injury. One of his family nicknames was "bowling ball." His head was large, perfectly shaped, and remarkably sturdy. When barely a year old, he stumbled head-on into an older toddler at a local pizzeria. The other kid went down like a bowling pin, with Bart hardly seeming to notice. By age three he loved to challenge his uncle or another willing adult to head-butt with him, invariably winning. In soccer, basketball, and baseball, all of which he played in middle and high school, he was a dogged defender, never shy about taking a hit. Opposing players just careened off him. He seemed nearly indestructible.

✦

Our first sight of Bart as an infant had been in a lounge at JFK airport's International Arrivals Building. A frazzled escort handed him to Dayle, saying only, "Here. Here's the strong one." In the excitement we had no chance to ask her to expand on that cryptic remark. With eleven children arriving on the flight from Korea, the lounge was jam-packed with glowing new parents, relatives, and friends milling around in dazed, happy confusion. Arriving home that evening, we began to get a feel for what she meant. At barely five months, Bart could sit up, crawl, and even stand with someone to help keep his balance. Big for his age, he sported huge hands and feet, and an unusually large head supported by a thick neck. Apparently well fed, he looked like a miniature Buddha. We later learned that foster mothers in Korea, for whom fat is beautiful, compete over who can best "plump up" their little charges.

✦

Earlier tonight, the police lieutenant told us that the car had wrapped around a tree on a narrow side road, a stone's throw from Main Street. The village speed limit is 30 mph, and one could hardly go faster if one tried. Surely Bart's solid constitution and rock-hard head would stand him in good stead. A letter from a dying uncle written later while Bart was in a coma boasted, "In a contest between a tree and your head, my money's on your head any day." Luckily the New Paltz Rescue Squad is one of the best in the region. Other towns around Ulster County send new recruits to train with them. The squad would take excellent care of our boy. We tried to take comfort from these and similar thoughts during the desperate ride to the hospital. Cell phone service is spotty in the mid-Hudson valley, but we managed to ascertain that Bart had been taken into surgery. That bit of news burst our fragile confidence. Brain surgery on a minor without even obtaining parental consent—it must be do-or-die. I began to exhibit an odd nervous reaction—rapidly shaking my head from side to side, much like a dog shaking water off its coat; as if trying to shake unbearable images from my mind's eye. Oddly, it seemed to temporarily dislodge the awful visions.

The evening had begun pleasantly. With our eleven-year-old daughter, Cassidy, sweetly dozing in the back seat, Dayle and I returned home from a Christmas party around 11:30 p.m. in holiday spirits. Sixteen-year-old Bart had spent the previous night at a friend's house and was scheduled to return home along with a couple of buddies to crash in his room. In rural Upstate New York, endless rounds of sleepovers are a way of life for teens. Coming up the driveway, as we noticed every light in the house on, Dayle sighed with relief, "Good, they're home." But upon entering we found only the dog, and on the kitchen counter a hastily scrawled note, "Went to Gary's." With Bart out, I felt obliged to check the answering machine, which blinked, "1 Message." It was from a lieutenant with the New Paltz police, asking us to call right away. Assuming what I thought was the worst, I worried that the boys had been arrested. The last couple of years Bart had led us on a very merry chase, in trouble at school and even a near run-in with the law. Lord knows what mischief the knuckleheads had gotten into. The dispatcher seemed reluctant to talk with me, saying I'd have to speak to the lieutenant, who apparently was unavailable. Finally, after a couple of agitating minutes on hold, another officer came on the line. Bart had been in an accident in the village and was on his way to Westchester Medical Center, some seventy-five miles south. Yes, he was alive. No, he couldn't say how serious it was, but he had been medivaced. Why take him to Westchester when there were five hospitals within thirty minutes of home? And by helicopter no less?

I hung up the phone, shouting to Dayle to call friends and ask them to come by for Cassidy. The Kennedys should plan to keep her at least overnight, maybe longer. Better pack her kit, just in case it was more than overnight. I kept a bag already packed for last-minute business trips and suggested that Dayle throw in a few things. We tried calling Westchester Med's emergency room. After several futile attempts we finally reached someone who at least tried to be helpful but was unable to find any record of a Bart Goldstein or Groudine-Goldstein. My mind was beginning to cramp a bit, and I struggled to give a detailed description. The voice confirmed that a young John Doe matching Bart's description was already in CAT scan. It seems he had arrived without any kind of ID. The neurosurgeon on call had been summoned. I felt both relief and dread—relief that we had at least located him; dread that Bart faced neurosurgery nameless and alone in some gigantic municipal hospital. My mother and sister, both with long and distinguished careers as nurses, had filled me with a reflexive horror of hospitals. Mom had been quite blunt, saying simply, "Stay out of hospitals; they'll kill you." I forced myself to take deep slow breaths through the belly to stave off the cold knot growing in there, whispering that Dayle should be ready to shove off the moment the Kennedys drove up. We knew Cassidy would be fine with them. If need be she could spend the rest of Christmas break with their daughter Lauren, her best friend. Dayle made a quick call to her oldest sister, asking her to stand by ready to make more calls if needed. Then she phoned our good friend Duffy Violante, formerly a nurse in a brain-trauma unit and now a massage therapist and healer, asking him to light a candle and say a prayer for Bart.

Somehow we arrived safely around 1:30 a.m. at Westchester Med, a sprawling campus of buildings centered around the main hospital with its heliport and emergency room. Struggling to control our feelings, we ran into the building and stumbled smack into Sean Daniels and his parents, Gwenn and John. Glad to see familiar faces, even haggard, shell-shocked ones, we all retreated to a deserted waiting area near the recovery room. We caught up a little, learning a bit more about the accident, and getting filled in about the condition of the other two boys who had been in the car, Sean and Kyle. Riding in the front seat, with the protection of seatbelts and airbags, they were both badly shaken up, but physically okay. Bart was riding in the back seat without a belt. There was no one from the hospital to speak with, so we killed some time by going to the registrar's office to clear up the question of Bart's identity. Every hour or so we'd call the recovery room to inquire about Bart. Each time was the same: no news. Each time I'd remind the nurse to *please* call us as soon as they learned *anything*, making doubly sure she had the extension number for the waiting room phone. And above all else, to please let the surgeon know we were dying to speak with him. It was a long night, but we were very lively and alert, high on adrenaline. My recollection is spotty, but I know we tried to keep things light, joking around, especially with Sean, who, though physically all right, seemed a wreck. A few scant hours earlier he had totaled his family car, dragging Bart's apparently lifeless body from the wreckage.

Finally, around 5:30 in the morning, we discovered quite by accident that Bart was already out of surgery. On a periodic trip to stretch our legs, we looked in at the post-operative acute care unit (PACU) and were astonished to find Bart inside. They hadn't bothered to call us. It was, after all, a large hospital with many waiting rooms. The surgeon had gone home to get some sleep, and no one was willing or able to give us an assessment of Bart's condition. Everyone seemed surprised that we hadn't been briefed by the surgeon.

PACU is kept locked to keep out pesky relatives and their germs. As the parents of a minor, we were buzzed in, along with "Uncle" John Daniels. Nothing in my experience prepared me for what I saw. I could not for the life of me recognize Bart. His entire head and face were swathed in bandages, leaving only small slits for his eyes. There were hoses snaking out of his mouth and nose, and, unbelievably, even a couple coming right out the top of his skull. The misshapen swollen mass of his head seemed held together by clear plastic tape, the kind used to seal cardboard cartons. Beneath the tape I detected staples, the large ones used to tack plywood. I resorted to examining his hands and feet to assure myself that this grotesque, lifeless creature was my precious son. His large feet and hammertoes made the identification conclusive.

Folks in PACU were kind and sympathetic, but shed no light on Bart's condition. Finally a doctor came in to check on Bart, examining his monitors, including the respirator, which was doing his breathing. Opening his eyes with her fingers, she shined a tiny flashlight at them. Bart did not seem to react to the light, and I thought I caught a hint of resignation in the doctor's eyes. We couldn't get her to divulge anything about his condition other than that he was in a coma, both natural and drug-induced. Later, passing us in the hallway and seeing our anguished expressions, she confided, "Listen, whatever happens, it's going to be a long, long haul for your boy." A cockeyed optimist, I took this as good news. At least she expected him to live a long time. By now we were beside ourselves, desperate to get a clear picture of the nature of his injuries, what had transpired during the nearly six-hour surgery, and, most urgently, his condition and prognosis. We asked the head of PACU as well as several hospital administrators to help us get a report from a responsible party, but with no satisfaction.

Finally around 8:00 a.m. an exhausted doctor in rumpled green approached us in the hospital lobby where we had huddled for coffee. He said Bart's surgeon had gone home, but that he had assisted during the operation and could fill us in. Bart had suffered a massive subdural hematoma, a large blood clot between the surface of the brain and its outer covering. The life-threatening clot had been removed, but his condition was extremely critical. There might be permanent injuries. He added almost as an afterthought, "We may lose him during the next ninety-six hours," then turned and walked off. We had sent the Daniels home at around 6:00 a.m. to get some sleep, so were utterly alone. Dazed, we sat down in the empty lobby and began to quietly weep. I felt my whole body surrendering to a rising wave of sobs when Dayle jabbed me hard in the ribs, whispering, "Joel, keep it together; we've lots to do." I snapped to it and we made a to-do list, then called our old friends Lou and Lisa Badalato who lived ten minutes from the hospital. Catching them leaving for work, we asked if we could crash at their house for a few days. Stunned by the news, they agreed to leave a key for us, giving us freedom to come and go as needed. Next I called my nephew Scott Marsel, a prominent internist in Florida. After tracking him down and giving him a quick update,

I asked him to stand ready at a moment's notice if questions, concerns, or decisions came up. He suggested that, once Bart stabilized, we might want to move him to a top New York City hospital, possibly New York–Presbyterian Columbia University Medical Center. We called the Kennedys and told them to expect to keep Cassidy for a few days and also to request prayers from friends in our Korean culture camp.

That morning Marlene Kennedy sent an e-mail to the Mujigae camp committee. Mujigae, a Korean heritage camp in Albany for adopted kids, had been an important part of our lives every summer since Bart was six. Her e-mail read, "Last night Bart Goldstein was in a serious car accident and was medivaced to Westchester Medical Center. His family has requested your prayers, whatever your denomination. Wouldn't it be great if we could surround him in an embrace of Mujigae love and positive healing energy? The next seventy-two hours are the most important. Please don't call the home; they are down at the hospital. Their daughter is staying with us for now. When I find out if he can receive cards I will e-mail you again."

The following day she wrote, "Bart is in the WMC pediatric ICU. His condition is pretty serious. He is in a level six coma. Right now a ventilator is helping him breathe, but he seems to be doing more of the work now. For the next thirty-six hours the focus is on keeping the brain swelling down. At the current time he does not seem to have any other internal injuries, which is good. When he first was admitted he needed an operation to reduce the pressure on his brain. The surgery took five hours and appears to have been successful. It is now a wait-and-see time. Dayle called and said that even if he comes out of the coma relatively quickly he will need to go into rehab and it may be a long haul. They have asked friends and family to pray for a speedy and complete recovery. Feel free to pass on info to Mujigae friends. We should know more in the next few days. You can always e-mail me." Marlene sent similar succinct messages, which became known as "Bart updates," every day or two for the next four months. The updates relieved Dayle and me of the necessity of speaking daily with the many worried people seeking information about Bart's condition. We received the e-mails as well, so in addition to cutting down wear and tear, it kept us abreast of what other people were hearing about Bart.

2
The Fellowship

With no beds available in the neurosurgical ICU (NICU), Bart, still technically a child, was "parked" for a few days in the pediatric ICU (PICU). With each newly arriving shift, startled nurses wondered out loud, "Are you sure he's just sixteen? He's huge!" With heavily muscled limbs, barrel chest, and outlandish headgear, Bart resembled a monstrous Roman gladiator—wildly out of place in a crowded ward packed with tiny preemies, critically ill babies, and shell-shocked young parents. After nearly a week, he was moved to the neurosurgical ICU. We were relieved to be leaving the PICU, where doctors seemed to furtively avoid our gaze, and when we did manage to corner them, to retreat into technical jargon and CAT scan talk. We barely understood what they were saying; only that Bart's brain was gravely injured in several areas. Until he regained consciousness and his neck brace could be removed, they couldn't be sure if he'd sustained spinal cord damage as well. The pediatricians were kind but guarded in the manner of those who've had lots of practice delivering hard news to parents.

The NICU had four beds to a room: rooms that were unusually cold and dirty, not at all what one expects in a hospital. Patients were pierced by a bewildering variety of tubes, sprouting from their skulls, noses and mouths, arms, stomachs, and urinary tracts. Plenty of opportunity for nasty germs to start infections, and the cold temperature was meant to reduce that risk. Tumbleweeds of dust and stains on the floor and walls were harder to understand, but the nurses claimed that cleaning fluids were too abrasive for use around these patients, most of whom were on respirators and in extremely critical condition.

It was difficult to tell a patient's age or even gender beneath harnesses of tubes and wires. Fresh from surgery, each would arrive in the NICU like some alien creature, head and face swathed in tape and tubes, attached by scads of wires to an array of medical devices and monitors. The monitors spit out a staccato series of bells, buzzes, and alarms, too noisy to sleep through. The clamor didn't bother the patients, most of whom were in coma. Grotesque thick tubes coming right out the top of their skulls reminded me of battery cables; smaller ones that drain cranial fluid were more like IV feeds. (Cranial fluid is clear and colorless.) Every two patients were assigned a specially trained NICU nurse, working twelve-hour shifts for three consecutive days followed by a couple of days off to recharge. I have a soft spot for nurses anyway, and these specialists are a rare breed. Routinely losing nearly half of their patients, they wage an unrelenting war against death with professionalism, humor, and care. Like a firefighter, their job is mostly tedium, punctuated by panic. Except they don't panic, even when fighting breathlessly to save a life on the brink. They are unsung heroes.

TBI afflicts all kinds, but the most common patient profile is a sixteen- or seventeen-year-old car crash victim. A couple of teens had died in NICU just prior to our arrival, and I was grateful to have been spared that horror. We'd seen and heard hysterical parents in PICU, and I wasn't sure I could bear more of that in this bizarre, hellish place.

Many patients were barely clinging to life. Already in my midfifties, I had never seen the last rites of the church, but was privileged to witness that sacrament twice in the NICU. There was a Hispanic man, Emmanuel, who had been mugged in the Bronx, hit over the head with a bat, robbed, and left for dead—murdered really, since he succumbed after five days. We could tell by the doctors' expressions that he was a hopeless cause. A stressed-out nurse, frustrated by her inability to communicate to his nephews the need to summon the family (they spoke only Spanish), finally blurted at them, "Don't you get it—he's dying!" Her other patient had passed away earlier that day and she seemed near the breaking point. Someone quietly suggested that she find a translator, although from the expressions on their faces, it was obvious the nephews had received her message loud and clear.

A forty-year-old woman, Linda, had tripped, laundry basket in hand, fallen down the basement stairs, and landed on her head. Trapped in her bed across from Bart's, she was declared brain-dead after a week. Her large, grief-stricken family gathered around her tenderly to pray and say good-bye, and then gave permission to discontinue life support. Her organs were donated to help several waiting patients. According to her niece, Linda had been a real prankster, the life of the party—something she and Bart shared in common. These losses were heartbreaking, and there was precious little we could do or say to comfort the bereaved. There was an eerie, palpable feeling that the grim reaper was never far from one's side. We felt as if we were in alien, enemy-held territory.

Sometimes patients joined our grim little circle for a few days, to begin recovery after removal of a brain tumor. These patients were generally able to sit up, sometimes even speak. One such short timer was Tina, Bart's neighbor for four days, a young twentysomething African American woman. Her father was with her most of the time and we all became friends in the spontaneous way common in NICU. We prayed for Tina just as her dad prayed for Bart. Then she was gone, discharged. Two days later she turned up back on the fifth floor, standing outside our door, head in hand, rhythmically rocking back and forth. Alarmed nurses thought she might be having some kind of post-operative setback, but when asked, she replied quietly that she had come by to pray for Bart. Another day a teenage girl, recovering from brain-tumor surgery, stopped her wheelchair in the hallway and stared long and hard into our room. Speaking only Spanish, and accompanied by her mother and pastor, she asked Dayle if she would mind if they prayed for Bart, an offer that was gladly accepted. Quiet acts of kindness are commonplace in NICU, making time there more bearable.

Of course, we tried our best to care for the other patients and their families through small but meaningful gestures, such as sharing our Lourdes holy water or tips on where to find something good to eat. In the NICU the brotherhood of man is no pious platitude, but a day-in, day-out, living reality. The same sort of fellowship has often been noted among combat troops, possibly for similar reasons. I dubbed the phenomenon that transforms ordinary folks faced with ultimate challenges into more caring, humane persons "the fellowship of the damned" and then eventually, just "the fellowship." Though rooted in tragedy, it was comforting to know that in this dark, frightening place the light of kindness and brotherhood still gently shined. In our numbed state of mind, it seemed odd and sad to realize that one's best impulses assert themselves most surely in nightmarish circumstances.

Upon returning to school after Christmas break, Sean and Kyle received a rough welcome from their classmates. Reactions ranged from cold, reluctant stares to piercing screams of "You killed Bart!" The boys retreated to the guidance office or back home. We were appalled to learn of their chilly reception, and grateful to hear that the varsity baseball and football coaches, Coach Defino and Coach Tegeler, had intervened to calm the waters, even holding a prayer circle for Bart in the gym after school. At the next home basketball game a few days later, a moment of silence for Bart was observed and the game dedicated to him. Skunked all season, the struggling home team managed to eke out a win. I whispered all these hometown doings into Bart's ear, editing out anything negative.

Life at WMC was dominated by the ICP monitor, which records intracranial pressure, the pressure of fluid within the brain. With swelling, pressure increases. Like any other part of the body, when bruised or beat up, the brain swells. Even slight increases in intracranial pressure are dangerous. A healthy person's readings are in the single digits. Pressures in the thirties are dangerous, while higher numbers usually result in permanent brain damage or death. We would sit at Bart's bedside all day, eyes darting to the digital readout above his bed. The ICP monitor was connected to a pressure sensor in his brain through a tube coming out the top of his skull. Alarm bells, buzzers, and whistles in the ICU are absolutely maddening, especially since we had no way of telling which ones were fairly routine, merely indicating, say, an empty intravenous bottle, from true emergencies. We gradually learned the ropes.

It mostly came down to ICP numbers. Bart's pressure readings were in the high twenties and low thirties for days on end. When they spiked briefly into the forties, we were overcome with breathtaking helpless angst. Trying to decrease brain activity and thereby lower ICP, the doctors repeatedly sent Bart into deeper levels of drug-induced coma. Dayle's cousin, Scott Groudine, a prominent anesthesiologist at Albany Medical Center, phoned everyday to confer with the doctors in the ICU. Then he'd translate the gist into layman's terms for us, adding his own perspective. Speaking with him was usually a comfort, but not always. He was terribly concerned about the high ICP readings and urged even deeper coma or other measures—whatever it took to lower the pressure. Even if Bart survived, the damage caused by post-traumatic swelling might be worse than the original injury.

About this time Dayle began giving Bart a daily Reiki session. Reiki is an ancient healing art involving the gentle laying on of hands that brings balance to body, mind, and soul. A natural method of healing, it can be combined safely with conventional medical treatments. During a Reiki session, the practitioner's hands are placed very gently on or slightly above the patient. The Reiki Master receives the healing energy through a higher power, sending it gently through her hands to the patient. I think of it as akin to prayer, or perhaps faith healing. Originating in Japan, the techniques have been around a couple thousand years. When Dayle had begun to study and then practice Reiki a few years earlier, I was very skeptical, but after experiencing the relaxation and release of the sessions, to say nothing of the wonderful effect on my chronically aching back, I became a believer. I have no idea how it works, any more than I'm sure how prayer works, but I'm enough of a pragmatist to go with the flow. Of course, it's no substitute for a skilled neurosurgeon.

A physical therapist visited the NICU every few days, so I asked her to teach me some of the basic exercises designed to prevent a patient's limbs from stiffening from disuse, and began to give Bart daily or sometimes twice daily sessions. Gently bending and stretching his arms and legs, I was doing something useful finally! His paralyzed right side seemed to loosen up a bit. Bart was still running a fever, which was a serious concern, and coughing to beat the band. A buildup of phlegm, apparently caused by the tube down his throat, gave him a really hard time, and threatened pneumonia. When a nurse or respiratory therapist would periodically suction his lungs, it was agonizing. Even in a coma, Bart seemed to find the procedure nearly unbearable. A daily trial, sometimes twice daily, it was excruciating to witness.

On the seventh day in the ICU Dayle absolutely insisted I go to work for half a day. After all, there was no way to know when this waiting for his ICP to stabilize would end. I went, relieved to be out of that madhouse. After making a successful pretense of following my normal work routine all morning, I got a page from Dayle. The neurosurgeon, Dr. Harter, was going to insert another tube into Bart's brain, a ventricular drainage tube. It would provide continuous drainage of fluid, relieving the pressure buildup. He was going ahead immediately with the procedure, which could be done bedside. I grabbed a cab for the hospital, hardly able to speak. The forty-minute ride was maddening. I begged and pleaded with God. "Spare the boy. I'll do anything you ask! Let him live. I'll never be angry with him again, ever."

✦

My own father usually reserved his worst anger for the ones he most loved. Sadly, I favor him in that respect. Bart especially had a way of unnerving me so that I'd work myself up into a white-hot fury. At those times Dayle worried that I'd "pop my cork"—have a fatal stroke or heart attack. I'd break into waves of screaming, which finally seemed to spend themselves, only to whip up another rolling boil all over again, hoarse and venomous. It was as if I just couldn't let go. Naturally, these angry outbursts never did any good, although there was the momentary satisfaction of striking back at a tormentor.

The first time I recall throwing such a fit at Bart was after returning from an exhausting trip to visit friends on the West Coast. We'd caught a red-eye from San Francisco, and two-year-old Bart's ears bothered him. Throughout the seemingly endless flight, he screamed and fussed with his famous set of lungs. I thought some passengers were going to mutiny and pitch the three of us out the emergency hatch. Finally arriving at New York's JFK airport we drove two hours back to our house, collapsing into bed around midday. Three or four hours later Bart climbed out of his crib and presented himself at our bedside, demanding, "Come on, Dad, get up. Let's do something." When I shooed him away saying I needed some more sleep he only got louder and more insistent. Finally I rolled over away from him in the forlorn hope that he might take the hint and go away and play for a while. Never easily discouraged, Bart grabbed the rechargeable flashlight from its wall mount and brought it down with both hands on my head. That got my attention, and I found myself in a blind fury, spitting out my father's favorite angry phrase, "Goddamn it to hell; goddamn it." It was the first time I completely lost it with Bart, though fortunately Dayle's wing was there for him to scramble under for shelter. To be fair, he was only two, and transcontinental travel with a toddler is always risky business.

At the end of eighth grade, Bart took the ninth grade math Regents exam a year early along with the rest of the students in the accelerated math program. Bart was gifted but never motivated in school. I threw a major conniption when he narrowly failed the Regents exam, then after claiming he didn't need tutoring, he failed it again in August, forcing him to repeat the course.

Fun loving and hilarious, Bart was an odds-on favorite to win the title of class clown when the awards were announced at middle school "moving up" ceremonies. A friend of the family put it exactly right when she labeled him a "loveable rogue." Barty boy was a spirited child, with a twinkle in his eyes, eyes that were restless and mischievous. A typical Bart prank: lounging outside the middle school at lunch, he spied a physical education class walking out to the soccer fields in neat order, just the way gym teachers love. Swooping down on the lead kid, he stole the ball and led the class on a wild goose chase around the far-flung school grounds. Bart was plenty fast and the class eventually gave up, but not before scattering to the four corners of the school's fields and playgrounds, infuriating the gym teacher. Like all his pranks, it was disruptive, but not mean. As a regularly summoned visitor, I got to know the assistant principals of Bart's schools on a first-name basis. Afterward, I usually lost my temper. On "moving up day," we learned that the school elders decided to drop class clown from the ranks of honors awarded upon graduation. As the picture taking and congratulations began to wind down, a goody-two-shoes girl, with an armful of awards, came up to Bart and sneered, "Gee, Bart, three years wasted." Bart was okay—always one to look on the bright side—at least he was finished with middle school.

By the time my taxicab screamed up to the hospital at 3:00 p.m., Dr. Harter had already inserted the ventricular tube. Dayle and I agreed that "work therapy" was a luxury we'd need to postpone until Bart had passed through his crisis. Drained, we retreated to the cafeteria for a drink when we both felt a slight flush and nausea. Rushing upstairs with a feeling of dread, we found Bart's ICP readings had dropped to the single digits, within the range of normal for the first time since the accident. What a relief! We decided to a take a few hours off and celebrate—eat out Chinese and stop at Lou and Lisa's to make a few phone calls. We learned that my brother David's psychic healers predicted that Bart would pull through, a great comfort to Dayle. For my part I was somewhat skeptical of psychic healers but didn't see how they could hurt.

A couple of days later, the ICU nurses came running up to us in the lounge—Bart's right eye had fluttered open! We were thrilled, though not really sure what that milestone meant. Dayle's cousin, Dr. Scott, said that it was a very big deal, the beginning of the end of the coma, so we were wildly relieved and happy. It was a couple of days later when Dayle actually saw him open his right eye, turn his head toward her, and squeeze her hand. She sensed pain and fear in his tearful eye.

> Excerpt from Dayle's daily log, dated Tuesday, January 8, 2002
>
> "This is a Great Day!! In fact, it was so great that I forgot to visit the chapel. When I came to visit and Cousin Arlene showed up, I was holding your left hand and you were pulling it over and Arlene was talking to you. I asked her if your eye was open. It was, so I came around to your right and we gazed at one another. I could tell you were watching me with recognition. We both had tears in our eyes. You were scared, wanted to speak, and were frustrated. For the first time at the hospital, I was able to reach your eyes and nose and kiss them. You and I were watching each other for over an hour. You finally fell asleep and I went to lunch. When I returned they had given you morphine for the pain, so I stayed an hour, left for Lou & Lisa and then returned at 5:30."

Friends and relatives were clamoring to visit, but we steadfastly declined. Why needlessly expose Bart and the other patients to germs? As far as his friends visiting, we'd let Bart make that call when he came to. We also felt that the sight of Bart would be more than young people could bear. James Chang, a longtime Camp Mujigae counselor then in his first year of medical school, insisted that he could bear up. After all, he'd already seen plenty of awful things in hospitals. Given James's medical background, and his status as a surrogate "big brother" to Bart, we relented. On Thursday, January 10, he visited with Bart for thirty minutes, quietly praying at his bedside. Getting up to leave, he was white as a ghost, looking about ready to pass out. It's different when it's someone you love. A few of my cousins, Arlene, Cheryl, and Barnet, just showed up at WMC, refusing to take no for an answer. Cheerful types, their visits helped break the chronic tedium and dread of NICU.

Gwenn Daniels was having a bad time, racked with guilt over allowing Sean to drive that night. I called John Daniels every couple of nights to give him a Bart update for him to pass around the school community. In return he kept me informed of school news. It seemed a kid made a wisecrack about Bart in the school cafeteria and was promptly knocked out cold by Kurt, one of Bart's buddies. We sent word to Kurt and other kids at school that we didn't want anybody getting hurt on Bart's account, although I secretly admired Kurt for sticking up for his helpless friend.

After a week or so in NICU we felt like grizzled veterans when a sixteen-year-old girl named Meredith was wheeled into the room, bedecked in the usual gear. Seems she had hitched a ride with a couple of liquored-up boys who promptly wrecked their car. Thrown from the vehicle, she sustained such severe brain injuries that the neurosurgeons were unwilling to operate. She was not expected to recover. We met Meredith's parents out by the elevators, quietly filling them in on the some helpful bits of information we'd picked up about how to navigate the hospital. It was a relief to be able to actually do or say something useful. Apparently when the doctors briefed her family on her prognosis, her uncle had fainted away right in the NICU. Meredith was from a military family, and they were clearly not crybabies, but what can you say to people who've just been told their child's case is hopeless?

Anyone with a gravely ill child knows the aching sense of helplessness. What can one do to help this precious child? There's busy work, thank God, arranging parking, meals, calls to relatives, babysitting for Cassidy. There's reading aloud at the bedside: the Bible, letters from friends, relatives, and classmates, hundreds of cards. Bart's entire English class wrote letters to cheer him up. There are daily trips to the hospital chapel where one can write a special request to God in the book appointed for such things, or read similar pleas from other anguished folk. Thoreau's famous remark came to mind: "Most men live lives of quiet desperation." Especially for those accustomed to framing plans and taking effective actions, you are rapidly brought to the maddening and finally humbling realization that there is nothing more you can do than to let your child know how much you love him and that you'll be there for him every step of the way.

Meredith didn't die. Clinging tenaciously to life, she even improved a bit. We urged her parents, Betty and David, to beg Dr. Harter to take on her case, since she'd been seen by another surgeon. David Harter, chief of Pediatric Neurosurgery, loomed large in our eyes, not only for saving Bart, but for his humble, humane ways. When I mentioned in my nightly call to my sister Judi how Dr. Harter would page me each evening with an update, apologizing for not getting to me sooner, she remarked, "Holy cow, a neurosurgeon called you to apologize? You better hold on to him, 'cause if you lose him, you'll never find another like him. Most wouldn't give God Almighty the time of day." On the contrary, when we saw Dr. Harter on the way to our frequent chapel visits, he'd invariably smile and ask us to put in a good word for him, claiming he needed it. He was the very soul of kindness.

After stubbornly refusing to die for a week, Meredith underwent neurosurgery with Dr. Harter. Somehow we were confident that she'd come through. Her injuries were extremely grave; half of her skull had to be removed to prevent post-operative brain swelling from killing her. It would be kept frozen, then reattached a month or so later. Afterward she began to recover more swiftly than Bart. She and her family spent nearly eight months with us, first in NICU, then at the rehab hospital, and finally in the outpatient clinic. Her stepfather, David was a marine non-com (noncommissioned officer), ramrod straight, sporting a crew cut, with a dash of laconic humor. Betty was a wisp of a woman, but with great inner strength. They became key members of the fellowship, and we watched after each other's kids as if they were our own.

Twelve days after the accident, Bart moved his right arm. Dayle called me at home, where I was supervising a quick "changing of the guard." After a week of babysitting Cassidy, Dayle's parents were leaving and her sister Cathy arriving to stand in for the next week. I was moving at high speed, wanting to return to the hospital ASAP, with barely a moment to spend with Cassidy, yet lots of minutiae to go over with ditzy relatives. Dayle's call caught me off guard. Bart had moved his right arm from its resting place at his side onto his stomach. She had seen it herself. No, it wasn't a reflexive action, but "voluntary." It was the first sign of life in a limb that until now had barely even evidenced the so-called pain reflex. I was thrilled, and hanging up I found myself crying in a quiet, happy kind of way. Tears of joy. I had never understood what that expression meant. It was the second time I cried during our ordeal, though not the last. I'm not a modern, cosmopolitan kind of guy who cries at sappy movies. I believe one needs to be strong and resourceful to navigate life's storms, and to bear up when things get really tough. Not that one should be grim about it. Humor is still the best defense against life's slings and arrows. Of course there are times when it's all too much, when even humor fails.

That night I slept in Bart's room. Soaking in the familiar sights, the smell and feel of him, I puttered around his trophy beer bottles, found his poorly hidden cigarettes and lighter, and spent hours leafing through old middle and high school yearbooks, photo collections from Mujigae, piles of ticket stubs from long forgotten ball games and Broadway shows. I fell asleep in the early morning hours feeling very close to Bart, as if somehow the "real" boy were in this room, not in the NICU. Over the next four months, from time to time, when the spirit moved me, I would spend a night down in his room. Everyone grieves in their own way. Until he returned home months later, Dayle never set foot in Bart's basement bedroom. Just going down to the basement to put out the garbage or do a wash was a trial for her.

✦

Bart began persistently rubbing his right foot with his left one and his right hand with his left, as if trying to waken the sleeping limbs. This seemed like purposeful behavior, and we clung desperately to anything positive. Sometimes Bart would respond to very simple commands from the doctors, other times not. The nurses said that he was showing signs of feeling some pain in his right foot, a sign of life returning. By now we had moved home and were commuting daily to WMC. Cassidy was feeling neglected, and it was time to stop imposing on Lou and Lisa. A four-hour round-trip commute meant we had fewer hours each day to spend in the NICU, which worried us no end. A friend of a friend of Dayle's sister was the head nurse for the NICU floor. She promised to stop in and check on Bart each evening after we'd left, which was some comfort. One night I stayed late just to see if she'd drop in, and thanked her for her kindness.

After three weeks at WMC I badly needed to return to work, for a change of scene and a chance to do something other than wait, worry, and pray. Work is occupational therapy. The routine and little rituals of work are comforting. People were ever so nice, though after expressing sympathy and concern and asking a few questions about Bart's condition, most seemed to find it hard to speak with me. It's tough to kibitz about the Knicks' losing streak with a guy whose son is in a coma. I'd experienced the same awkwardness myself around people suffering some great personal loss. After a day's work in New York City I'd take the Metro-North Railroad to Dobbs Ferry station then drive hurriedly to the hospital. One night, finding the main lot full, I parked in one far down the campus. Running through the lots, slipping on the icy pavement, I careened around a Jeep Cherokee parked directly in front of the hospital's main entrance. Breathlessly anxious to see Bart, I found my path blocked by a uniformed guard who sternly admonished me to move my car, since it was in a no-standing zone. I blankly sputtered, "What?" The guard replied, "Listen, you can't park there; it's a safety hazard—this is an emergency loading zone." "What are you talking about?" I replied, still not comprehending. "Listen, I saw you get out of the Jeep. Now move the damn thing, or for damn sure I'm gonna ticket you." Struggling to contain my frustration, I told him pointedly that I was parked down the road, and what's more I didn't drive a Jeep. He said he'd seen me plain as day with his own eyes. Did I take him for a fool? Somehow I managed to stammer, "Fine, tow the damn car for all I care!" as I brushed past him into the lobby and up to the NICU. I got a good laugh at this escapade, as did Dayle and our pals in NICU. I had struck a blow against mindless bureaucracy! This incident often came to mind in those days, always bringing a smile when I needed one. Amazing how small things like that can give you a lift.

Periodically Bart would disappear from NICU for a couple of hours, usually for a CAT scan or other diagnostic procedure. They needed to check on swelling as well as secondary damage—ischemic activity, or mini-stroke-like events—in other parts of the brain. Dr. Harter confirmed that there were indications of a number of ischemic events throughout Bart's brain, though as usual, we really didn't know what to make of that information, other than to worry. Nurses and doctors and respiratory therapists kept trying to wake Bart up so they could assess his breathing and what else might need to be done.

When we weren't talking or reading to him we'd try to put comedy shows on TV, so Bart could have some laughs. We felt sure that in some way he was processing what went on around him. Dayle, always at Bart's side and totally in touch with him through her daily Reiki sessions, threatened to use country music to jar him back into consciousness. Whenever the kids got too rambunctious in the car, Dayle could invariably reestablish order by threatening them with country music, which she loved and they hated like it were poison. If she followed through with her threat they would hoot and holler, beg and plead with her, even claiming that exposure to country music amounted to child abuse. One afternoon, while sitting at his bedside, Dayle watched a fresh-faced young doctor remove the staples from Bart's head.

3
The Snow Angel

The report from the adoption agency in Korea, along with a small photo, described our infant daughter as "bright yet mild." Mary Graves, director of Love the Children, said she was serene, a child who would restore balance to our family, harmonizing Bart's excessive yin with her own gentle yang. She would tame his wild heart, turning him toward the Useful and the Good. At the airport six-year-old Bart fell in love with her at first sight, remarking with deep conviction, "Gee, she loves me already!" Later, watching her emerge from a bath in the kitchen sink wrapped in a white towel, he whispered wide-eyed, "She's like a snow angel." (She had arrived home midwinter.) Apparently grieving for her foster mother, Cassidy was very reserved the first few months, never smiling except for when she was with Bart, who loved to make her laugh by outrageous, hilarious mugging. She was so gentle and mild that sometimes you could almost forget she was around, with an uncanny knack for soothing people's nerves without saying or doing a thing, just by being there. In preschool and later elementary school, teachers soon noticed this knack and we were forced to write annual letters requesting that they refrain from seating her with the most disruptive kids in class, something that unfailingly helped teachers manage their classrooms. After all, it wasn't fair to Cassidy.

In a quiet, seemingly effortless way, she was the happiest child I'd ever known. All things pleased her. She was never bored and would silently build, glue, sew, fold, draw, or otherwise occupy her ceaselessly busy fingers. Mary Graves, who had grown up in an orphanage herself, was uncannily right about things. Bart settled down noticeably after Cass arrived, becoming much less the complete Ninja Turtle and more the perfect big brother, doting on and protecting his snow angel. In his eyes Cassidy could do no wrong, and he became her unfailing advocate. If Dayle or I corrected her for some minor offense, we'd invariably have to deal with Bart adamantly arguing her case. Nagging concerns about his racial identity rapidly faded. Bart asked me, in all seriousness, if they were twins, they looked so alike in his eyes. In fact they look no more alike than Arnold Schwarzenegger and Gwyneth Paltrow, except, of course, they're both Korean.

At barely three years of age, Bart complained that his eyes looked different than ours, and for that matter, everybody else's. We rushed out and found a countywide support and playgroup for families like ours, and we even helped start a Korean heritage day camp with the help of a local Korean church in Poughkeepsie, but there seemed to be a lingering hurt deep in his heart that he couldn't let go of, until Cassidy. Within months of her arrival, Bart's first grade class created a large mural depicting the town of New Paltz. On open school night, while dutifully admiring the mural draping the wall of the first grade wing of the school, we noticed that atop town hall a Korean flag was boldly flying—no American flag, just Korean. Biting my lip to keep from laughing, I asked Bart which part of the mural he had painted. With a self-satisfied grin he piped up, "Town hall! Ya like it, Dad?" I did indeed. That night signaled the end of Bart's rejection of his racial identity and the beginning of his nationalistic phase of Korean boosting. Never one to be wishy-washy about anything, he became overbearing at times. "Did you know Chan Ho Park is Korean?" "You know baseball is Korea's favorite sport?" "Do you know Korea ranks highest in math scores?" We hoped he'd eventually strike a balance.

Cassidy was eleven at the time of Bart's accident. Our first impulse was to shield her from the worst, never remotely suggesting that Bart might die of his injuries. (In fact, the first few days he had only a 20 percent chance of recovering.) We rented her the movie *While You Were Sleeping*, a romantic comedy in which a key figure is in a coma throughout most of the film. When he finally wakes up he's as good as new, if a little confused. Cass's school principal, doubtless well intentioned, assured her that his own son was "supposed to die" after a car accident, but instead had fully recovered. For almost a month we kept her away from Bart, but her quiet insistence, plus our sense that she badly needed to see him to assure herself that he was really alive, finally persuaded us to let her make a visit. We also vaguely hoped that she might be able to wake him. If anyone could reach him, it was Cassidy. So Dayle, accompanied by Marlene Kennedy, went down to WMC with Cassidy. As usual, Bart slept nearly all day. Overwhelmed, Cassidy never uttered a sound. There's no way of telling whether he felt her presence. I do know that when periodically his eye would droop open we would hold up pictures of familiar people—photos of grandparents, friends, summer camp buddies, aunts and uncles—hoping to lure him back to the waking world. His eye just seemed glazed over, giving no sign of recognition. The only picture that drew a hard stare was the large school picture of his sister. Try as we might to protect Cassidy, like all of ours, her life changed forever. The memory of that day's visit especially haunts her.

4
No-Fault

The Daniels' auto insurance company called repeatedly within days of the accident. New York State has so-called no-fault insurance that automatically covers medical expenses of accident victims regardless of who was at fault for the accident. It was becoming obvious that the resources of no-fault would soon be depleted and that more money would be needed to meet Bart's long-term medical expenses. We had absolutely no idea what might be in store for Bart and us. I met with Bruce Blatchly, an attorney friend with an adopted Korean daughter, about prospects for suing to gain additional funds. Thankfully, the Daniels' insurance included $500,000 in liability coverage. Blatchly assured us that the insurance money would be available. There was just no telling how much more would be required to see Bart through a possible lifetime of disability. He suggested two additional potential income streams to pursue. One was the Village of New Paltz. The street on which the accident had occurred was poorly lit, poorly curbed, and poorly drained. It was covered with a smattering of gravel and boasted a series of tight hairpin curves and no warning signs whatsoever. Sean had crashed into a tree at the first hairpin curve. The street was, as anyone could see, an accident waiting to happen. The Daniels were another possible target of a lawsuit. We told Blatchly to explore the possibilities of suing the village. With each new class of sixteen-year-olds rumbling onto the local roads, that lousy street was a continuing hazard. A lawsuit might rectify that. Besides, the village was bound to have adequate insurance, and we might win some money to help with Bart's care.

✦

We decided to forgo suing the Daniels. Dayle was adamant about that. They were not people of means, and we didn't see the good in ruining them financially over what was fundamentally an accident pure and simple. Hard-working folks with kids to put through college, they felt miserable enough about their part in this mess, and there was no point in furthering their misery. We trusted that somehow we'd have the resources to meet Bart's needs. About that time we went out and bought a couple of good cell phones, something we'd been dawdling about for years. We could no longer afford the luxury of being out of touch.

The pulmonary specialist would dash by Bart's bed every day, insisting that Bart would benefit tremendously from a tracheotomy; since then his breathing would be assured and he'd be able to move on to rehab. It was a regular mantra with this guy—do a trache; do a trache; do a trache. But we were against it. Poor Barty was going to have to live with a handsome scar smack down the middle of his head. Teens are so self-conscious anyway, why burden him with another unsightly scar at the throat? Give him time, he'll come to. Bart had started to breathe for himself for long periods of time—up to four hours. Of course he was always attached to the respirator by tubes snaked down his throat and nose, so if he stopped breathing on his own, the respirator would pick up the slack. To avoid the necessity of a trache, Bart would have to regain consciousness and be responsive to simple commands. Days and weeks went by without Bart reaching those twin milestones. Though he seemed unconscious most of the time, when doctors tortured him by repeatedly asking him to wiggle a finger if he could hear them, he finally managed a weak middle finger salute. I was very encouraged. Somewhere inside, Bart still had attitude. He'd need that to fight his way back. After three weeks in hospital, I confided my anxieties about the trache to Dr. Harter, especially the way the respiratory guy kept pushing for it. I'd guessed they needed the bed. Harter smiled and took me around the shoulders, assuring me, "It's Bart's bed as long as he needs it." What a guy!

One evening down in the main cafeteria for a coffee run I noticed a young woman in a jumpsuit with flight insignia on her shoulders. Curious, I asked if she'd been involved in Bart's rescue. She replied that she had indeed and was up to see him frequently, even helping transport him to CAT scans. She always tried to look in on her passengers. As she was a darkly beautiful Hispanic in her late twenties with a dazzling smile, I asked her if Bart had ever seen her, but she said he had always been unconscious. Only half-joking I told her to try to wake him up, since he'd be really glad to see her!

Dayle and I had never even heard of TBI before Bart's accident, but we were learning fast. Social workers handed us brochures and pamphlets, and we were flabbergasted to learn how often it occurs and its societal costs, to say nothing of its awful toll on victims and their families. Every twenty seconds, someone in the United States sustains a traumatic brain injury, defined as "a blow or jolt to the head or a penetrating head injury that disrupts brain functions." The severity of injuries ranges from mild to severe. Mild cases often involve a brief period of mental confusion or momentary loss of consciousness. Concussions at football games are typical examples. A severe injury involves an extended period of unconsciousness or amnesia, often resulting in short- or long-term challenges to independent functioning. Although TBI is not a household word, what it refers to is common as dirt. According to the Brain Injury Association of America, 1.7 million persons sustain a TBI every year in the United States. To get a sense of just how large that number is, consider that each year in the United States there are approximately 179,000 new cases of breast cancer, 44,000 new diagnosed cases of HIV/AIDS, 11,000 people who sustain traumatic spinal cord injuries, and 10,400 new cases of multiple sclerosis. The number of persons struck by all of those dreaded conditions combined constitutes less than one-sixth the incidence of TBI.

Of the more than million and a half new victims of TBI each year, 1.2 million are treated in emergency rooms and released, 235,000 require further hospitalization, and 50,000 of those die. The principal causes are falls (28 percent), motor vehicle accidents (20 percent), and assaults (11 percent). Increasingly, blasts are a leading cause of TBI for active duty military personnel, becoming the signature injury of our troops fighting overseas. Males are about 1.5 times as likely as females to sustain a TBI. The highest risk age groups are ages birth to four years old (falls) and fifteen- to nineteen-year-olds (vehicular accidents). Elderly people are particularly prone to falls. TBI is the leading cause of death and disability among teens, far outstripping drugs, suicides, and other causes combined. With Bart and Meredith representing auto accidents, Linda representing falls, and Manuel assaults, our little group in the NICU was a microcosm of the overall TBI population. 1.7 million TBIs a year! Joseph Stalin, not my favorite person, is believed to have said, "One death is a tragedy, a million deaths is a statistic." Every last one of those 1.7 million is someone like Bart or Meredith, Linda, or Manuel.

For the victims, especially those with severe injuries, TBI's effects are often profound and lasting. The Centers for Disease Control and Prevention estimates that over 5.4 million Americans currently have a long-term disability as a result of TBI. That's slightly more than 2 percent of the population! Since the brain is involved in so many functions, TBI can affect a person physically, cognitively, and emotionally. One may suffer memory loss, lack of concentration, reduced ability to process information, seizures, paralysis, vision problems or even loss of vision, migraines, loss of smell or taste or sensation, speech impairments, anxiety, impulsive behavior, depression and mood swings. You name it, TBI can foul it up. Victims are at increased risk of epilepsy, Alzheimer's disease, Parkinson's disease and other brain disorders, including subsequent TBIs. The estimated cost of these injuries and aftercare is over $48 billion per year. We felt like "greenies" in a strange new sinister world.

Twenty-nine days after Bart had first been put on a respirator Dr. Harter reluctantly concluded that keeping him on it longer risked permanent damage to his esophagus and voice box. It was time to pull the tubes out of his nose and throat. They would also need to insert a tube into his stomach for feeding, which would replace the intravenous drip. The trache would make it easier for Bart to cough up phlegm and for nurses to suction his lungs. Once the intravenous drip and respirator were gone, he would be ready for rehab. So Bart would face surgery again and be left with more unsightly scars. Worried and sad, we couldn't see a good alternative, so agreed to let them go ahead with the surgeries, which were considered quite routine. A general surgeon would do the stomach tube, or "peg" as the nurses called it, and the respiratory guy the trache. Dr. Harter would attend both procedures. Bart wasn't going under without Harter there to supervise. The peg insertion was scheduled for 1:00 p.m. and the trache for later the same day. The hour or so waiting while the peg was inserted was pure torture. Bart was still sedated when he returned from the operation, which was "pristine" according to a friendly resident doctor. When Bart stirred he was obviously uncomfortable—itching, scratching, coughing, and tearing at the neck brace with his good left hand. We waited through dinnertime and then early evening, growing steadily more anxious about the upcoming trache. Finally around 8:00 p.m. we collared our favorite neurological resident, Dr. Simon, and asked what was delaying Bart's surgery. It seemed Dr. Harter had been up the previous night for emergency surgery on an infant, and he had been in hospital ever since. Bart was "on deck" so long as Dr. Harter could stay awake. Harter's dedication and sheer endurance were the stuff of legends. Dayle quipped that it was small wonder he was so thin—he never had time to sit down to a decent meal, what with surgery often going on for eight hours or more at a clip. We both wondered how exactly he took bathroom breaks during all that time—the mysteries of medicine. Then all of sudden, Bart was wheeled to the elevators and swallowed up again. Before very long he was back, ventilator tubes attached right through his throat, below the neck. At least he was resting soundly. Dayle and I, racked with angst, kissed his sleepy head and left for home.

Next day Bart seemed more conscious and alert, seemingly watching a half hour or so of the Knicks game on TV, but refused to give Dayle eye contact, something she had grown to expect and count on. Perhaps he blamed Dayle for his condition; there was no way to know. It seems with TBI, as the medical staff frequently reminded us, it's never steady progress, but two steps forward, then one step back. There are periods of consolidation, and then no way to tell what to expect next. Kyle's parents, Debra and Randy Thompson, visited Bart, who managed to stay awake for nearly four hours straight—a record. When he became frustrated or disinterested in what was going on around him, he'd show his displeasure by pulling the sheet over his head. When Randy started to sob in the middle of talking to Bart, he was promptly dismissed with that silent but eloquent gesture. Though technically emerging from the coma, Bart continued to sleep at least twenty hours a day. Awake he was miserable, scratching at his neck brace and pulling at his tubes. After a month they finally removed his collar, having established by X-ray that there were no injuries south of his head. That was wonderful news. Responding to what became ceaseless tube pulling that threatened to undue the trache, the nurses put a Velcro restraint on Bart's left hand. When we were around, we undid the cuffs, and gently held his hand instead or diverted him away from the trache.

Westchester Medical Center had a large cadre of chaplains, with two of them, Rosemary and Ann, covering the NICU among other responsibilities.

They just seemed to connect with us naturally. Warm, loving persons, they had that special knack of giving comfort to weary desperate folks. It's a true gift, one at which I often marveled. I'd rather corner a rabid raccoon in the attic than have to comfort people struggling with grief, panic, and heartbreak. And they remained cheerful as well, which truly amazed me. I would be terrified in their shoes. Rosemary especially was a hands-on sort of chaplain, stopping by Bart's bedside to pray nearly every day. We ran into Ann or Rosemary in the halls, by the elevators, in the cafeteria—they seemed to be everywhere and were always glad to see us. They were great listeners—calm, steady, cheerful, the very soul of loving kindness. Some families eschewed the services of the chaplains, for whatever reason. I felt sorry for them, remembering the old adage, "God is speaking to you. Are you listening?"

5
The Fellowship Grows

The day after Linda died a new patient was rolled into the spot across from Bart. Though missing the usual harness of cables and tubes atop his head, there was something even odder about Griffey's appearance—the right half of his skull seemed to be completely caved in. Turned out the skull bone had been surgically removed to prevent massive swelling and the resulting pressure from killing him. The docs hoped to reattach it later. His wife, Dotty, a registered nurse, set up shop in an armchair next to his bed. Like my mother and sister, she was paranoid about hospitals and determined to "special" him around the clock. As far as I could tell, she never left his side except for necessities. We became close quickly in a NICU kind of way. Friendly and outgoing, she chatted up a storm, becoming our most reliable source of information about how Bart was doing after we left for the night, which was a great comfort. Only in his midforties, Griffey had suffered a massive stroke and was not given much chance of recovery. Unlike most NICU patients, he was conscious and could even speak a little, sometimes even responded to questions. His usual response was an upbeat, smiling "Yep!" It became his trademark. Dayle and I and even Cassidy at home took to answering questions with a loud "Yep." It was touching to see Griffey, so terribly stricken, keep a sharp eye on Bart. Dotty and Griffey both said that Bart was a fighter and was going to make it. Like other members of the fellowship, they would transfer to Helen Hayes Hospital for rehab, where we would spend months together. Dotty and Griffey joined Betty and David as Bart's guardian angels. Somehow, after hearing their voices for weeks while in coma, Bart felt very close to them all when he eventually began to wake up.

✦

Bart has charisma; he's so full of life that the place seems to resonate with his energy. He's the loudest, the funniest, also the most empathetic and generous. At barely a year old, we enrolled him in a Gymboree play class where one day a classmate hurt himself and was wailing away. Bart stumbled over to him and gently patted his back. The toddler's mother, struck by the empathetic gesture, quipped, "That's it. Bart will cheer you up, Alex." Bart has deep feelings, which he wears on his sleeve. Before the accident he would say, "Love you, fam," most every time the family went for a drive, and he always kissed Cassidy atop her head when he sat down to dinner. He was still easy to hug and kiss at sixteen. But cross him and he was implacable. A couple of teachers had made his shitlist, and he hated them with relish, harping on them until it drove us crazy. This trait of not letting go, which we later learned is called perseveration, became much worse after the brain injury.

✦

Finally the big day—Bart's transfer to rehab—was at hand—January 31, a month and two days after the accident. Though barely conscious for a few hours each day, with the trache in place to assure his breathing, he was ready to begin the process that promised to return him to life. The doctors, nurses, aides—everyone—claimed that rehab was the "happy valley" that could bring him back. Naturally we were thrilled and a little apprehensive. Could the change of venue really work miracles? There's always the nagging doubt about the devil you don't know. We'd heard the program there was like boot camp, with therapies all day long—speech, physical, occupational, recreational—therapies everyday, some twice a day. It was hard to imagine Bart, still in a dream state, mute and bedridden, with his right side practically lifeless, coping with such an ambitious workload. But there he was going, ready or not. I went to work that morning, since he would be in transition all day. First there was a lengthy discharge from WMC, then an ambulance ride to Helen Hayes Hospital for admission. Dayle stayed at WMC waiting to follow him over the Hudson River to his new home. Now he'd be on the west side, "our" side of the Hudson, and only an hour and a half from home. I kept in touch by phone with Dayle throughout the day. As usual there were problems with our medical insurance coverage. The insurance company held up the transfer for several hours until they could get preauthorization, an all-too-familiar snafu. We'd given all our information to the social workers at both hospitals days earlier and received assurances that the move was preapproved. I had taken the precaution of checking directly with both the insurance company and the hospital to make sure that Helen Hayes participated in our plan. After an agitating day, especially for Dayle, Bart was ensconced in the trache room at rehab.

Just fifteen minutes prior to his transfer from WMC, Chaplain Rosemary found Bart, who was on his gurney waiting for the ambulance to Helen Hayes. She'd meant to stop in earlier and pray for him as part of her daily routine, but had missed him in the predischarge shuffle. Of late, she'd taken to singing an old Greek hymn that she'd recently recalled, forgotten since childhood, whenever she spent time with Bart. As she took his hand and began to sing softly and pray, she experienced something ineffable, as if Bart were praying *with* her even in the coma. Though impossible to clearly explain, it was a defining moment in her ministry. Ever since, she's felt a special connection with Bart, who she believes taught her how to hear the prayers of persons in coma, a knack that's proved invaluable in her work. She still prays daily "with" Bart. A couple of years later, Bart met Chaplain Rosemary—for the first time as far as he was concerned—and she wept to see and hear him up and about. Astonished, he quipped in typical Bart fashion, "I have that effect on women."

6
The Circle of Prayer

What began as a request for prayers from friends and family grew into a circle of well-wishers of all types and faiths, spanning the globe. Our friend Caroline had hosted several foreign guest students and we soon began to get e-mails from a Buddhist monastery somewhere near the India-Tibet border, informing us that on Bart's behalf, prayer wheels were spinning in the foothills of the Himalayas. A Muslim friend in New York City promised that his mosque would pray for Bart regularly. Aunts and uncles were saying regular prayers at their synagogues, as well as arranging for special prayers on Bart's behalf to be inserted into the Wailing Wall in Jerusalem. Chasidim were contacted and their rabbis enlisted in the effort, informing us that their prayers were best made using his Hebrew name. Bart is a tough name to translate into Hebrew, but together we found an approximation. Our kids were raised Greek Orthodox, and Greek friends in the United States and Greece pulled out all the stops. Never one to be outdone, Bart's godfather sent relics from their most sacred monastery at Mount Athos. Dayle's cousin arranged for Catholic nuns in western Canada to say a healing mass for Bart every week. My brother enlisted an evangelical church down south as well as a pair of prominent psychic healers, Ricky and Gail Kriesberg, to work on Bart's behalf. He also wrote a very moving poem. A college football coach in New Jersey who also ministers at a Baptist church brought his Newark congregation into the circle. A former coworker, an emeritus minister of a Baptist church in Harlem, weighed in with his congregation.

There was more. Bart's godmother, very active in Alcoholics Anonymous, enlisted her entire chapter in the good work. Before we knew it, prayer circles at every church in or around town were including Bart. We often learned of this by chance. An acquaintance would call about Bart, saying he had heard of Bart's accident from the pulpit at a church we'd never heard of. Some of our friends from Camp Mujigae are members of local Korean churches and they spread word to sister churches in Korea. Likewise our adoption agency lent a hand in spreading the news. To this day we occasionally bump into complete strangers who have prayed for Bart. On a visit to the local state college in town to inquire of the special education department about a companion to pal around with Bart on weekends, the department chair asked me when Bart's accident had occurred. When I replied that at Christmas it would be two years, she smiled and exclaimed, "Why I've been praying for your son all along." As near as I could figure, Bart had played basketball with a boy from her church. The boy's dad was a deacon. And so the circle of love spread. A business friend's Haitian secretary brought her Voodoo congregation aboard.

As a long-time volunteer and board member at the local YMCA, I called Jack Young, the executive director, to ask for a leave of absence or to offer my resignation from the board if need be. He declined my resignation but passed along a request for prayer to the board and staff of the Y. Of course the chaplains we met in our journey through the hospitals all became very involved with Bart and prayed for him daily, often at his bedside. Other members of an informal fellowship whom we gradually met and befriended during our time in and around hospitals included Hindus, Muslims, Christians, and Jews. We all prayed for each other. That first night of the accident our friend Duffy held an all-night prayer vigil, lighting candles to help him focus. He lit a candle for Bart everyday for years, joking that he wished he held stock in the candle company. Dayle's cousin, an astrophysicist, decided to pray for Bart. Well known as a freethinker, he wrote that he had chosen to be an optimistic agnostic.

There is no way to measure the effect of such prayerfulness. Dayle and I were deeply moved by the outpouring of love for Bart and our family. Especially in the darkest moments, we felt supported and comforted. Without faith our ongoing ordeal would have been too bleak and unbearable. At times it felt as if prayer was the only resource we had. Bart himself seems to have been moved, showing remarkable inner strength and a positive attitude, with hardly a trace of bitterness or self-pity. For a teenage firecracker like Bart to bear up so well under what has seemed to him like endless heartbreak was a small miracle that we attributed partly to prayer.

7
Helen Hayes

Helen Hayes Hospital was a relief after the horror of the NICU. Nestled atop a hill overlooking the Hudson River in sleepy West Haverstraw, New York, the hospital is reputed to be one of the finest rehabilitation facilities in the nation. Named after its great benefactor, the actress Helen Hayes, it has the ambiance of a fine private institution, although it's actually operated by the State of New York. Rehab is different from acute care. The feeling and pace are almost leisurely. Nobody seems stressed out. In fact the staff was downright friendly, relaxed, even jovial. Perhaps most striking was the layout and decor—immaculate spacious rooms adorned with pictures, drawings, and displays of photos and cards. Patients were given bulletin boards, which were crowded with all sorts of memorabilia from life at home. A sweet young aide was posted to watch Bart so he didn't remove his trache or stomach tube. The restraints that had often been attached to Bart's good left hand for the same purpose in NICU were conspicuously absent. They were inconsistent with HHH's philosophy of rehabilitation. We were very impressed and relieved.

Ensconced in his wonderful new digs, surrounded by a virtual shrine of pictures and cards from home, Bart was still fundamentally in awful shape. That fact was driven home with shocking power when Dayle and I came to visit next morning. Though apparently conscious, he shrank from us, wild eyes blazing with paranoia but no apparent recognition. We tried to offer him some comfort and company, our hearts full to bursting. It was a true low point, almost as bad as the early days. Whatever wishful thinking we had engaged in (which was quite a lot really) evaporated in the teeth of this hard new reality. Obviously it would take more than a change of scene to coax Bart from this waking coma.

Especially frightening to us, Bart seemed to be regressing, losing even the faint, wavering signs of alertness that had fed our hopes. We badgered the attending neurologist, who finally agreed to try a spinal tap to relieve the cranial pressure somewhat. It resulted in increased alertness, which faded rapidly and was entirely gone within a day. Was the dread ICP building up again in his skull? Was this hydrocephalus? Was it just a reaction to a change of place? No satisfactory answers ever emerged.

Bart was very much in a waking coma, a condition we had never heard or dreamed of previously. He often seemed to be awake, but was mostly unresponsive to verbal or visual cues. He was sensitive to pain, as evidenced by his tearful grimace when nurses administered daily injections of blood anticoagulant directly into his abdomen. Watching his silent scream was horrible. The shots were meant to counteract the dangerous effects of being bedridden long-term. Later, when he began learning to walk again, the physical therapist offered him a carrot—if he could take a hundred steps, they would stop giving him the shots.

We had no idea what he could see, but suspected double vision, a common side effect of serious head injuries, one that usually clears up over time. He often put his good arm across his face in a way that covered his left eye. When we could get him to watch TV, he invariably covered one eye. Nurses remarked, "Oh, he's probably got double vision," but no one knew for sure. There was no way to ask him, since with trache tube in place, Bart could not speak. Asking him to write down answers was out of the question. We were warned that he might not be able to speak even after the trache was removed, since aphasia, or brain-based muteness, was fairly common with this sort of injury. Meanwhile he mostly didn't seem to understand, follow, or even pay attention when we spoke to him. Physically, his left hand was quite active, often playing with his trache or stomach tube, or the tube to his urine bag. He kept us all hopping trying to discourage such fiddling. But the fiddling, agitating as it was for us, seemed like the sort of thing our Barty boy would do anyway. Sometimes the nurses would have to be summoned to reinsert or reattach the tubes. They often got a spray of urine or stomach contents for their trouble.

Bart was not serene. His left leg would restlessly toss around, especially when he was asleep, seemingly trying to wake up his right leg. Though he sometimes could move his whole right arm from one resting place to another, he didn't seem able to do anything with his right hand, which hung limply. Over several weeks his limp right hand froze into a permanent clench. The staff said that was tone built up in the muscles. It was controlled by the brain, and there was nothing for it. Most agonizingly by far, there was just no way of knowing what he was thinking or feeling about anything, though we could sense in some unspoken ways that he was frightened, angry, and sad. Who wouldn't be, with needles jabbed into your stomach while you lay helpless and mute? Hell, he probably had only the foggiest idea of what was happening to him. The docs assured us that he would never recall the accident or aftermath, and it turns out they were right.

Reading through brochures obtained from social workers and nurses, along with some online reading and conversations with the New York Brain Injury Association, we began to get a clearer picture of what Bart was probably experiencing and of what we might look forward to. Most patients follow a general pattern of recovery after a severe brain injury, although there are wide variations, and not everyone recovers fully, or at all. Healing may progress through four stages.

Stage one, colloquially referred to as a coma, is well established in the public imagination. The patient is unresponsive. There may be some reflexive, random movements of the limbs for no apparent reason. During stage two, early responses, the patient starts to respond to things that are happening to him, but responses are inconsistent or slow. The patient may turn toward a sound, follow something with his eyes, or pull away from something hurtful. Early responses may include following simple commands, such as gripping and releasing hands or sticking out the tongue. Upon arrival at Helen Hayes, Bart was still categorized as stage two.

The next stage is called agitated and confused—a label that promised cold comfort. While responding to cues more consistently, the patient will be confused about his or her whereabouts and about what is happening. Memory and behavior problems are common. Confusion often leads to screaming, cursing, biting, or striking out. Although unnerving, this difficult stage is a step toward recovery. Finally, at stage four, higher-level responses, the patient can complete routine tasks without difficulty, but still has issues with problem solving and making judgments and decisions. Patients may not understand their own limitations and may place themselves in danger. They seem more like themselves, yet there may be personality changes. Novel or stressful situations likely will be hard to manage. There are a near-infinite number of shades and degrees of all of these stages, especially the final one, which often take years to work through. Many patients never make it all the way. Some reach stage four but their responses remain automatic rather than spontaneous and natural. We'd leaf through the booklets during the long hours in hospital trying to imagine what these stages really meant for Bart—how we'd handle them, how long they'd last, how fully he'd come back, how changed he might be at the end of the line.

Around Bart we kept up a lighthearted, upbeat pose, relating events from home, doings at school, news events, especially of his beloved Knicks who were having an awful season, the first of many. We got a book of jokes and read aloud to him, along with daily Bible readings and rereadings of letters and cards from friends and relatives. My sister sent a teddy bear, which we named Giggles. Giggles often laughed hysterically at readings from the joke book. Repetition is essential with brain injury. Before long I knew long Bible passages by heart. My favorite was Isaiah chapter 40, the part that says, "Even the youths shall faint and be weary, and the young men shall utterly fall. But they that wait upon the Lord shall renew their strength. They shall mount up with wings, as eagles. They shall run and not be weary." I couldn't tell if Bart heard or comprehended the words, but they comforted me, and I hoped that at some level they reached him too.

Our fellowship expanded again at Helen Hayes. "Scoobie," a young man with profound injuries, occupied the bed directly across from Bart. He and Bart shared the same birthday, so somehow we felt especially close to him and his family. Originally from Pakistan via Guyana, his young wife and two preschool-age children, his mother and father, and brother-in-law kept a constant vigil around his bed. Large Arabic prayer banners draped his bed and wall. His brother-in-law related how Scoobie, barely twenty-five and faced with mounting family and business responsibilities, had decided to sell his beloved motorcycle as part of a more grown-up lifestyle. The day the buyer was due to come over and take possession, Scoobie and friends had decided to take one last spin for old time's sake. He'd crashed his bike at high speed and been taken to a local hospital in Connecticut rather than to a level one trauma center like

Westchester Med. Extensive neurosurgery followed, but the damage was so massive that his brain was effectively "mashed." He was not expected to regain consciousness, but with a trache in place had been shipped off to rehab. The sight of his little children, hardly more than babies, trying to get their dad's attention and recognition was pitiful. Scoobie's mother and wife were both very beautiful, their quiet sadness and dignity making them even more so.

In the bed alongside Bart was Joe Milano, a rotund, jovial Italian paterfamilias with a gaggle of children and grandchildren practically always around. He had suffered both a stroke and heart attack, so was in very precarious health, but was conscious and could even speak. A man's man, he became very fond of Bart, saying he was a "real thoroughbred, always kicking around in his bed like a high-strung stallion." Blessed with a fine sense of humor and warm loving nature, he enjoyed the unstinting devotion of his huge family. A couple of times when he had panic attacks, his grown daughter would climb into bed with him and he'd fall asleep in her arms with a smile on his face. After a few weeks, he was well enough to graduate from the trache room to a semi-private room down the hall. In the brain recovery wing, only patients in the trache room were allotted a full-time dedicated RN who was stationed around the clock in the room. We missed Joe and his wife, Jan, so much that we would wheel Bart down to visit with them daily. Although still mute, Bart knew that they loved him and was always eager to visit.

Joe Milano's old bed was soon filled by Siri, a twenty-three-year-old biochemist who had mysteriously been struck down by an aneurism in her brain stem, leaving her mostly paralyzed though fully alert. Her husband, Pavan, and her parents were constantly by her bedside. I could see the exhaustion and bewilderment on their faces when they first wheeled her into the room, so I went over to introduce myself. Her dad, shaking my hand like a pump handle, repeatedly said, "Hello, I am Rob. I'm from India." I thought that an odd thing to say and chuckled to Dayle later that he must be a little paranoid about being taken for Pakistani, it being only a few months after the September 11th terrorist attacks. Later we learned from Pavan, who spoke better English, that his in-laws had just that afternoon stepped off the plane from India and taken a cab directly to the hospital. Rob was literally from India. They were wonderfully devoted parents who stayed at their daughter's side for the next five months. We all became close friends. Being surrounded by so much tragic loss, especially in young people like Scoobie, Siri, and their families, brought to mind the ancient wisdom commending us to be kind, since most everyone you meet is fighting a hard fight. When Meredith and her folks showed up a few days later, and then Griffey and Dotty to boot, the brain unit at Helen Hayes really felt like a big family.

8
Boot Camp

It was small wonder that the rehab program at Helen Hayes was nicknamed boot camp. You might be in a waking coma, but there was no lazing about in bed dreaming your life away. Patients were up early, fed, dressed, and working in therapy by 9:00 a.m. There were three morning sessions—physical, occupational, and then finally speech therapy. In the afternoon, the grueling cycle was repeated again. Initial goals for Bart were quite modest. After a month flat on your back, you can't just pop up and walk. In physical therapy the goal was to get him sitting up in a specialized wheelchair. To accustom him to an upright position, there was a tilt table. He'd be strapped to it and then gradually raised from horizontal to vertical. Occupational therapy focused on getting him to respond consistently to simple requests. Since he couldn't speak with his trache, the speech therapist worked on assessing his readiness to speak, his management of secretions, the condition of the flesh around the trache, which is prone to infection, and getting a handle on his ability to understand speech. Worrying about relatively small things like the condition of his trache diverted our attention, helping us to avoid worrying about the less manageable big picture.

We usually arrived at the hospital at lunchtime, so that we wouldn't distract Bart from his work. Even in his dreamlike state, parents on deck were a distraction. By lunchtime he was utterly exhausted from the morning's sessions. As long as the trache was in place, his meals remained predigested fluids siphoned through the stomach tube. We noticed rapid and alarming weight loss, as if he were disappearing before our very eyes. Formerly a strapping 180 plus pounds, he barely tipped 138 when they weighed him on a device similar to a deli scale. We were really worried, badgering nurses and orderlies to give him extra cans of nutrients, to stop the wasting away. He stabilized and even gained a couple of pounds, but he still looked like a stick figure. Bart's energy level was extremely low, especially unnerving in a boy who had been just shy of hyperactive. He tired so easily that therapy sessions were often cut short, since a therapist could step away for a moment only to return and find Bart soundly dozing. The doctors prescribed Ritalin to increase alertness and energy. Routinely prescribed to calm down hyperactive kids, the drug apparently has the opposite affect on severely brain-injured people. His endurance increased and he was somewhat less likely to fall off at the drop of a hat.

Wheeling Bart about in his chair, stick-thin legs out front, head floppy style, spittle dribbling down his mouth, was hard to take. But we assured ourselves and him that he'd be up and at 'em soon, though his right side remained stubbornly unresponsive. During lunch break the therapists would leave the large therapy room where most of the hard work took place and brief us on daily doings. They were wonderfully dedicated young women, and very fond of Bart. His physical therapist, Shawn, "the Jewish girl with an Irish name," really connected with him. Her job was to get him walking. Progress was slow going and not too encouraging. The neurologist in charge cautioned us to keep our expectations low in light of the severity of Bart's injuries. We took an instant dislike to him, sensing that he was just going through the motions, not really interested in Bart as a person. Some of the other families felt similarly. It seemed that patients were pretty much just grist for his mill. Remarkably, the nurses and therapists all worshiped him as the most brilliant man they'd ever met. Just shows you that professionals and laypeople often have an entirely different perspective.

The social worker left a note asking us to visit her, explaining that the no-fault insurance money had been exhausted at Westchester Medical and that our private insurance would be completely depleted after sixty days of rehabilitation. We would need to file for Medicaid on Bart's behalf to cover the additional anticipated medical costs. I was astounded. We spent almost $10,000 per year in premiums for health insurance, yet the plan wasn't going to nearly cover the necessary expenses. Seems the plan had a lifetime cap for rehab benefits—with the cap set well below what can be anticipated in the event of serious TBI. I was pissed. Medical insurance is great unless you really need it, then forget about it! Fuming, I learned from the rest of the fellowship that everyone was in this same lousy boat. It felt like the social worker was really more of a bursar's agent; her main concern seemed to be seeing to it that the hospital's bills got paid. Somehow the title social worker had suggested something more compassionate. On top of everything else, her office hours were remarkably restricted (apparently due to budgetary cutbacks) so that it practically seemed like she was available every other Wednesday and Friday between the hours of 3:00 p.m. and 3:15 p.m. If you were looking for advice or solace in wading through the vast medical bureaucracy, you'd have to look elsewhere. Passing by her closed door everyday, festooned with upbeat aphorisms and cartoons, I felt a little bitter and disappointed, but smiled, remembering the song from *My Fair Lady* that declares that God expects us to help our neighbor, but "with a little bit o' luck, when he comes around you won't be home." My sister Judi, a retired head nurse, had some useful advice about Medicaid and related issues.

9
Sadness or Euphoria

Sometime during our first month at Helen Hayes the adrenaline finally ran out. Dayle and I had been on a fight-or-flight footing. We hadn't seemed to need much sleep or food and lost weight so effortlessly that we joked that we didn't need no stinkin' special diets—we had the "Anxiety Diet," which magically melted pounds away. Now ebbing adrenaline was replaced by exhaustion that swept over us irresistibly. Weariness, both physical and psychological, settled in just as we were realizing that we were in for a very long haul. Up until then we were in a hard battle, but now it dawned on me that we faced a long drawn-out war of attrition. I've always been a military history buff. No sooner had I gotten my first car at seventeen, than a friend and I took a road trip to Gettysburg to carefully retrace, step by step, the three days of that great battle. I'm ashamed to say I even stole a rock as a souvenir from the breastworks around Cushing's battery, where Pickett's men and the Confederacy reached their high tide.

Unlike the Civil War, TBI wars have no decisive battles. Instead they are protracted contests of endurance - daily grinds, some agonizing, most just tedious. There's never a cease-fire or armistice. You may wake up feeling under the weather, or like sleeping in, or a little blue, but rise and answer the call to arms just the same. No metaphor is perfect. We weren't literally at war, but it felt in many ways the moral equivalent. A battle, even a long one, is too short of duration and too immediate to represent the struggle with TBI. Wars, on the other hand, may go on for years and involve many disparate campaigns, often fought on different fronts simultaneously. There are usually noncombatants and allies, always enemies, and, of course, casualties. We were very grateful for our friends in the fellowship, who made "campaigning" more tolerable. Yet at quiet times driving home at night from the hospital, we often felt very alone. Other folks, busy rushing home from work, maybe chasing the almighty buck, or relaxing with a friend, or whatever else, cannot possibly understand this long, lonely way. Gradually, with time and experience of many others besieged with TBI or struggling with autism, cerebral palsy, mental illness, and other lifelong challenges, my perspective changed. I understood that there are plenty of folks with hard rows to hoe, seemingly invisible—to find them just knock on any door. Still, there were mornings when I'd have given anything to roll over and hide in bed all day, or even better, to have a shot at a decisive battle, do-or-die, to finally best the enemy or die trying.

An extrovert first and last, Bart no sooner learned to wheel himself about in his chair than he became the nurses' constant companion. Parked mutely by the nurses' station in the trache room he watched everything that transpired—as medications were dispensed, phone calls taken, visitors briefed. If a nurse attended a patient at bedside, Bart rolled right along—though he sometimes was ejected for privacy reasons. A simple device was rigged to keep him from leaving the trache room. An adjustable vertical pole attached to the back of his wheelchair could be raised to a height higher than the doorjamb. Bart would periodically make a break for it, only to find his way blocked by the crashing pole. With his short-term memory terribly impaired, he'd make for the hills again and again every few minutes.

After a couple of weeks he was allowed to roam outside the trache room, and soon the entire north wing of the fourth floor—the neuro-rehab wing—became his domain, with the main nurses' station, centrally located just outside the trache room, his favorite hangout. He'd roll through the swinging doors and plant himself closest to the action. As one of only a handful of youngsters in the wing (the vast majority of patients were older stroke victims), he was a favorite of the nurses, orderlies, aides, and most patients. When the nurses made their evening rounds, Bart tagged along to help. Many patients came to expect him and wondered aloud if ever he missed rounds. Always a party monster, even in his mute state Bart had a friendly, expressive face. A shadow of his old self, he still exuded something that reached people at a gut level:

youth, humor, and playfulness. Patients remarked what a sweet a kid he was. Of course many people were moved by seeing a young fellow dealing with such a crushing injury.

One old lady especially, Margery, seemed to come to life, beaming whenever Bart rolled by. She had been easing out of her car seat when she was struck by a passing vehicle and fell on her head. Tragically, her son had predeceased her and her only other living relative, a cousin, lived in California. No one ever visited, so we all tried to keep an eye on her. She was a lovely, dignified old lady, seemingly stuck at stage three—agitated and confused. She sometimes claimed that Bart and she were to be wed when they "got out of this place." Frequently she would carry on imaginary conversations with her son. Once, in a moment of apparent lucidity, she yelled at some nurses working on Bart, "What the hell's the matter with you? Can't you see he's just trying to get his life back?" We were stunned. The next moment she was lost again in private reverie.

Boot camp ended each day around 3:00 or 4:00 p.m., and the trache room filled with patients, families, and visitors. There was a good deal of socializing, as we'd check on other members of the fellowship and catch up with their families. Meredith's dad, David, reluctantly accepted that his marine helicopter unit was shipping off to Iraq without him. With Meredith still not out of the woods, his commanding officer had ordered him to stay behind. That order proved a boon to both Meredith and Bart, since he had a wonderful sense of humor and knack for motivating young people. Before long he had Bart playing catch with the small beanbag from occupational therapy. We were thrilled that Bart could manage to catch the bag with his left hand. David even organized wheelchair races for the young patients. Bart, wheeling with only his left hand, was not a strong contestant, but David didn't take no for an answer. If I had tried to get Bart to race around the wing, he'd have sulked and refused. But he followed David's lead, trusting David from the early days.

Each night as we prepared to leave, we'd roll a large-screen TV/VCR unit to the foot of Bart's bed and set up one of his favorite movies. He's always loved films and had a large collection of videos at home. Although we'd brought in a bunch to select from, he invariably chose *The Matrix* or *X-Men*. We learned from the nurses that he usually drifted off to sleep within a half hour of our departure.

✦

Raised in an orphanage, Mary Graves, venerable founder of Love the Children adoption agency, dedicated her life to finding "forever homes" for others. Mary had forgotten more than most people ever knew about adopted kids, and she warned us to expect a period of depression when Bart arrived home. After all, he'd been rudely uprooted from his foster family only hours earlier, arriving at JFK "a stranger in a strange land." To our relief, baby Bart seemed to hit the ground running. In the video of his arrival at the airport lounge, he seems a little jet-lagged but curious and ready to play. By the time we got home a few hours later he was showing definite signs of eagerness to party and soon earned a reputation as a party animal.

Videos made over the next couple of years—and there were plenty as befits a first child—often show him dancing, snapping fingers over his head, smiling, laughing, and generally being the life of the party. He was gregarious, enjoying all kinds of people, including old folks. His foster mother was an elderly grandmother, and he had slept for months on floor mats alongside five or six of her family members. He thrived on different people's company so much that Dayle and I sometimes quipped, "If you can't be with the one you love, then love the one you're with." But if you assumed, in the absence of outward signs of depression, that he had no strong feelings of attachment to his foster mother, you'd be dead wrong. His feelings were intense, but buried deeply and not easily expressed. We began to appreciate this better when at eight months of age he was learning to wave bye-bye. Though a quick learner and always eager to entertain, he flat out refused to wave. If pushed to do so by grandparents or other well-meaning relatives, he'd bawl. This eccentric behavior went on for years. We just got used to the fact that Bart wouldn't wave or in any other way say good-bye, not even casually. Once, his grandparents admonished six-year-old Bart about this lack of good manners and he blurted out, "If I say bye-bye, you might die." The grandfolks just thought that a peculiar thing to say, but we discerned something deeper lurking behind his stubbornness. When he was twelve, as we were leaving him in his bunkhouse at Frost Valley YMCA for a first time at sleepaway camp, Bart whispered, "So long," as we kissed him good-bye. It was a first.

Adopted kids are special; their feelings of loss run deep—the loss of a biological mother and family and of an original life, real or imagined. Not every child reacts as Bart did, since he felt more strongly than most about practically everything. Whatever void Bart felt was partially filled by Cassidy, his snow angel.

Some things about our children we only learned because of the accident and its aftermath. Bart and Cassidy knew how to keep secrets as only siblings do, and they knew how to keep a united front against the common enemy. But Cassidy shared some secrets with us while Bart was in hospital, probably as a way of keeping his presence alive. She also began to listen to rap music and to crave some his favorite foods, pouring salt on them just as he had. It was touching to see her unconsciously aping him. The year of the accident they had been taking the same school bus for the first time ever, something they had both been excited about. A sixth grader just entering middle school, Cassidy was riding the same bus as the high schoolers. Elementary school children were on a later schedule and so took separate buses. While Dayle and I thought they were riding the bus together, it turned out the reality was a little different. Cassidy waited for the bus alone at the end of the driveway, as Bart watched like a hawk from the porch, smoking a cigarette. After she was safely aboard, he'd duck back inside, take a quick shower, and be out in time to be picked up by a friend driving to school. The story made perfect sense. Bart was always alert to ways of creatively skirting the rules. At the same time, he'd never dream of letting his little sister wait for the bus by herself in the dark. He was, if anything, excessively protective. I asked Cassidy if Bart had told her to keep this arrangement secret. He had not.

A month after arriving at Helen Hayes, Dayle took Bart for a spin around the wing, stopping in to see Joe and Jan Milano and several other regulars. Parking him in front of the TV in the small lounge, she excused herself to visit the bathroom just down the hall. When she returned, Bart's sneakers were right where she had last seen them, but Bart wasn't in them. Somewhat anxiously, she retraced her steps back around the ward, which is triangular in shape, with the nurses' station in the center. Bart was nowhere to be found, so she hurriedly enlisted the staff, who put out a full all-points bulletin. Heart in her mouth, Dayle raced around the floor, catching up with Bart a couple of minutes later. He had wheeled to the other end of the building, where he was doggedly trying to open a stairwell door. It was a real scare, yet every time she retold the story and came to the part where she spied Bart's sneakers, neatly placed in the TV room, but no Bart, we always cracked up hysterically. Our lives took on a schizoid quality—one moment in panic, sadness, or anger, the very next moment hysterical laughter, or dancing the tarantella over some small improvement in Bart's condition. A working title for this book was *Either Sadness or Euphoria,* which pretty much sums up the tempo of life with TBI. After his attempted breakout, the nurses installed an electronic alarm under Bart's chair. If he started through the wing's exits, it set off a shrieking siren. On our weekend tours around the hospital grounds, we'd occasionally forget to turn it off. After jumping out of our skins, we'd have a good laugh.

10
Picking Oats from Manure

My father-in-law spent nearly four years of World War II in the India-Burma theater as an army air corps recon photographer. Although extremely reluctant to speak of his war experience (his plane was shot down twice), he did nevertheless share an image that has stuck with me like a cocklebur. He recalled starving beggars intently following the leisurely amblings of sacred cows. With every new dropping they would scramble to dig any undigested oats from the fresh steaming pies. That image has always served as a metaphor for making the best of meager things, for finding something worthwhile in the most unpromising situations. Our habitual dread was lightened by the occasional "oat" that fell onto our path.

Dayle returned one night from Helen Hayes Hospital with a nasty black and blue mark on her right upper arm, whispering to me that Bart, apparently hallucinating, had thrashed out, seized her with his strong left arm, refusing to let go. She was only extricated with the timely intervention of a couple of aides. We agreed that Cass's planned weekend visit was best postponed until after Bart was in his right mind. At dinner I gently explained to Cassidy that her brother, in his state of confusion, might accidentally hurt her, so she would have to wait awhile before visiting him again. We'd let her know when it was safe.

"What?" she said as if she hadn't heard right. I slowly repeated myself, only to hear her burst out, "I'm going. I don't care if he hurts me. To hurt me he'll have to touch me, and that means he'll know I'm there." Meeting only stunned silence on my part, she repeated doggedly, "I'm going." I was overwhelmed. Was that my sweet, shy, mild baby girl? We both wept as I quietly agreed. "Yes, of course you're going." After all, how can one resist the power of love, fearless and sublime? Although he stared at her long and hard without any apparent recognition, a response that badly rattled poor Cassidy, Bart never hurt or in any way threatened his snow angel.

11
Don Bosco

Is there anyone so secure in faith, or so lacking imagination, that they have never doubted whether God is a loving father who cares for his children? He certainly seems to show his love in strange ways, with so much suffering in the world, most often falling on the innocent. I don't pretend to have an answer to this theological puzzle, though I have struggled with it. They say that God is a mystery that we can never fully understand, but must in the end accept on faith, or not. Someone told me that the nearest way to get our arms around our relationship with God is the following metaphor. Anyone who's ever had a beloved pet dog knows what it's like to love a creature rather strikingly different from us and to be loved quite unconditionally in return. We may be sure that old Ranger loves us and that we reciprocate, without supposing that he really understands our innermost thoughts and nature. Ranger doesn't know whether we're Republican or Democrat, pious or atheist, bookish or ignorant, what we think about baseball's designated hitter rule, or a thousand and one other things by which we define ourselves. While our dog's understanding of us is quite primitive, the bond of love between us is none less real. In this doubtless unflattering metaphor, we are the primitives, and God the higher being to whom we are bound through love, but whom we hardly begin to understand. I wouldn't want to press this metaphor too hard, but it has helped me sometimes.

Like when I encountered another anguished parent, wheeling her chair-bound child around the HHH grounds. Roughly Bart's age, Steve was speechless, barely responsive, periodically chirping and screeching incoherently. His mother asked furtively about the pending visit of Father Sudac, a renowned healer, mystic, and stigmatic believed to cure even hopeless cases. Dayle, Cassidy, and I were planning to attend his healing service at Don Bosco's retreat, down the road from the hospital. We'd already been to see the old Italian priest at Don Bosco's, leaving him a large picture of Bart and receiving his promise to hand it to the stigmatic for his blessing. Steve's mother confessed that she was not Catholic, and had no faith left. She hated doctors, distrusted priests, and didn't know where to turn. Her son had been trapped like this for years and years, with little or no improvement. Who was I to tell her to believe in the face of such hopeless tragedy? Should she go, she asked. Helpless, I told her, "Well, I don't see how it could hurt." Why should my son get better and hers languish? Because I pray, and she doesn't? Is her son less worthy of God's tender mercy than Bart? At such times it's painfully obvious that God is unfathomable.

✦

Croatian Catholic priest, mystic, bearer of all five marks of the stigmata, Father Zlatko Sudac was coming to Don Bosco's retreat in Stony Point, barely a mile up the hill from Helen Hayes Hospital. His visit caused a bit of a stir around the hospital, where many patients and families faced desperate fights. Carrying pictures of several patients who could not make it to church or send representatives, we arrived two hours before the healing mass was scheduled to begin, hoping for good seats. To our surprise, the large parking lot was jammed, and we had to park a quarter mile down the road. The retreat's church, no larger than a small parish church, was standing room only. We threaded our way about halfway down the left aisle finding a place to stand against the outer wall. The local priests were leading the assemblage in rounds of Hail Marys and the Lord's Prayer. We joined in for what must have been scores of repetitions, as the church, already jam-packed, continued to fill. After another hour or so, we were pressed literally cheek by jowl. The repetitive chanting from thousands of voices had an almost hypnotic effect, especially in what was becoming a sweltering mass of humanity. Someone pointed out that there were twice as many people gathered out front of the church, where loudspeakers had been rigged. We were so closely packed that one could hardly shift one's weight, and Cassidy complained that her feet hurt, asking plaintively when we could go home.

As the appointed hour approached, to our astonishment, a couple of very large women waded through the crowd, toward the front pews, which were reserved for the handicapped. They literally ploughed slowly through the tangled mass of supplicants, like icebreakers through a frozen artic sea. I thought it impossible for them to pass, but pass they did, pressing us all hard against the church walls. When they reached the closely packed pew, they simply sat on top of whoever was already seated. People spilled off the pew at both ends. Dayle and I looked at each other in dumb amazement. If it had been a movie theater, there would have been a riot, but stunned supplicants, on their best church-going behavior, simply yielded to the heavy-handed barbarity. I was musing on the remarkable spectacle of these obese ladies and their bizarre notion of Christian behavior when Father Sudac slipped quietly onto the platform.

Barely thirty, thin, with long flowing black hair and a full beard, he appeared to me rather Christlike. Although he understood English, he chose to speak through an interpreter. I suppose he spoke Croatian; it sounded very Russian-like. Speaking softly but confidently, he assured us that we did not need priests or the church to find God's healing power. Nor did we need him. The priests seated behind him on the stage seemed to squirm in their seats slightly as he spoke. He went on to say that we need only open ourselves to love—love that is all around us, in nature and in ourselves. He gave several down-to-earth illustrations from everyday life. God is love and keeps the world together. Yes, we'd rejoice and join together to ask for healing, since coming together is good, but the main thing is to throw off our indifference, let down our defenses, and admit love into our lives. He went on to ask God to heal those in pain, illness, and suffering; thanked us; blessed us; and was gone. I was deeply moved, my heart filled to the brim.

We'd been standing still in dress shoes for over three and a half hours. Cassidy said later that she wanted to run out of church screaming, she was so miserably tired, so numb that she hadn't been able to hear Father Sudac's words. The service ended around 11:30 p.m. Dayle and Cassidy took communion that was offered at three or four spots just outside the church, and we left, utterly blitzed. Cassidy caused a small ruckus when taking the communion wafer from her mouth, she asked, "What's this?" Greek Orthodox communion is served with delicious thick, challah bread, and she'd never seen or tasted the special wafers that Catholics prefer. The priest serving communion had a conniption, supposing that Cassidy was going to abuse the consecrated host. He practically shoved it down her throat. Then we were gone, riding home in silence, lost in private thoughts.

Father Sudac's visit was on a Thursday night. The next Sunday morning, Bart began to move his right foot around in bed, lifting and bending it for the first time. We were so thrilled that we literally danced a tarantella around his bed, though Bart seemed unfazed, as if he'd been doing it all along. Tuesday morning we got a frantic call from Shawn the physical therapist. Bart had managed to take a few steps, albeit with support from a couple of aides. Had his leg responded to Father Sudac's blessing? God only knows, but we were very grateful, inspired, and hopeful.

Dayle was first to see Bart walk. There he was, smiling sheepishly, with a beaming Shawn supporting him on one side and an aide on the other. He crept along the hallway for a dozen steps. The staff was absolutely thrilled, in sharp contrast to Dayle. The sight of her boundlessly athletic boy shuffling along like an emaciated nursing home patient was heartbreaking. It was so unsettling that she barely managed a weak cheer for him before going off for a good cry. But Bart was smiling and pleased with himself and we kept up our perennially upbeat front. In a couple of weeks he was walking down the length of the hall, hanging on to the handrails. Once an aide insisted that Dayle come quick and see Bart picking up a Spalding ball. After what seemed an eternity, with many false starts and ungainly near misses, Bart managed to bend over and pick the ball up from the floor. These small victories were bittersweet. Encouraging signs that Bart was making progress, they were painful reminders of how much had been lost and how far he had to go. For the most part Bart faced this twice daily grind of therapies alone.

There was the time Katie, the occupational therapist, asked me to join her in the therapy room for a demonstration of a game of Jeopardy. They had devised a simple game—they would read a card with a word and picture, for example, "mitt," and Bart would have to place it into one of three bins marked "baseball," "football," or "basketball." Besides the word, there was also a large picture illustrating the sport as well (e.g. Michael Jordan flying to the basket next to the word "basketball"). They found that sports were the only subject to which Bart would attend. Katie read the card aloud while showing it to Bart. He was unable to place it. After a couple more cards were all met with the same puzzled expression, she removed the football category and tried again. This time Bart successfully matched "free throw" with "basketball." Katie seemed pleased. I rooted Bart on but was so agitated that I was finding it hard to sit still. In sixth grade Bart had won the sports trivia contest at the town's summer rec program. Coach D had awarded him a trophy and a set of baseball cards. This Jeopardy game was pretty hard to take, even though I understood it was a necessary step on the road back.

With no therapy on weekends, we fell into the routine of getting Bart up and out into his wheelchair to see the sights of the hospital. Regular stops included visits to the public cafeteria, the gift shop, the chapel, the various wings and common areas. Sundays the hospital's auxiliary presented live entertainment in the huge lobby area—a local rock band playing 60s hits, or a swing band, sometimes country western. That day there was an oompa band playing, and we positioned Bart's wheelchair right up front, so he could get a good view of the goings-on. We sat on either side of him, aware that the music was not the sort he'd most enjoy, but figuring it was something to do, as well as good music therapy. The next thing we knew a class of developmentally disabled adults came in to join the fun and a few of them got up on the dance floor, as the spirit moved them. Most had Down syndrome or some other obvious signs of disability. What they lacked in technical skills was more than compensated for by the absolute joyous abandon with which they danced. Although initially a little put off by the spontaneous intrusion, I thought to myself that their dance must be as pleasing in God's eyes as the finest efforts of the American Ballet Theatre. Bart grew increasingly agitated as the music and dance built momentum. Dayle sensed his distress and asked him if he wanted to leave, to which he nodded vigorously, tears streaking down his face. We were aware that the old-school music, combined with the vision of "Helen Hayes Flashdancers" may have been hard for Bart to witness—perhaps he took them for a premonition of things to come. Dayle quietly assured Bart that he'd soon be out of the chair and out of the hospital, that he'd regain his old life. What lay behind Bart's tears, we could only guess. Fear at what was happening to him? Longing for his old life? Confusion about what it all meant? Though I kept it to myself, I was nearly overwhelmed by grief and sadness at my poor boy's pain.

The next weekend we tried something different. Instead of going to the concert, we brought in his Walkman. Bart loved the film *Almost Famous.* A big fan of classic rock, he owned both the movie and the soundtrack. Set up in one of our favorite lounges, we helped Bart get comfortable with the headphones, wondering if he'd even remember how to operate the Walkman. He fumbled with the controls a little with his left hand, but soon seemed to be impatiently pressing the forward button. When he came to track thirteen he settled down to listen, gently bopping his head to the rhythm. The track was Elton John's "Tiny Dancer," which plays a big part in the most memorable scene of the movie. Watching him happily sway to the music was great—dramatic proof that our Barty boy was still in there, rockin'on. Music therapy would be a big part of bringing him back. We started to bring in his favorite CDs—he had a large Led Zeppelin collection—but he always seemed to pick up when listening to "Tiny Dancer." Ever since it's been my all-time favorite rock song; I must have heard it a thousand times.

✦

My old mother had seen plenty of hardship and heartbreak in her time, though she kept it to herself. Her parents had left pogrom-torn Lithuania to seek a free religious life in the Holy Land. Orthodox Jews, they settled in Jerusalem where my mother was born the third of eight children raised in genteel poverty. When she was still in grammar school her aunt, uncle, and several cousins were hacked to death in a minor jihad called by the local Muslim cleric. Reeling from the horror, her parents packed the family and made the steerage trip to the United States in 1929. In the old country she had worked from age five at piecework, then in America as a licensed practical nurse back when the certificate could still be earned through hands-on experience. She eventually married my dad, whose family had come from the same area in Lithuania. As a refugee, immigrant, and nurse she had suffered greatly and seen worse, but never spoke of it, or practically never. We could only guess the *veltshmerz* (Yiddish for "world's grief") she'd witnessed from occasional remarks. I remember her often saying, shaking her head as if to clear away an unwanted image from her mind's eye, "It's a great life if you don't weaken." It was one of her favorite sayings, and I always thought she was its author until as an adult I met other old-timers who used it as well.

Once, after my sister lost her firstborn child, the family's first grandchild, my mother modified it, saying, "It's a great life if you don't waken." At times like those she added in a whisper, "Life is like a sentence, which we must serve." As a teenager hearing this declaration, I was shocked, even revolted, convinced it was nothing more than old-world nay-saying and tragic sense of life. As an American for whom all things are possible, I was eager to leave old world *veltshmerz* where it belonged—back there. I occasionally wondered what kind of heartbreak could lead a strong and brave woman to such a conclusion, but being young and thoughtless, I didn't wonder too hard. By some strange quirk, all of my mother's children grew up cockeyed optimists, a trait that has sometimes wreaked havoc in our lives, but without which really hard times would have been unbearable.

12
Friends

We'd been telling Bart about the boys' impending visit for days. With TBI, everything old is new again, and ideas require many, many repetitions to sink in. He seemed to perk up a little at the mention of Gary, Kyle, and Sean. Kyle's parents had been visiting Bart for some weeks, along with the Daniels. He sometimes picked up a little for them, but nothing to write home about. Finally the big day was at hand, and the boys, looking quite nervous, were in the dining room, where we were wheeling Bart. Fully dressed, Bart was looking good to us but must have been a shock to the boys. He sported a huge scar, nearly an inch wide, running clear down the middle of his head from his hairline to the back of his skull, then around the left side to his ear. A trache tube protruded from his neck, and his right hand was perpetually clenched. Wheelchair bound, shorn of forty pounds, he was a gaunt shadow of his former athletic self. His manner must have seemed even more bizarre. Sometimes he appeared to be absent, other times easily distracted by the slightest thing. Most often, one couldn't quite tell if he heard or understood what was said. John, playing host to the four boys, suggested they adjourn to the TV room down the hall. Someone came up with the beanbag used for occupational therapy, and before long Bart was throwing the bag at the boys with his left hand, especially picking on Kyle, who had always been a favorite butt of his jokes. The boys were all laughing, and Bart was smiling widely. He was even faking his throws, sending the boys cowering for cover. The boys tossed the bag back gently, and Bart often caught it. The sort of hilarious, madcap fun that was trademark Bart, it was also the first time since the accident we'd seen him really enjoy anything. We were elated. The whole thing gave us a little more hope that somewhere trapped inside was our Barty boy.

Lord knows how we would have enticed Bart out of his lethargy without the boys. The power of friendship is transforming. Their visits were probably never easy for them. But John Daniels persisted in bringing them, time and again, often three times a week. John was motivated by genuine sorrow and guilt for his and Gwenn's part in the accident. We were so pleased and moved by the boys' visits. The effect on Bart was as dramatic as if they'd given him a blood transfusion. Often glum, listless, and vacant, he would be stirred by word that his friends were on their way and allow himself to be dressed and set into his wheelchair—up and out to greet them.

It wasn't all fun and games. One evening, relieved to know the four boys were tooling around the premises with Bart's wheelchair, we were relaxing over a cup a coffee with a few guests when one of the boys came running. There was trouble; come quick. I ran up the four flights to find Bart in front of the double-sized elevator doors, practically floating in a huge urine puddle. Apparently his diaper had overfilled and burst, onto him, the wheel chair, and floor. The boys stood around in dumb shock. I told them to stand fast and hurriedly rolled Bart back to his room, calling for a nurse to help clean him up and an orderly to mop up the hallway. I stayed with Bart, whose face was ashen, asking him if the boys could come and visit with him in his room. He closed his eyes shaking his head no. I retuned to the visibly upset boys and established that they wanted to continue their visit. Thanking them for hanging in there, I ran breathlessly back to Bart again to assure him that his friends were still there and wanted to visit some more. Eyes still closed, he raised his hand and waved me away. Sometimes, there is nothing for it. Even your best, frantic efforts can't achieve a satisfactory outcome. My heart ached for Bart, and his sad, mute face haunted me through another sleepless night.

✦

They had been threatening to come for weeks. The high school principal and even the district superintendent kept calling to arrange a visit to Helen Hayes. The delicate task of politely declining their offers fell to me. Bart's prior dealings with both were strictly of a disciplinary nature, and given his delicate mental state, Dayle and I were afraid the mere sight of these authorities might freak him out. After all, he was still pretty much in a fog, a near-dreamlike state, and they might well appear to him as nightmare figures. I had high regard for both of them, but there was no way we could risk a setback. Dayle was adamant, saying they'd come "over my dead body." After thirty years of marriage, I wasn't sure if she meant her dead body or mine. Principal Clinton took it well enough and may have even been relieved to be off the hook. There was considerable pressure within the school community for an official visit so I recommended they send a delegation of coaches. Bart loved the coaches, and in spite of his high jinks the affection was reciprocated.

The plan was to meet the coaches at Helen Hayes, to guide them though their first contact, and help manage the initial shock of seeing Bart. But there was a snafu, and by the time we arrived at noon that Saturday, the coaches had already come and gone. Betty and David and later Siri's husband, Pavan, gave us a good account of the visit. They'd brought gifts, including a book of readings on endurance and faith, and a basketball signed by Bart's entire high school class. They also left a memory book in which visitors could write greetings, in which each coach had written cheerful, encouraging messages. The senior member of the delegation, Coach Defino, had been Bart's gym teacher on and off since first grade, coaching him in summer rec leagues as well as basketball and baseball in middle and high school. He was accompanied by Coach Tegeler, who was Bart's modified basketball coach in middle school and gym teacher in high school. Defino was in his thirties, with young children, his protégé Tegeler still in his midtwenties. Both were great coaches and fine men, role models, and mentors to Bart, who had often said that he wanted to "be like them when I grow up." Bart didn't immediately recall their visit, but the gifts seemed to help him. An emerging feature of life with Bart was that one was never quite sure what he actually remembered, since he often bluffed, too embarrassed to admit obvious lapses of memory.

13
Birthday Boy

Each autumn, just as the kids were readying to start back at school, we'd ask them, "What was the very best thing you did this year?" The answer was invariably, "Camp Mujigae!" Even the years we visited Florida or vacationed on the Maine shore, the answer was always the same. It would be impossible to exaggerate how much our kids love Mujigae or how important it has been in their lives. For Bart, whose racial identity was a sore point until Cassidy's arrival, Mujigae resolved any lingering doubts he may have harbored. The camp draws three hundred plus Korean adoptees from throughout the Northeast, especially Upstate New York, many returning year after year. When they "age out" at seventeen campers often return to work as counselors or staff. Now in its twenty-sixth year, the camp is staffed almost entirely by former campers. For five magical days at the start of each summer, Parsons Child & Family Center in Albany is transformed into a Korean village. Preteens and teens sleep overnight on campus, while younger campers return to their homes or hotels each night. Instruction is offered in everything from folktales, calligraphy, and Hangul (the Korean language) to Ssireum (Korean sumo wrestling), tae kwon do, and traditional farmers' dancing. There are lots of social activities, like bowling, dances, karaoke, and carnivals. Instructors recruited by the Korean Presbyterian Church of Albany work year-round preparing curriculum, sewing handmade costumes for traditional plays, and making banners and lots of other fun stuff. Camp is organized into six separate age groups, ranging from "rising stars" to "seniors III." Under the watchful eye of the mandu king, the kitchen crew feeds upwards of five hundred people at a time. Working out the schedule of classes for the various age groups, all running simultaneously, would leave an army logistician cross-eyed. All of it—food, facilities, dorms, instruction, nursing care, and entertainment—is done by volunteers.

Dayle and I had done our bit, helping for years on the camp committee, culminating the summer prior to Bart's accident when I served as camp director, and Dayle as coordinator of volunteers. Somehow everything works out beautifully, though it often has the look and feel of a six-ring circus. The final day of camp, family day, finds a thousand blitzed campers, parents, volunteers, and instructors deliriously dancing to the hypnotic sound of farmers' drums in a grand finale. Then, like the village in *Brigadoon*, it all abruptly disappears—mess tents, flags, campers proudly flying their group colors and singing camp songs, drummers—all gone without a trace, only to return faithfully the following summer.

Each year by mid-June Bart and Cassidy began showing signs of Mujigae fever, happily surrendering to the joys of anticipation. They would dig out old camp yearbooks, pour over photo albums, retell stories, and sing camp songs. Everyone got caught up in the spirit. When the big day finally arrived, we'd drive up to Albany, happily shouting camp cheers and speculating about whether that year would be the best Mujigae ever. After five days and near-sleepless nights of camp the kids were so wiped out that they'd usually be asleep before the car cleared the campgrounds.

Bart's seventeenth birthday was fast approaching. We wanted to throw him a party, a festive event, yet nothing too overwhelming. We arranged to use the public cafeteria downstairs, with catered pizzas and an ice cream cake from Sweet Lou's, and invited a dozen of his high school friends. Other than the regular threesome—Sean, Kyle, and Gary—none had seen Bart since the accident. We were a little nervous about how the first contact would go but decided to plunge ahead and hope for the best. We also invited his two best friends from Mujigae, Ashlee and Kaili. A couple of years older than Bart, they had been friends forever. A large picture of them hung prominently in Bart's bedside "shrine." His feelings for these two girls, sometimes affectionately referred to as the "Mujigae babes," were a combination of true friendship, Asian racial solidarity, and good old-fashioned romantic longing. Just a little too old for him, they were forever out of reach. Each summer at camp Dayle and I remarked that at least Bart had great taste. If he brought home a girl like either of those two, we'd be thrilled. Fun loving—otherwise Bart would never find them attractive—they were warm, bright, hardworking, loving, conscientious young women—among our all-time camp favorites. If that weren't enough, they were gorgeous to boot. Campers routinely requested them as counselors since that assured a great time. Cassidy, who had them as counselors one year, loved them as much as we did. As soon as he was old enough to be a counselor-in-training, Bart teamed up with one or both of them (they were already junior counselors) to run a "color group" of younger campers. Bart was well known on campus as a wild and crazy guy—typically, he had won the karaoke contest with an outrageous routine the previous year at camp. On the other hand, he was a seriously devoted counselor. He felt deeply that the little guys just coming up deserved the same sort of fantastic experience he'd enjoyed as a young camper at the discovery and explorer camps. The little kids adored Bart, swarming around him wherever he went. He could hardly sit down to eat, or try to make time with a girl, without a couple of little ones plopping onto his lap. Heaven help you if you didn't do right by his campers—whether you were another counselor, a parent volunteer, or camp big wig—you'd sure as hell hear from Bart, who did not suffer fools gladly.

Friendships forged at Mujigae proved lasting and true. James Chang and his younger sister, Jane, visited Bart at HHH where Cassidy and Jane staged wheelchair races, to the delight of all. James had last seen Bart in a coma at Westchester Med and was relieved to see how far he'd come. The Chang sibs had spent overnights at our home, and Jane, a couple of years Bart's junior, had even joined us one summer on vacation in Maine. They were practically like niece and nephew.

Ashlee and Kaili arrived for the party an hour early, which was perfect. Wonderfully natural and affectionate, they whisked Bart off to the lounge, chatting, laughing, and hanging all over him. With the trache freshly out, Bart was in his glory, trying his best to make himself understood in a hoarse, cracking whisper. He must have sounded pretty weird to kids accustomed to his usual thundering, boisterous voice. When I went down to check on the pizza delivery, I found Gary, Kyle, and Sean sitting around in the lobby. I mentioned that the Mujigae babes were upstairs, and they practically fell over each other rushing the elevators—they'd seen pictures. Before long the fourth floor lounge was a loud, happy, rocking place. Just before seven o'clock, we asked everyone to come down to the cafeteria, where other guests had gathered. Besides the kids, a few parents showed up, probably because they didn't want their kids driving alone to Helen Hayes, more than an hour from New Paltz. The kids all sat at one huge table, with the birthday boy at the head. After an invocation and a few toasts, everyone settled down happily to their pizzas. The reactions of high school pals who were seeing him for the first time varied from seemingly fine to apparent shock. Bart, who looked great to our eyes, was still in a wheelchair, was speaking in a cracking, barely audible remnant of a voice, and could hardly follow a conversation.

After an hour or so, Bart rolled off by himself and motioned me over. He had to use the bathroom. I wheeled him across the lobby to the restroom, helping him into the stall. He was agitated, and I held my breath, hoping to get back to the party without an outburst or an accident. Bart was still relearning bladder and bowel control, and I was worried. Thankfully things went smoothly. Back in the cafeteria ice cream cake was served and birthday gifts opened. Lots of photos were shot with his pals, many in vintage goofy poses favored by Bart. By nine o'clock, an exhausted Bart bid his guests good night. It was hard for him to let go of Ashlee and Kaili. Their gift to him was a beautifully framed collage, made from dozens of pictures of Bart and them at Mujigae, from the early years up to the present. They had loads of photos to choose from, since the three of them were usually inseparable at camp.

Driving home that night, we were pleased with the party but exhausted from the anxiety of worrying over how things could have gone awry. It was hard to shake nagging worries about how Bart would fit in when he returned to school in five months, worries heightened next day when we learned that he didn't recall the party. That came as quite a shock. We had drifted into one of our periodic optimistic hazes, and that revelation definitely served to snap us out of it. When we brought him photos of the festivities the following day, it seemed to jog some memories.

14
Signs of Life

The nurses liked Bart, but Mary in particular doted on him. Nearing retirement, she had raised three now-grown sons, and Bart's plight touched her deeply. She was fond of saying to him, "When your momma's not here, I'm your momma." When Bart senses you love him, he'll give you the shirt off his back. Wherever Mary went, Bart rolled right along, her constant companion. TBIers go through some pretty strange stages during emergence, and she had seen it all. Sometimes they have uncontrollable urges to take off their clothes, and a couple of times Mary found Bart rolling happily down the hall in his birthday suit. Griffey's wife, Dotty, who looked in on Bart regularly, had also reported finding him buck naked out and about. As a nurse, Dotty took it in good-natured stride. When Bart started to relearn toileting skills, Mary would find him contentedly using the corner of his room as a urinal—and worse. But nothing fazed Mary, who was of the old breed. When the trache tube was set to finally come out, we all wondered what Bart's first words would be or whether he'd be able to speak at all. It's common for the first words to be a stream of profanities, and Bart did not disappoint. He hurled bloodcurdling curses at Mary, who was just delighted to hear him speaking at all. She called us at home, so we could hear for ourselves, but she couldn't get him to perform on demand. Thankfully the "drunken sailor" phase lasted only a few days. For some strange reason, I always expected him to speak. It never seemed a real possibility to me that he might have aphasia. The idea of a silent Bart was just not conceivable.

Several of the ward staff were from the Philippines, including a pair of nurses who were brother and sister, Noel and Flora, and the ward's orderly,

Moses. They all went above and beyond for Bart, saying, "He's one of our own," meaning Asian. Moses helped with the heavy lifting, getting Bart in and out of bed, into the bath, and so on. Even cleaning up Bart's mess in the corner didn't dim Moses's sunny disposition or his expansive affection for Bart. A pretty nurse's aide, Angelina, was the first person Bart consistently smiled at after the accident. She beamed as she showed him smiling sheepishly, exclaiming, "He loves me like a momma." I knew my boy and assured her that was not the way he wanted to love her. To my amazement, next day she showed up with her fifteen-year-old son, although she herself appeared to be no older than her twenties. Another regular was Father Snodgrass (no kidding), an Episcopal priest, who came around once a week to visit Bart. A kindly older gentleman, he loved to relate how, after his stroke, he'd been nursed back to life in this very ward. He was a relentless Helen Hayes booster and an upbeat kind of guy. A couple of times our family attended services in the small hospital chapel, where he blessed Bart hands-on.

A few weeks prior to his discharge date, I visited Bart in his private room. He had graduated from the trache room into a private room down the hall. There I was greeted by a flustered and distraught speech therapist. Unlike veterans Shawn and Katie, Lisa was fresh out of college and earnestly finding her way through the labyrinth of TBI. Lisa informed me that Bart, who had begun speaking a few weeks earlier, had apparently lost the knack. She had read of similar cases and had examined him for a cause without result. She was going to recommend that an eye, ear, nose and throat specialist be called in to do a thorough workup. Closing the door behind her when she left, I looked Bart straight in the eye and asked, "Why did you do that to Lisa?" Grinning, he hoarsely whispered, "Because I can." The gag was vintage Bart, and though he was still too dopey to truly have a twinkle in his eye, I took heart that he was finally showing signs of life. I almost relished the thought of being called to the assistant principal's office in response to some prank he'd pulled. Katie, a feisty blond occupational therapist, came in to fetch Bart for her session. I warned her about the voice ploy, but she swished him out the room, assuring me, "Oh don't worry, Bart will sing like a bird for me." He was still grinning with satisfaction.

✦

A couple of weeks after the birthday party, the Rickards, among our closest Mujigae friends, drove up from Philadelphia in a heavy rainstorm to celebrate belatedly with the Bartman. Each summer from ages ten to fifteen, Bart and his friend David Kennedy returned home with the Rickards after Mujigae to spend a week at the St. Aloysius sports camp, run by yet another Korean adoptee, Sam Wallace. The fearsome threesome—David Rickards, a year younger than Bart, David Kennedy, a year older than Bart, and Bart—all bunked at the Rickards', in what was in effect a weeklong house party. Along with the Kennedys we'd drive down to Philly at the end of the week for a huge cookout and post-Mujigae gabfest. We'd all dissect that year's camp and brainstorm for next season. Bart loved the entire extended Rickards and Wallace family and came to view Philadelphia as a home away from home. David Rickards' nephew, RJ Schmidt was also a Korean adoptee, much younger than our boys, but they all often slept down the block at the Schmidt house where David's older sister, Jenny, was a tolerant and adoring host.

Sam Wallace and his wife, Paige, were both older Koreans, having been adopted in the immediate aftermath of the Korean War. Their two sons, Shill and Bryson, were biological children of adopted Koreans. It sounds more complicated than it really is. What it amounted to was a wonderfully accepting Korean affinity group where Bart felt truly at home and at ease. The Rickards were vacationing in Florida at the time of the original birthday party, but insisted on visiting Barty as soon as possible. David's mom, Tisch, his older sister, Jenny, and David drove four and a half hours through a storm arriving at Helen Hayes late Saturday afternoon. In their honor we threw a mini-birthday party again in the public cafeteria. Bart seemed more relaxed and fluent than usual with them, especially with David, whom he affectionately called "Rickards." Their devotion to Bart was very moving and inspiring. It meant a lot to Dayle, Cassidy, and me, and of course to Bart. Thank God for photographs; with their help, Bart was able to remember their visit.

The Mujigae boys shared a special bond, forged by years of happy camping and post-camp hanging out. Of course, not every encounter was happy. When Bart was fifteen, he, "Rickards," and David Kennedy were lazily hanging around on a summer's evening in the predominantly white suburb of Drexel Hill when a police cruiser stopped to challenge them. When Rickards replied that he lived a few blocks away, the officer demanded to see the boys' IDs. Only Bart was carrying one, but his high school student card, which read Bart A. Goldstein, was not a photo ID. The officer, clearly suspicious of Asian teens, sharply asked Bart, "Who's this Goldstein guy? Where's *your* ID?" Bart angrily insisted that he was himself, but to no avail. And with that, the boys were in the squad car, on their way to the station house on suspicion of loitering and God knows what else. Rickards managed to convince the cop to stop at his house and check with his folks. But as luck would have it no one was home. Just as the squad car pulled away from the curb for the station, Rickards spotted a neighbor, who readily vouched for him. The officer, somewhat reluctantly and without a hint of apology, drove off, presumably to keep Drexel Hill safely white. The boys were quite steamed up about this incident, and there was talk about letters to the police commissioner and mayor. In the end after thorough venting, we hoped they'd learned a sad but necessary object lesson. They would have to be aware of and prepared for racism from police and other authorities. Sharing angry, hurtful experiences only served to deepen the bonds of friendship and brotherhood that had been forged at Mujigae.

✦

Several weeks prior to his discharge date of May 1, we began taking Bart on field trips. The first was very brief—to Sweet Lou's ice cream parlor just up the road. Bart already loved the handmade gelato, which we'd brought to him many times at the hospital. A bear of a man, Sweet Lou had retired from a long career as a professional rugby player in Italy. Originally from the area, he had retuned to his roots armed with an outstanding recipe for Italian ice cream. Dayle and I had stopped in for his equally good espresso every day for months, so Lou knew all about Bart and was almost as excited about the field trip as Bart. A youth coach as well as player, Lou understood teens and gave Bart the royal treatment, offering advice and encouragement on everything from sports to girls. He became one of Bart's favorite people, and a stop at Sweet Lou's became a mandatory part of every field trip. We went far out of our way to visit Lou for years after Bart's discharge. Invariably, upon returning to the hospital after one of our field trips, Pavan would greet Bart with a big hug then ask the $64,000 question—what flavor ice cream had Bart eaten? Bart never could remember, but it was good fun nonetheless. Eventually Bart settled into the habit of always ordering lemon sorbet, and so finally he was able to get the answer right. That sort of practical shortcut, such as always ordering egg foo young at Chinese restaurants or a chicken wrap at a diner, becomes a feature of life with TBI.

The next weekend we stowed the wheelchair in the trunk and went off to the local mall. Wheeling him around was an eye-opener. It's amazing the obstacles chair-bound people face in everyday situations. In brand-name stores we'd visited dozens of times, we now found it damn near impossible to make our way to the merchandise. Sensing his sadness, Dayle promised Bart that some day soon he'd be driving to the mall with his friends, hanging out, and making his own way. He seemed to gather himself up, and next thing you know he was walking along slowly, holding onto Dayle's arm. We instructed Cassidy to sit in the chair, hoping the experience would give her a different perspective. She complained that people were looking at her weirdly, and they were, too. After a short time Bart became fatigued and resumed wheeling around, but he agreed to buy a new pair of shoes—Nike basketball sneakers, a hopeful gesture.

The first field trip back to our home was nerve-racking. Bart's bedroom was in the basement, which meant he'd need to negotiate narrow wooden steps. No way would he tolerate anyone spotting him on the way down. Since he couldn't recall his AOL password, we awkwardly stumbled around on the computer trying unsuccessfully to arrange for a new one. That evening, after we'd dropped him back at Helen Hayes, I managed to log him onto AOL, only to find myself swamped by buddies thrilled that Bartman was back. I replied that soon enough he would be.

Bart's fuse was short. The least bit of frustration would cause him to let loose a storm of verbal abuse, often followed by a round of door slamming. Of course, he was generally well behaved around others, reserving his ire for Dayle and me. Cassidy, increasingly put off by these frequent, unprovoked outbursts, remained exempt from them. She was still his snow angel, but a wedge was growing between them, driven by his uncontrollable anger. Door-frames and handles gradually gave way under Bart's rough treatment, and I refused to replace them, even removing a couple of door handles to make them harder to slam. Other times Bart was so listless and enervated that he'd put his head down and fall asleep midsentence. This was our introduction to the twin demons of disinhibition (inability to suppress or inhibit impulsive behavior and emotions) and adynamism (lack of energy and ability to self-start actions), both typical of TBI. They would be long-term guests.

15

Day Hospital

May 1, discharge day, was looming large. The date was determined entirely by bureaucratic considerations, mostly Medicaid reimbursement schedules, rather than by any objective changes in Bart's condition. Hospital beds were expensive, so he was being shipped home to continue intensive rehab on an outpatient basis. Still in rough shape, he was rated on the cusp between level 3 (agitated and confused) and level 4 (higher-level responses) coma emergence. His attention span was short and he was easily distracted by the least little thing. Memory was so shaky that he might ask five times in as many minutes, "Where are we going?" His understanding was only a little better. We'd noticed on field trips that his distance vision seemed very poor; he couldn't recognize familiar sights as we drove down Main Street in New Paltz, not even favorite haunts like the Plaza Diner. Twice daily he downed antiseizure medications along with antipsychotic drugs meant to reduce angry outbursts. Physically, he was a little sounder. The therapists had warned us that gross physical movements, like walking, often come back first, well before fine motor control. Bart's right hand was still hardly working. Mental and emotional control is often the last to return, if it ever does. He was ambulatory, getting around without a cane or walker, though he tended to walk into things, and his balance wasn't great. If thirsty, he might check the fridge ten or twelve times an hour. Had he forgotten that he'd just checked? Or was it just something to do, something to break the boredom of nothing to do? We felt as if we were living with a caged animal. All the energy that previously had burned off in athletics was stuck simmering below the surface.

✦

A doctor friend of ours had once given us a gift of a book titled *Raising Your Spirited Child*, quipping, "Here's a book about Bart." About twelve at the time, Bart was a lovable handful. The author explained that about 15 percent of kids are spirited—meaning they feel and experience everything more intensely than the rest of us. They notice and care about things most of us don't even experience, like the feel of their socks, or how the labels on their clothes rub against their back. Bright and very active, but not so hyperactive as to be outside the range of normal, they have boatloads of energy to spare.

After a typical day at school followed by hours of grueling practice (soccer, basketball, or baseball according to season), then dinner, Bart would plead to be driven to the college's athletic "bubble" to play pickup basketball. That didn't leave much time for homework, but Bart was a quick study and didn't care about grades. People were initially drawn to Bart by his hilarious sense of humor and then fell under his spell, held by his boundless, boisterous energy. He would literally "boogie till he bounced." It was like living with a force of nature. Returning home from Helen Hayes, he lacked the upper body strength to put a basketball up to the rim; we lowered the rim to its lowest setting, and then he barely could manage. Worse, he lacked both the physical and psychic energy to play. If goaded, he might try one basket (dribbling was out of the question), shake his head saying, "I stink," and retire inside. Remarkably, he didn't seem depressed by any of this, probably because he forgot the whole thing in a few minutes, a rare advantage of TBI. Dayle and I were not so blessed.

Some youngsters are graced with natural athletic abilities, excelling at every sport they turn their hand to. Joe Namath and Jim Brown come to mind. Bart wasn't like that. He had a fast burst in the 100-meter dash in track for the middle school. But his reaction times and eye-hand coordination were barely average. The fact was he had lazy eye syndrome, something we suspected when first oohing and aahing over the picture sent from the orphanage in Korea when we were matched. His left eyelid seemed to droop a little. When at age nine we finally had it diagnosed by an eye doctor, we were assured that it would never be a serious problem, since Bart's brain had adjusted well. To my later regret, we didn't seek a second opinion. The net effect of this visual defect was that his depth perception was poor, affecting everything from judging a pitch in baseball to making a three-pointer in basketball. Bart was never a great hitter, but remarkably was a fine fielder with the rare gift of judging a fly ball. Never able to do it myself, I'd marvel how at the crack of a bat, Bart was flying to the precise spot in the outfield, often making a shoestring catch. In basketball he was not a great shooter, but with good dribbling skills and very fine court sense, he played guard. A crisp, accurate passer, he had many spectacular assists to his credit. He loved to drive to the basket, only to pass off the ball at the last second, sometimes behind his back. On defense he was a bear, often taking a hit for the team. In soccer he mostly played midfield where he'd use his speed to set up plays.

All his coaches agreed—Bart was a "gut" player who dug deep and never held back. On a couple of occasions we saw him on the sidelines at soccer games, puking his guts out, while begging to be put right back in the game. He lacked the natural athletic grace and polished foot skills of the some of the boys, but was second to none in heart. Bart really loved to play. At play, especially basketball, he seemed most alive. He'd play anywhere, anytime. Friendly and extroverted, he'd deal himself in wherever—even vacationing in French Canada, where the language barrier proved to be no obstacle. Somewhat of an introvert, I've always admired his easy knack for just popping up and saying, "Mind if I play?" With his wide eager smile, he was invariably welcomed. On a family picnic, ten-year-old Bart managed to join a bunch of college men playing pick up soccer. For him it came easy.

Play was his perfect medium. He strongly preferred pickup ball to organized team sports. Even though he worshipped the school coaches and enjoyed the team spirit, he found the long workouts drudgery. To him "play" was the operative term in "play ball." He always had a great time, but was truly pissed off if his team (Catholic Youth Organization, town league, or school) lost. Bart was not easygoing about anything—especially play. He was one of those kids who kept up a constant bantering chatter among his teammates. Athletics were the ideal outlet for Bart, satisfying his intensely social, outgoing personality, while meeting an urgent need to spend his boundless energy. At play he was beautiful.

Although I thoroughly enjoyed teaching him to throw and catch, and to make a layup, I was never much of an athlete. My favorite recreational activities were hiking, bicycling, horseback riding, tae kwon do, and when I was younger, skiing and mountain climbing. We exposed Bart to all of these, but for the most part he found them solitary and boring. (To honor his Korean heritage, we forced him to earn a black belt, but after that day he never again donned his dobok.) The ancient Greeks said, "Even the gods bow to necessity." Though I lamented this temperamental difference, I figured to make the best of things by getting more involved in team sports. Having played a bit of "choose up" softball and baseball as a kid, I picked up again, in my midforties, playing friendly pickup softball games along with Bart in the park. Those were wonderful, hilarious times, though my poor old aching back was always miserable the next morning. We started going to Yankee games, and I'm still an avid fan.

✦

At the Helen Hayes pre-discharge conference the therapists made it plain that Bart could never be left alone at home, even for a moment. If he wandered off, he might get lost or worse. They suggested we install alarms on all the doors that would trigger if he tried to make a break. Sleeping in his basement room or even just walking stairs without assistance was out of the question—in fact we needed to padlock the basement door. Someone needed to be nearby when he slept, in case of seizures or other emergencies. To avoid falls in the shower, a special seat would need to be installed. He might well need help showering. They painted a very frightening picture of life at home. In the end we installed a new locking handle to the basement door, and Dayle and Bart set up shop in the living room, Bart on the foldout futon, Dayle on the sofa. Bart refused to use the shower seat we bought, so we returned it.

I was downright frightened by the prospect of Bart's homecoming. No matter how badly things went at Helen Hayes, we got to go home at the end of the evening. There was time and space to unwind. How would life with Bart at home work out? I knew it was best for him, but wasn't sure how I'd bear up under the constant pressure. I learned, and we all learned, to walk on eggshells around Bart.

With Bart sleeping in the living room there was literally no privacy. With no nurses to follow around, he traipsed after us wherever we went, even into the bathroom. He seemed to have lost all sense of privacy or social space, sort of like a 180-pound preschooler. He was always very extroverted, and now we were the only people available. There were a couple of other surprises. He couldn't tolerate abbreviations, even well-worn ones like "Mickey D's."

Everything had to be fully spelled out. I never noticed how often we use abbreviations until they were pointed out. If someone happened to say CIA, Bart would loudly object, "What? What the hell is CIA?" Yogurt at TCBY was a trial. The really odd thing is that he seemed to understand the abbreviations perfectly, but couldn't tolerate hearing them. TBI does some pretty bizarre things, which as a dyslectic, I can appreciate better than most. His enunciation was poor, especially when tired. But if we couldn't understand his slurred words, we made an educated guess, since asking him to repeat himself often brought a nasty snarl. We slowly discovered other eccentric behaviors. If a ballad came on the radio, Bart would take Dayle around and start dancing the foxtrot. It was the sort of goofy prank that was vintage Bart, but he did an awful lot of it now. But better dance and laugh than cry. One Friday night, while his classmates attended the junior prom, Bart danced round the living room with his mom and then hit the futon early, his mother quietly weeping on the sofa.

✦

Helen Hayes had been a mixed bag. Nurses, therapists, and other staff were mostly wonderful people—caring, competent, really superb. The administration, on the other hand—social workers and medical staff—were indifferent. When we came to collect Bart on May 1, we met the department's neurologist for the very first time. The good doctor had managed to stay scarce enough that we'd never actually seen him during three months of daily visits. To us he was just a smiling picture on the bulletin board and an elusive, hard-to-pin-down voice on the phone.

The Day Hospital was worse. An intensive outpatient program developed to serve recovering stroke victims, the Helen Hayes Day Hospital is an entirely separate operation, with its own wing and distinct staff of therapists and medical specialists. A renowned program, it is much more intensive than ordinary outpatient services. Patients spend three to five full days a week in something very comparable to rehab's boot camp, only on a more advanced level. For instance, speech therapy was no longer one-on-one but set in a classroom with several patients getting ready to return to school or work and learning to cope with a more complex, demanding environment. In addition to speech, occupational therapy, and physical therapy, Bart had regular counseling sessions with a psychiatric social worker. The stroke survivors, all older folks, loved the program.

The teens—Bart, Meredith, and a couple of others who had preceded them—were not as keen. Bart for one hated Helen Hayes like it was poison and was miserable spending three days a week there. He became increasingly hostile and uncooperative. During the long drive over he would be lost in glum silence. Parking at the Day Hospital entrance, we could never be sure what to expect. Sometimes he balked, stubbornly sitting in the car. We'd go in without him, letting the heat of the summer sun eventually drive him into the air-conditioned facility. The therapists were mostly very young, with no clue how to engage and motivate Bart. He outright refused to work with the first couple of OTs. We inquired about having Katie from upstairs working with him (he'd have jumped through hoops for her), but that was apparently out of the question. The medical director and neuropsychiatrist acknowledged that their staff had no special training in working with teens—or more precisely, that funding had been cut, along with the training. Accustomed to working with highly motivated, mature stroke victims, the staff were stumped by surly, angry teens. It stank. Their only suggestion was to increase Bart's antipsychotic meds—in effect pacification by stupor. We refused, instead lobbying successfully for Dave, the recreational therapist from upstairs, to work with Bart in place of OT. With a mix of humor, compassion, and strength, Dave commanded Bart's attention. They played soccer and basketball together. It was good therapy.

Getting Dave to work with Bart was a hard-won coup. Bart had been working with a sweet young OT, freshly out of school, who won him over by playing soccer with him outside on the spacious lawns. Bart seemed happy to oblige. Then one day she pushed her luck, trying some word recognition and other cognitive exercises. I saw her running into the waiting area, trembling like a leaf. Bart had thrown the exercise worksheets to the floor, screaming at her and backing her into a corner, she confided to me between sobs. The poor girl was scared stiff. Mortified, I tried to apologize and comfort her, at the same time seething inside that there was no one in this joint who could handle Bart properly. No sooner had she left, in tears, than Bart confronted me, demanding to know what she had said about him. Before I could gather my thoughts, he grabbed my upper arms with all his might, pushing me backward, muttering curses, his face purple with rage. I gave way, moving backward to escape his vice-like grip. We danced across the full length of the lobby, until I was backed against the wall. By now I was yelling at him to stop this crap and get a hold of himself, on the verge of using a tae kwon do self-defense technique to break away, when Betty came along, asking Bart to give her a hand with something or other. Abruptly he let go, traipsing off after her. Thank God for Betty. Breathless and shaken, I noticed a New Paltz special ed teacher and a school psychologist walking through the lobby doors. They had been sent by the school district to evaluate Bart's readiness to return to school. After introducing themselves, they explained that they hoped to observe Bart's next therapy session, which happened to be speech. Still a little dazed as well as stunned by the lousy timing of their visit, I waited to hear the visiting delegation's verdict, my mind's gears pretty well stripped.

After an hour or so, the older of the two women came over, a sweet, kindly, sympathetic, expression on her face, whispering, "You don't really want him back in a classroom setting, do you?" I think I startled her a bit with the intensity of my reply. "You bet we want him in class, even if special classes. He hates this place. How's he gonna make progress here? He needs to be in familiar surroundings, around people who know and love him. Then he'll give his best. He's dying to be back in school. The whole family feels the same. Now make it so." Would that it were so easy! The folks at the Day Hospital felt that Bart, who had not made much progress, hardly reaching a single milestone of the program, would be better off in some kind of residential setting, perhaps a nursing home. For their part school officials were not so sure they could manage Bart or that he was up to the rigors of school.

We had to sign releases for the hospital, saying we were acting against their advice in returning him to school, and lobby hard for his acceptance at school. Sometimes the experts have their heads up their asses. We were determined to keep the bar up, to set difficult but attainable goals for Bart, and then raise the bar again and again. After all, who knows for sure how far anybody can go? You've got to have a little faith. These bureaucrats are not mean spirited so much as driven by statistical models of probable outcomes, without taking into account the character of the boy, or of his family. After that day, all the Day Hospital OTs refused to work with Bart, but his sessions with Dave, the intrepid rec therapist, remained the highlight of his day. For weeks, my left arm that he had gripped with his strong right hand showed five distinct black and blue finger marks. The Day Hospital lasted from May 5 until the end of August, every day a hard fight, without much to show for it.

✦

That summer we traveled down to New York City to the SUNY State College of Optometry to consult with a distinguished professor of neuro-ophthalmology. (A rare breed indeed, the most esoteric of medical specialties, these doctors complete residencies in both neurology and ophthalmology.) Bart was constantly bumping into things, and we suspected that vision as much as coordination played a part. The exam took all day, since Bart fatigued easily, requiring long rest periods. At the end of the day the sweet, sympathetic young professor told us that Bart suffered from hemianopia, or blindness to his right side in *both* eyes. While his eyes and even optic nerve were fine, the area of his brain that processed visual images was damaged. This brain blindness would either clear up spontaneously on its own or persist as a permanent condition. It was untreatable, though special lenses were available to somewhat expand the remaining field of vision. What remained of his field of vision was less than that of a one-eyed person. Dayle and I rode home quietly mulling what this new revelation would really mean for Bart's chances of regaining his life. As whipped as he was, Bart hadn't even bothered listening to the doctor's prognosis. An unsinkable optimist, I refused to accept that such a common condition, apparently afflicting 15 percent of stroke and TBI victims, could be untreatable. The doctor had actually used the term "intractable" in response to my questioning, which really got under my skin. That night I launched an all-out Internet search on hemianopia but was frustrated and annoyed to find that there seemed to be nothing for it. I repeated the exercise most every night for years. Meanwhile, we managed to get Bart an appointment with a low-vision specialist to see about special prism lenses.

16

Ready or Not, Here He Comes

They say that marathon runners focus on just the mile at hand, rather than an unfathomable distance ahead. The advice that "tomorrow morning this will all be over" had always served me well, whether for a tooth extraction, tonsillectomy, or other predictable crisis of growing up. After nine months of agony, there was still just no way of knowing when Bart would be restored and all this would be behind us. Mercifully, the true time line of TBI emerges only gradually over time, as if on a need-to-know basis. In NICU the medical staff seemed to concentrate on the first three months. Then as one arrives at rehab, it's the first six months that hold the key. In the Day Hospital the focus is on the first year as the time most healing occurs. After that first year has passed, the doctors say that, especially in a young brain, good healing goes on for at least two years, then six. In the beginning we took the time frames rather literally, at least as rough estimates. While Bart was at HHH, I comforted myself with thoughts like, "At least we're halfway home. It can't possibly be worse than what we've already been through. Just hold on for another three months or so. Keep it together for that long." I e-mailed several friends that "Bart should be out of the woods in six months or so," and I believed it too. There were nagging worries when after three months he was still wheelchair-bound and speechless, but I thought perhaps one day he might just snap out of it. How else could he recover in six months? After nine months and facing Bart's return to school, I knew it would take the full two years and realized soon after that six was more likely. In the end one relinquishes deadlines and tries to live day by day, accepting rather grudgingly that the outcome is in God's hands.

Of course God helps those who help themselves, and we were determined that no stone be left unturned in the search for remedies. It became our obsession, our mission.

In early June, just before Regents exams, the high school threw a "Bart dance," the first-ever such event in honor of an enrolled student. It was billed as a fund-raiser to buy Bart a new computer. (Ours was ancient.) When initially approached by the school administration, I was staunchly opposed to the idea. It seemed to suggest that Bart was destitute, which was not at all the case. Then one of the school hall monitors phoned our home to caution us against "false pride." Mrs. Z, popularly known as "Terminator 3," had notched her belt with plenty of run-ins with Bart and particularly adored him. She insisted that the kids felt a strong need to do something to help. Chastened, I finally relented. When the big night arrived, a dozen boys, looking somewhat sheepish, showed up at our house to escort Bart. The principal, assistant principal, and many teachers were on hand, plus a couple hundred students, mostly from Bart's grade. It was a very moving evening, though the guest of honor tired so easily that we had to leave before nine. Afterward, we stopped at Village Pizza with a few of the boys. A college town, New Paltz boasts no fewer than eight pizza joints, but Village was Bart's favorite. When time came to settle up, the owner flat out refused to accept money for the pies and soda, saying only, "It's just good to see Bart back." I was learning the true meaning of the admonition that it is better to give than to receive. We had been taught at momma's knee to be generous. But it's much harder to graciously receive, though I've had a great deal of practice these last years. That night at the pizza shop, I noticed with concern that none of Bart's closest friends except Doug had bothered to tag along.

As a kid I hated Hebrew school. An undiagnosed dyslectic, I was a failure at reading in both English and Hebrew and was in the slow class until fourth grade. We were drilled on the seven levels of *tzedakah,* or charity. The lowest level of charity is done in a way that exalts the giver and demeans the receiver. Lending a hand to someone in need and then bragging in a self-congratulatory way to all and sundry and reminding the receiver at every chance is operating at the lowest level. While better than doing nothing, it's a poor sort of tzedakah. The highest kind is done purely for love of goodness, with both giver and receiver remaining completely anonymous. A practice common in the Jewish Pale of Settlement throughout Eastern Europe always struck me as a singular example of perfect tzedakah. When one loses a family member, there is a prescribed period of mourning, or shivah, during which work is prohibited. The rabbi visits the bereaved family's home, always leaving behind a mourner's box for the duration of the weeklong shivah. The box is filled with money—more than enough to support a family for a week. If a family is too poor to do without wages, they take what they need from the box. If a well-off family loses a loved one, they add money. Nobody knows who took and who contributed, or how much. The result is optimal—the poor manage to keep their shivah obligation without undue hardship or the indignity of public begging. The community accomplishes this without anyone being tempted to crow, since no one can be absolutely sure who gave and who received (except presumably the rabbi, whose lips are sealed.) Never an attentive religious student, some things still managed to sink in, and the lessons of tzedekah stuck like a cocklebur.

Midway through summer Bart caught me in the basement with an armful of laundry. He had been spending more and more time down there lately, watching TV, flipping through old middle and high school yearbooks, or just napping. Blocking my way, tears in his eyes, he implored, "Dad, can I pleeeese move back into my room?" Fighting back my own tears, I nodded. "Sure." If he couldn't handle sleeping alone in his own room, how was he ever going to manage going back to school in a month?

17
In the Wind

No sooner had Bart been discharged from Helen Hayes than we realized the pivotal role John Daniels had played in the boys' frequent hospital visits. Absent his ramrodding, the friends' visits dropped off so abruptly and unexpectedly that we were astonished. A few weeks after Bart's homecoming I needed help putting up a dog pen and thought to call the boys to ask their help. They practically fell over each other to come and lend a hand, but still didn't call or visit Bart. In his first few months home they made a total of four visits, after that, never again. Kyle had Bart over for the Super Bowl after Bart called and asked. (It was a tradition to watch the Super Bowl at Kyle's.) Afterward Bart told Dayle that he missed the Thompsons awfully. Kyle's wonderful mom, Debra, connived to have Bart over two more times to watch some TV and spend a couple of hours with Kyle. Since Kyle seemed put out by the visits, Debra even offered to host Bart sometimes "with or without Kyle." We declined her good-hearted offer, sensing that being at Kyle's sans Kyle would be even harder on Bart. Like Bonnie Raitt says in her song, "I can't make you love me."

Sometimes, when you least expect it, good things happen. We had practically forgotten about Doug, Bart's only close friend not involved in the accident, since John Daniels never invited him to ride along to the hospital. Of course he had attended Bart's seventeenth birthday party at HHH along with a dozen other friends. Alone among them, Doug visited Bart faithfully every week, until graduation the following June, less frequently that summer, then made what we thought was his last appearance just as he was about to start at the local community college. Doug's visits were an unanticipated godsend.

We never understood why Doug hung in there while others faded so entirely, although we often puzzled over it. Dayle speculated that Doug, who has had scoliosis since middle school, understood what it was like to be faced with a major medical challenge and so empathized more readily. Doug had always worked, initially at his dad's hardware store, then after it burned down, at a local produce store. Perhaps he was just a little more mature. Of course he wasn't burdened by guilt, since he had no part in the accident. The boys' behavior puzzled and disturbed us no end, partly because it was a constant source of frustration for Bart, who ran into them every day at school.

If they had been a few years older, the boys may have been more mature and responsible. But adolescent souls are fragile, and prey to small things. Constancy in the face of awful pain and loss, compounded by guilt and embarrassment, is perhaps more than one can expect. The spectacle of the new Bart was a reminder of their own vulnerability and mortality, things that youngsters simply aren't prepared to face. We knew from others within the larger TBI fellowship that thirtysomethings who suffer the catastrophe of TBI often have better luck with friends. Attaining a certain critical age, sometime in the midtwenties, is a necessary condition for mature behavior.

Grudgingly I acknowledged this developmental fact. It is, after all, what makes teenagers different. Even if they are adult-sized, their brains' frontal lobes, which control higher cognitive functions, do not fully develop until around age twenty-two. And though I knew full well that in their shoes Bart would have behaved as badly, I couldn't help seething with frustration and anger when faced with the everyday reality of Bart's near-total social isolation. Even the disturbing insight that, at their age, I would have behaved no better, didn't slake my resentment. After nearly a year, it finally dawned on me that my feelings were more appropriately directed at the boys' parents. As a teenager I surely would have fled such a tragedy, but my parents would have intervened, insisting I do the right thing. For them, duty was paramount. When I was barely fourteen and already working a weekend and after-school job, I earnestly asked my dad what he thought I should be when I grew up. He answered quite matter-of-factly, "It doesn't matter what you do for a living, as long as you're a *mensch*" (a decent responsible person of admirable character). I felt that if the roles were reversed, I'd have dragged Bart kicking and screaming if need be to visit his injured friend. That it was inconvenient, distressing, boring, or a thousand other things would not have mattered. Still, in quiet moments there were nagging doubts. Faced by an implacably stubborn Bart, in desperate flight and rebellion, would I really have done any better than the other parents? Probably not.

But no amount of soul-searching or insight into the adolescent mind could banish my recurring indignation at the cavalier way in which the boys brushed Bart aside and moved on with their lives. Gary especially got under my skin. On the eve of Bart's discharge from the hospital we had sent him an e-mail thanking and congratulating him on being such an important part of Bart's healing. Although he dropped Bart more swiftly and completely than any of the others, Gary continued to congratulate himself, bragging to all comers that we'd credited him with being a wonderful friend. It really felt like he'd pulled a bait and switch.

It may seem odd, but I had no problem forgiving the boys and Sean's parents for their parts in the accident. Dayle seems to have forgiven them instantly and permanently. It was, after all, an accident pure and simple. Sure, people made bad judgments all around, which set the stage. Bart should not have gotten into the car with Sean at all, no less in the back without a seat belt. Sean should have known better than to tool around at night with friends, barely a fortnight after receiving his license. Most crucially the Daniels should not have permitted their son, still wet behind the ears, to cruise around town with a car full of buddies. John Daniels had refused Sean's request but Gwenn Daniels relented, to her bitter regret. The street was dimly lit, with poor signage and banking, and a series of hard, sharp curves. At the wheel, distracted by loud, boisterous buddies, it was all too much for Sean. He misread the road, overreacted, then panicked and wrapped the car around a tree, not thirty yards from Main Street. In an instant all our lives were changed.

What is an accident really? Some people like to say everything happens for a reason, or even happens for the best, but I don't buy it. We make choices, do things, sometimes impulsively, sometimes thoughtfully, no matter. Other people are busy making choices and taking actions as well. Nonhuman factors also play a part in some outcomes—weather, wild critters, the phases of the moon, an endless list of possible causal influences. How many times has a fatal crash been precipitated by a yellow jacket flying through the open window of a speeding car? I guess we'll never know. We live and breathe and act in this causal stone soup influenced by too many factors to fully comprehend, much less control. When we collide with other people who are blithely doing their thing in unfortunate ways, we call the outcome an accident. When there is a happy result, we call it coincidence or kismet.

To see the hidden hand of God in all this is to saddle him with a needless burden. To suppose every yellow jacket is on a mission from God is rubbish. Our own free will, expressed through choices and actions, compounded by imperfect knowledge, seems the simplest, surest explanation. When people peddle platitudes like things "always work out for the best" or "are meant to be," they're just sanctifying whatever shit happens. I feel like screaming back Jack Nicholson's line from the film *As Good as It Gets:* "Go sell crazy someplace else; we're all stocked up here!" Don't get me wrong, I don't pretend to understand how it all sorts out. Important insights, deeper compassion, even a new closeness with God—these sometimes emerge from the ruins of tragic events. I don't doubt that for a minute and am grateful. But it sure seems more like a crapshoot than a preordained perfect outcome. Sean went on to total another car in a one-vehicle accident less than a year later, flipping it over a couple of times, walking away again with nary a scratch. Are we to presume that God favors Sean but not Bart? Isn't it simpler and more honest to admit that we haven't a clue how it all sorts out than to suppose that God has his fingerprints on every little thing that transpires in this vale of tears? I sometimes feel like the priest in Auschwitz remembered for his kindness and for a prayer uttered in a moment of supreme angst, "Dear God, if you exist, please help us! And dear God, even if you don't exist, please help us!"

Pushed hard enough, it makes more sense to suppose that God doesn't exist than to suppose that everything happens for the best. Perhaps atheists are right after all, and God is a human creation, the personification of our deepest longings for moral order and connectedness. I'm not sure how to reconcile God's nature, all powerful and good, with the world as we experience it. I have close friends who are agnostics and atheists, and they're among the finest folks I've ever known. Judged on the basis of moral behavior and character, they'd pass anyone's test for rectitude. One can be a good person with or without belief in God. So why believe? Whatever one believes, in God, or in something else—science, nature, progress, whatever—whichever way one turns, it still seems a choice, a decision, a leap of faith. There are lots of reasons to believe in God, none entirely compelling. If there were such a once-and-for-all proof of God's existence, carrying the same force as a proof in geometry, then there would be no need for faith. Knowing God would be easy as knowing the Pythagorean theorem.

For me, the best reason to believe in God is found inside, in one's heart or conscience. The still, small voice remains radically different than everything else we experience. Conscience does not illuminate how things actually work in the world, but rather how things ought to. It seems to point to a moral law beyond the world that science discovers and describes. A law of science describes how objects generally behave, for instance, force equals mass times acceleration. Our inner voice doesn't describe how we actually behave but how we should behave, not what we in fact want, but rather what we would wish to want. The laws of physics seem fundamentally different in kind than the laws of the heart.

Is there another reality beyond the one we stumble through everyday, beyond what we can touch and see and feel, even beyond the discoveries that science unfolds? If so, that other reality is God, and conscience the best clue we have about his nature and how he calls upon us to live. That there is something totally "other," apart from the world of everyday experience and science, is a pretty odd thing to accept on the face of it. But no more startlingly odd than the contrary position—that everything results from random forces, particles, waves, or strings in motion. What of the lives of the heroes and the teachings of the prophets? What of the Psalms, Shakespeare's sonnets, Michelangelo's *Pietà*, the Brandenburg concertos, the Salk vaccine, and the discovery of the double helix? Are all, in the end, results of purely natural processes fully comprehensible ultimately in terms of physics? Perhaps our highest achievements and aspirations, including the contents of conscience, can be explained naturalistically by their survival or adaptive value? Or are our better angels a reflection of God's nature? I choose to believe the latter, though I can't prove it.

✦

That summer we were lucky enough to be invited guests of the Namath/Dockery football camp. Broadway Joe and my employer John Dockery have sponsored the camp each year for over forty years. Friends since their playing days on the Super Bowl–winning 1969 Jets, they hold a weeklong camp for school-age players the first week of summer. In its forty-first year, the football camp extends dozens of scholarships to promising young minority athletes. Namath and Dockery have a blast with their young charges.

Bart and I, along with three of his buddies, were heading up to Massachusetts for the day. It was a two-and-a-half-hour drive, with Bart sitting in his customary place in the front passenger seat and Gary, Kyle, and Doug crammed into the back. Garry was so sick we had to pass him an carsick bag en route. But he wasn't going to miss a chance to meet Joe Namath. Stopping midpoint for a coffee break on the Massachusetts Turnpike, Bart became agitated in the bathroom, saying I didn't have to wait for him, he could find his way back to the car—he wasn't a baby, you know. When he finally found the car, he was flustered and muttering curses to himself. I held my breath, hoping his friends could divert him from the predictable outburst. We arrived at the sprawling rural campus just before Sunday clinics were to begin. Dockery gave us all a warm welcome, speaking with each boy personally, telling them how much he admired them for being loyal to Bart and reminding Bart how lucky he was to have them as friends.

While Broadway Joe's exploits are too well known to require comment, John Dockery's life is no less remarkable. One of seven children of hardworking Irish immigrant parents, Dockery rose by dint of talent, hard work, and a couple of lucky breaks to become a Super Bowl winner, sports broadcaster, and business leader. Born and raised in Brooklyn and educated at Catholic schools, he excelled academically but found his true expression through athletics, earning varsity letters in baseball, basketball, football, and track, being named All-City in both baseball and football.

Dockery was slated to continue on the traditional Catholic school route to an athletic scholarship until his high school coach and mentor John Paterno (Joe's brother) urged him to aim higher and try for the Ivy League. As a nervous seventeen-year-old, Dockery went up to Cambridge on an athletic scholarship, wondering if he could survive Harvard's academic rigors. He thrived, while earning letters in football, baseball, and track. Captain of the baseball team as well as top base stealer in the Eastern College Athletic Conference, on the gridiron he played safety and halfback, making All-East and All-Ivy.

After graduation, Dockery was signed by the Red Sox to play AA ball. Although he had always dreamed of playing in the majors, he couldn't manage to hit a slider or curve in the pros and was released after just two seasons. At only twenty-two, he already felt like his life was over, and he slid into a funk. Once again, his high school mentor, John Paterno, gave him the push he needed, calling the Jets' legendary coach Weeb Ewbank to arrange a tryout for young Dockery. John recalls, "I was standing on this pile of dirt trying to stop Don Maynard and John Saurer from catching passes thrown by Joe Namath. I held my own and was signed for the taxi squad. Fortunately, I was activated for the 1968 team that made it to the Super Bowl. I spent five years in all with the Jets." Talk about timing—Joe Namath's prediction for the 1969 Super Bowl, and living up to it, was one of the great moments in pro-football history. After the Jets, Dockery spent a couple of eventful years with the Steelers before hanging up his cleats.

With help from his wife, Anne, a Dublin-born actress, he got a tryout with Channel 5 sports and won a spot as field reporter, and eventually anchor. His career as sports announcer spanned ten years with CBS where he covered both college and NFL games, then NBC where he did Notre Dame football and the Olympic games around the globe. He won an Emmy for his coverage of the Tour de France. John remains involved with football as field announcer of NFL Monday Night Football on Westwood One radio.

Dockery's parents had owned and operated a small family business in Brooklyn, where John learned the values of hard work and thrift, honesty, and loyalty, principles by which he runs his own business, Cambridge Corporate Services, providing facilities management services to Fortune 500 companies.

Dockery has remained fast friends with many of his schoolmates from Brooklyn Prep, Harvard, and the NFL, and has always been extremely involved with a host of charitable causes. Two of his all-time favorites are the Abilities! and Brother Rick Curry's National Theatre Workshop of the Handicapped. Recently he was inducted into the Catholic high school hall of fame. John balances his Cambridge responsibilities with sports commentary and good works, to make for a very full and active life. His older daughter is a veterinarian, and his younger daughter is working on a PhD in psychology. Both are Harvard grads. He and his wife reside in Brooklyn, where his Horatio Alger story began.

Dockery's mother was devoted to his younger sister, Margaret, who struggles with cerebral palsy, and John shares that devotion, giving him keen insight into the role family plays in coping with chronic medical conditions. He repeatedly reached out to Bart just when he needed a word or gesture of encouragement, quietly and without fanfare. Though I'm dead sure Dockery never attended Hebrew school, he intuitively grasps the principles of tzedakah and practices the very highest type.

The highlight of the visit was watching Namath lead the quarterback clinic, followed by posing with him for pictures. Namath was down-to-earth, friendly and kind to Bart and his somewhat awestruck friends. The next day I rushed the film to a one-hour developer; then overnighted the 8x10 glossies back to camp, where Namath graciously inscribed one for each of the boys. A suitably framed photo of Bart, Joe Willie, and me hangs prominently in our den, inscribed, "Hey Bart, I enjoyed our visit. Good luck, pal! Joe Namath X12." A similar picture of Namath, Dockery, and Bart and his crew hangs in Bart's room above the TV. The day was an unforgettable highlight, made more so by the mementos festooning our walls.

As fine a day as it was, there was a churning undertone of dread growing in my gut. I worried about a likely outburst from Bart—he had come close when I handed him his midday dose of Risperdal; only his friends' joking around had saved the day. It wasn't so much the outburst itself that I feared as the resulting fallout on his friends. He was already terribly socially isolated. In fact we had organized this outing as an opportunity for him to spend quality time with them. My fretting was compounded by the sinking feeling that they were inevitably drifting apart. Distracted by these sorts of worries, on the way home I drove off from a fueling stop with Doug still in the gas station bathroom. After that incident I asked our family doctor for something to help with my nerves. The anti-anxiety medication Buspar became my "father's little helper" for the next few years. Though temperamentally immune to depression, I had discovered my proclivity for high anxiety.

18
School Days

Our attorney, Bruce Blatchly, asked for a Bart update. This is the e-mail I sent to him just as Bart was returning to school.

> Bart continues to make progress, but slowly. His gate and posture are similar to a stroke victim's—his right hand is somewhat clenched, and he walks slowly. His balance and ability to move through obstacles is impaired. He has an overall "right side neglect"—meaning he mostly forgets about his right side altogether. He has to be reminded to use his right hand for such functions as eating or computing. His right hand lacks the fine motor control necessary for such tasks as writing cursively or dribbling a ball. Physically, his greatest deficit is the cut in his field of vision. He's blind to the right side in both eyes. Effectively, he sees only a little more than half the normal range of sight. Prism glasses have corrected this slightly, but without major improvement in his field of vision, driving an auto is doubtful. Depth perception is noticeably weak, and walking down stairs or pouring juice from a pitcher is awkward at best. He has persistent fatigue and sleeps at least twelve hours a night, with bouts of exhaustion during the day. He is on stimulant medicines to help with this problem.
>
> Cognitively he continues to make progress. His long-term memory and recollection of general knowledge is at an early elementary school level. IQ testing and WIAT (Wechsler Individual Achievement Test) testing seem to place his general IQ at around 68. This should

continue to improve over time. His short-term memory has been practically nonexistent, but is beginning to improve as well. Without short-term memory improvement, learning new things is near impossible.

Bart was discharged from Helen Hayes Hospital's day program of therapy at the end of August and began school this week. His IEP (Individual Education Program) calls for a short day (10:30–2:00 p.m.), frequent rest periods, special ed classes, occupational, physical, speech, and vision therapies in school, and a one-on-one aide to help him navigate the halls and take notes for him. It also calls for regular counseling sessions with the school social worker. He will probably also need additional physical therapy outside of school.

Emotionally he is fairly even, although he is on medication to prevent angry outbursts that occasionally have been triggered by tiredness or frustration. He is especially frustrated by his vision problems, which make reading difficult and tiresome, and ball playing awkward. Considering everything, his spirits are pretty good. Fortunately his friends continue to visit him, although less frequently. Now he gets to see friends and socialize a little at school each day, which helps. We're arranging for a Marist College student who majors in special ed to visit Bart a few hours a week and act as a mentor/companion. It will be some time before Bart can keep up with his friends, so we are concerned about depression in future. Ironically, the more he recovers, the more he is aware of his disabilities and the greater his frustration with his relative social isolation. Bart is an intensely outgoing and gregarious person, and does not tolerate solitude well. We do whatever we can to encourage his socializing with his friends, but he has neither the stamina nor independence to do much in the area.

One could write a book about the trials of children with special needs in public schools. Parents of kids with learning disabilities will know what I'm referring to—the Committee on Special Education (CSE) meetings, the negotiations and compromises over how much support your child receives, the team meetings with special ed teachers and therapists, the revisions to the plan, and so on. It was a real eye-opener for Dayle and me, who had previously never given a moment's thought to special ed, except maybe to grouse a little about how large a tax bite it took from the school budget. New Paltz, unlike most rural upstate towns, has a good school system, but to our amazement and delight we discovered it had a first-rate special education program, boasting several master teachers along with dedicated therapists and aides. So after a series of meetings, conferences, and testing, Bart was slated to return to school, ready or not.

Of course, school would be different. The day was abbreviated. No way could he make it through a full session. His classes were in the special ed department, and he was assigned a full-time, one-on-one aide. Regular sessions of physical, occupational, speech, and vision therapy as well as counseling were worked into his weekly schedule. Most therapies were integrated into classes, though a few were timed just before or after school. He would attend regular gym classes, with the assistance of his aide and a physical therapist. Special gym classes had been discussed, but we rejected that idea. Bart would rather struggle to keep up with his peers than be isolated with kids who had severe physical and developmental disabilities, many confined to wheelchairs. Dayle would drive him to and from school, as the only transportation available was a special ed van with a lift for wheelchairs. Bart was fronting well, hardly showing a hint of the heartbreak he must feel, and we wanted to spare him the embarrassment of arriving at school belted into a seat on a special van. He was slated to carry a fairly demanding academic load: English, science, and American history. Since no special ed math class was being offered that year, math tutoring was arranged. We had no idea how he would manage all that but figured the stimulation would be good for him. A little extra worry was infused into the picture when the CSE made it plain that if Bart couldn't manage to pass these special courses, he probably couldn't remain in a school setting.

He was encouraged to take frequent breaks, every fifteen minutes if need be. So, with little fanfare (but much prayer and lighting of candles), Bart returned to school after a nine-month absence. Though he had previously attended the school for two and a half years, he could no longer find his way around without guidance from JR, his dedicated aide. Between classes the hallways were wildly overcrowded and deafening, making navigating even tougher. He tried slipping away on his own, but quickly became lost and confused. In class, after fifteen or twenty minutes, he'd drop his head down and snooze. A warm relationship developed between Bart and his counselor, a young school social worker named Dave Rosenthal, who was himself adopted. Always ready to treat a fellow adoptee as a brother, Bart quickly opened up to him, confiding that he was self-conscious about eating in front of his friends. His right hand was so unreliable that he often made a mess of things. JR arranged for him to buy easy-to-handle lunches in the cafeteria, mostly sandwiches and wraps. Dining presented another thorny problem. Bart was not happy having a grown woman traipsing about after him and was eager to blow her off, especially in the cafeteria, where everyone meets and greets. Yet JR was responsible for steering him to the nurse's office at lunchtime for his second dose of Risperdal, without which he'd be too emotionally volatile to continue with classes.

Barely a month into school, with the honeymoon clearly over, Bart blew up at JR in the cafeteria, cursed her out, and refused to walk with or acknowledge her the remainder of the day. Bart turned up at the nurse's office on his own, only to find that he'd already taken his meds. JR, a local woman who had graduated the same high school, certainly earned her keep bird-dogging Bart. We felt sorry for her. Meanwhile, cafeteria time grew increasingly problematic. Nobody invited Bart over to dine with them, and he seemed reluctant or unable to just deal himself in. The old ease and self-confidence was shot, and his peers didn't know quite what to make of him. They observed his aide, and couldn't help but notice his confusion and short temper. So he was truly the odd man out. This sort of problem can really eat your heart out—as there's practically nothing to be done. We spoke with Coach Defino and Coach Tegeler about convincing Kyle and Gary to eat with Bart. In profound denial, Bart still thought of them as his best friends. The coaches came through, and the boys started to dine with Bart on certain days. With the ice broken, a few other boys, including Sean, came forward, volunteering to eat with Bart on other days. The school administration helped out by arranging for some of the guys to switch lunch periods so they'd be able to join Bart. Surrounded by buddies, lunch became Bart's favorite period, as always.

We'd get a pretty good picture of how school went by reading Bart's memory log in which teachers, therapists, and especially JR accounted for his day, including homework assignments. Bart seemed to be trying hard to keep up in class. Once prompted, he worked faithfully on homework assignments, though Dayle or I had to read the textbooks aloud and transcribe his answers. The work generally was review for him, roughly equivalent to seventh or eighth grade level. Most other kids in his classes didn't have acquired learning disabilities; their conditions were congenital, so for them the material was brand-new.

Of course, with TBI, everything old is new again, but not in a predictable way. Some things he remembered perfectly, others not. We were often surprised by what was lost and what still intact. His math tutor found that while Bart had forgotten even the most rudimentary math facts—like three plus two equals five—he still remembered how to solve quadratic equations. Bart always had an excellent vocabulary, partially due to being an avid reader. He'd read every one of Crichton's novels, most of Stephen King's, plus stacks of sports, wrestling, and rock 'n' roll magazines. Our remote home in the mountains did not get cable access until Bart was in his early teens. Without TV to mesmerize him, he read himself to sleep. Needless to say, no sooner had the cable installer left our house than he assumed the position in front of the TV and has been a faithful devotee ever since.

We dug through the basement cedar closet to find old math flash cards, and played math games at dinner or driving in the car. Helping him relearn elementary arithmetic was a little awkward. Bart was embarrassed to find he didn't recall the sum of five plus seven, or loads of other similar facts. He'd stammer, "I feel like I should know this," and hazard a guess. Slowly, over the course of that first year back in school, with tons of repetition, he managed to relearn basic math facts. To everyone's relief, as the materials became more advanced, his comprehension improved. He had a real tough time with multiplying and dividing fractions (then again, who doesn't?), did better with decimals and percentages, and better still with elementary algebra. To this day, we can't predict with precision what's there and what's gone, either in his general knowledge or his personal memories. Months after his return home, I was speculating about how proud of him his grandmother and grandfather would have been. His face went purple as he stammered in a husky whisper, "You mean grandma's dead?" My mother had died more than a year prior to the accident. His memory of the months immediately preceding the accident seemed to have been wiped clean. I felt awful—my mother and he were close, and here he was losing her all over again.

Dayle and I shared many bottles of red wine wondering about the strange nature of Bart's losses. While his excellent vocabulary remained mostly intact, he no longer seemed able to fathom common expressions like "a piece of cake" or "waking up on the wrong side of bed." He could still tell a simple joke, but often didn't get ones told by others. We came up with the metaphor for TBI of a shattered mirror. Some pieces are hopelessly smashed to bits, while other larger shards still reflect perfectly. If a larger piece happened to hold, say, knowledge of the 2000 NBA All-Stars, then while on that subject, you'd never suspect that the overall mirror was shattered. Many people who met Bart for the first time remarked how normal he seemed. Of course, if they spent a few more minutes chatting with him and came suddenly to the edge of that shard, they were in for a rough ride.

A week or so after returning to school, Bart insisted on going to the season's opening football game. He regularly attended home games in previous years, as do most high school kids and near half the town, but had never bothered with away games, so it was with some surprise and concern that I drove up to Kingston's Dietz Stadium, the closest thing in Ulster County to a professional venue, with artificial turf and some two thousand seats.

Bart seemed tired and listless during the half-hour drive, so we sat in silence, except for rap music blaring on the radio. Too bad—he had practically outgrown rap in the months before the accident, progressively shifting back to alternative and classic rock. He had practically collected the complete Led Zeppelin. But that was forgotten now, and we were back to the music he had loved at fifteen—rap. What a drag. I dully wondered about how long it would take him to outgrow it a second time.

New Paltz was facing its traditional nemesis, Wallkill High School. It was a big game, and there were several hundred excited New Paltz fans in the stands. We joined them, finding seats near parents of several players as well as Bart's former karate teacher, Sensei Mike. Most hadn't seen Bart in nine months. After some hugs and pats on the back, Bart and I settled down to watch the game, which was nearing kickoff. Several of Bart's friends, girls whose homes he had been to for sleepover parties last year, walked right by us without batting an eye. I wasn't sure Bart had noticed them, but I was damn sure they had studiously avoided noticing him. It was going to be a very tough time for poor Bart, if even old friends walk on by without so much as a "fair thee well." Inwardly cringing, I held my peace.

Both teams were on the field, captains, coaches and referees moving toward the coin toss, when New Paltz head coach Tom Tegeler, a giant of a man, abruptly turned and strode swiftly from the field and up into the stands. He'd gotten wind that Bart was there, and climbed up and gave him a huge bear hug. Then, arm around Bart's shoulder, quietly confided to him that he was so nervous about the opening game that he was near ready to puke. The next moment he was gone and the toss and game ensued. After twenty minutes or so, bushed, Bart asked to go home.

In one simple gesture, under full public scrutiny, Tegeler, Bart's middle school basketball coach, a former minor league baseball player and local sports legend, had demonstrated that he had his priorities straight. An act of kindness and solidarity put Tegeler in our hall of fame. The memory of that night often gave me comfort over the next three years, as it would unfailingly come to mind every time I ran into Coach at the high school. I retold the story many times, and it's become part of our family folklore. You can imagine how astonished I was to learn years later that Coach Tegeler, in the excitement of the big game, had forgotten the whole thing. That really shouldn't have surprised me. People in the habit of doing them don't dwell on their acts of kindness.

> Excerpt from Dayle's note to herself, Monday, October 28, 2002:
>
> "Today I feel a bit f---d up. B can drive me crazy with not being able to get things done and have some privacy. Then, what really throws me over the edge is bringing him to school and Sean, Kyle and Matt are signing in . . . only Sean said hello and they all avoided him. That's such a heartbreak for me that I had to go directly to church and say some prayers. So while I sit here, awaiting my oil change and tire rotation I read about faith . . . learning that it's a choice. Which, in fact, it would have to be. I don't want any bitterness to erode my spirits. I just have to keep faith that B will continue to heal and move onwards toward a better life. (However, the daily routine of reality makes it tough just the same.)"

Three years after it was written, I discovered that note while cleaning out the car's glove compartment. I know too well the recurrent heartache I felt over Bart's loss of friends, but never realized how hard it weighed on poor Dayle. Whenever I complained to her about it, she seemed to take a conciliatory and forgiving attitude, frequently expressing her sympathy for Gwenn Daniels, whom she felt was tormented by guilt.

Little Buddha

Bart with mom, fresh
off the plane

Family awaits Cassidy

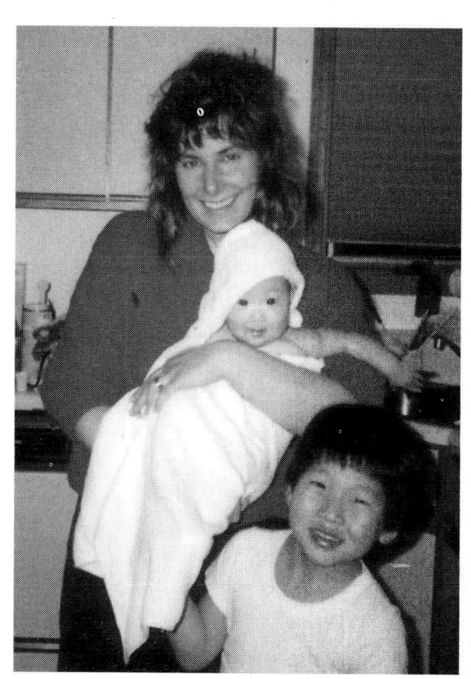

Bart's snow angel
arrives home

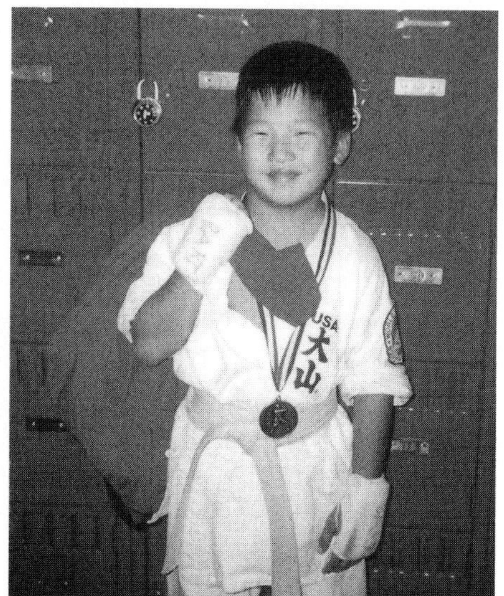

Loveable rogue

Camp Mujigae

Bart and his snow angel
all decked out

With Bart and Cass

Bart and Cassidy prior to accident

Bart's surgeon, Dr. David Harter

Bart in wheelchair

Seventeenth birthday party with Mujigae friends, Ashlee (left) and Kaili (right)

Bart on his first trip to Namath-Dockery Football Camp

Kayaking in Maine, 2003

Bart and campers at Mujigae, 2004

High school graduation

Bart and Cassidy on Corfu

With Bart on Corfu

Bart with Joe Namath and John Dockery (courtesy of Bill Kelly)

With Bart and Cassidy, 2009

19
Unintended Consequences

"Want to give God a good laugh? Tell Him your plans."
—Mother Teresa

Economists sometimes refer to the law of unintended consequences. What it means is you don't necessarily get what you intend—rather you get all of the consequences of an action or policy, including some unintended ones. It is probably the scientific basis for the old saw that the road to hell is paved with good intentions. We knew that our boy was too immature and impulsive to be driving on his own at age sixteen. So Dayle and I challenged Bart: work and save $2,500 and we'd match it and go buy a fine used car. Since Bart had no money, we figured with a little luck on our side he'd be seventeen before he'd squirreled away that much cash. By then he'd be a year older and more mature, have another year of supervised driving under his belt, and hopefully be roadworthy. Of course, we hadn't fully worked out all the unintended consequences of this approach, like his being a passenger in other boys' cars. We had of course extracted from him a promise to always wear seat belts.

✦

A month after the start of school, I managed to secure tickets to a Nets-Mavericks game, inviting Doug and Kyle to join Bart and me for the Saturday night contest. On the two-hour drive down to the New Jersey Meadowlands, during the game, and afterward returning home, the boys hardly spoke a word. Previously these guys would have been riotous—blasting music, cracking up, talking trash. Now they were at a loss for words. Bart wanted desperately to keep up with the guys, with their new girlfriends and cars, but the old life of the party was near tongue-tied. The boys seemed equally dumbfounded by the new Bart. I felt a heavy weight of care, worry, and sadness. How would Bart manage this tough slog back without a band of brothers at his side? And how would the family cope if he lost hope and despaired? I knew that somehow we couldn't let that happen. By hook or by crook we'd have to keep him busy, preoccupied, and on a positive tack. Because he was naturally an upbeat sort of guy, his predilection would be to look on the bright side of things. His sunny disposition was jarringly at odds with an increasingly frequent tendency to perseverate or return repeatedly to a negative idea, making it all the harder to take, as if each time the old fun-loving Bart tried to come out, he'd get his tongue tangled in a web of negative vibes.

The next weekend the family went to see *Guys and Dolls* at the local college. Everyone, including Bart, loved it. We made a point of requesting right side theater seats in deference to Bart's blind side, something that has since become second nature. We sit far right in any auditorium, even when Bart's not along. Habit is king over all.

An old friend, Jan Stivers, professor of education at nearby Marist College and a parent of Korean adopted kids, had advised us on getting Bart back into school with minimum fuss and optimal support. Well-known in the school district, Jan had taught several key members of Bart's team, including the school psychologist. So we turned to her again for help with a looming, delicate problem: how to keep Bart happily occupied on the weekends. His former friends were now in the wind, and he was spending way too much time alone in his room or pacing the house. He desperately needed to get out with young people, maybe even play some ball. Jan arranged for Bart to meet Brian Johnston, a senior at Marist doing student teaching in the local schools. After he had visited Bart at home a couple of Saturdays and it was clear they had hit it off we let the two of them drive across the river to Poughkeepsie where Marist College, and most of the interesting stores, malls, and movies are located. Brian was a rare find. Easygoing and sports-loving (he came from Boston, but Bart grudgingly forgave his membership in the Red Sox Nation), he even loved rap music as much as Bart. They often made CD mixes of their favorites songs. Working with Bart was valuable experience for Brian as a young special ed major, and he was truly a natural. They hung out, played video games, went to the movies, even gradually began to shoot some hoops. It was wonderful for Bart, and as a bonus afforded Dayle and me four or five hours of respite each week. Brian was the first of four successive Marist special ed students who served over the next three years as Saturday companions. As Bart became more nearly "normal" they progressively included him in their regular activities, including get-togethers with friends. Marvelous people, first and last, the final one, Pete Demarco, turned out to be cousin to one of Bart's oldest and best friends from Camp Mujigae. What a small world.

Each morning Dayle faced the daunting task of waking Bart for school. He slept like a log—it was scary. Besides, never an eager student, he was especially glum about facing a day filled with JR and special ed classes. When they arrived at school, Bart still beefing about not needing JR to tag along after him, he'd invariably be greeted at the late sign-in desk by one or another of the coaches, who would take him around like a long-lost brother. What a great way to start the day! Bart never understood that without JR to assure his safety, the district wouldn't allow him on school premises.

Later that year when he discovered the Special Ed character featured on Comedy Central's *Crank Yankers*, Bart became a huge fan, doing a very credible impression. Thank God, he never lost his sense of humor, though it regressed to grade school level. Being funny was so core a part of his identity that he often asked that first year home, "Am I still funny?" He was—in a crude whoopee-cushion kind of way. It was a way of hanging on to a vital part of his old self. We all had plenty of good belly laughs, with Bart even occasionally able to poke fun at himself. One time he insisted, quite convincingly, that ever since emerging from the coma, "Sometimes I see dead people." Turns out he was spoofing the movie *The Sixth Sense*, but for a few unnerving moments, he really had us going. After all, who knows what kinds of hallucinations he had or might still be having? We rolled on the floor laughing. I'm no elitist when it comes to humor—if it feels good, it is good. Bart invented a couple of signature sayings, including a funny way of sing-songing "wa-haaa" meaning something like, "Hey, I'm a little crazy, so don't bother me." Sometimes we'd all yell it out the car windows. (Everyone but Cassidy, who was too reserved for that sort of thing.) Even now, if Dayle nags me too much, I'm liable to belt out a loud "wa haaa" to mark my territory. Bart also loved to use "boo-yah" as a verbal exclamation point. (Much like TV's Jim

Cramer's greeting on *Mad Money*). To his morning complaints about school, we'd reply, "Hey, it beats the hell out of Helen Hayes. Boo-yah!" Frowning, he'd nod halfhearted agreement.

His short-term memory was gradually improving, but not fast enough to prevent a series of losses at school. Since he couldn't remember the combination to his gym locker, he resorted to leaving it unlocked. In the first year he lost three watches and a couple of jackets, including a brand-new winter coat from L.L.Bean. Dayle tore the school apart trying to find that fine coat, but with no luck. I couldn't worry much about lost stuff, but I dusted off my old winter jackets and looked for sales on watches, buying three at a time at J.C. Penney. They were important tools, indicating the date and day of the week, as well as time. Without a watch, Bart would ask the date and time at least fifty times a day. With a watch, he was more self-reliant. Very gradually he became aware of asking repetitive questions and began to preface them with, "I know I probably asked this before, but what's today?" With increased awareness came increasing frustration and embarrassment over his poor memory. It was a punishing cycle he would experience again and again. As memory and cognition continued to improved and the fog lifted, he was forced to confront his losses afresh, each time with a progressively clearer sense of their full meaning and impact. So every new breakthrough carried a built-in downside.

Each of us grieved the loss of the old Bart at our own pace and in our own way. Elisabeth Kübler-Ross in her book *On Death and Dying* explains that when we lose a loved one, we normally go through five stages: denial, anger, bargaining, depression, and finally acceptance. But in spite of its prevalence in popular culture, this explanation of grieving is wrong, or at least incomplete. Acceptance is not the final stage. The last stage might be called positive engagement. Even after you've fully accepted the reality of the loss, the pain of it can still go on for a long, long time. After all, one has to learn to cope with a whole new set of realties. Old habits, ways of relating, and expectations of what one can expect of others can't be shucked off easily. One must relearn to navigate the world without the familiar loved one by their side. To finally move beyond grief, each of us had to find ways to value and embrace the new Bart in his own right, not as a mere shadow of the old. That final stage, embracing the new person or situation fully, without regrets or second thoughts, is really tough. But the family can never finish grieving and truly heal without it. Bart's grieving was even more complicated, as he repeatedly mourned the loss of self, casting about desperately trying to find some shreds of value to cling to. For her part Cassidy seemed to founder, unable to gain any traction with this last, hardest leap—finding and affirming value in the new Bart.

✦

The school district had assembled a wonderful team of specialists—teachers, aides, therapists, and coaches. But the occupational therapist, Cathy Noonan, got under his skin, and Bart began to carp about her with numbing regularity. We were a little surprised, since we expected Bart to cut her a little extra slack because she was an older woman. Even as a baby, he seemed drawn to old folks. We speculated that this preference might be due to the warm love of his foster mother, an elderly grandmother. When the original "match pictures" arrived from Korea, there was Bart, fairly bursting with life, perched on the lap of a terribly tired-looking, old woman. The contrast was comical. But Bart cut no slack for Cathy Noonan, complaining that she treated him like a little kid, frequently patting him on the head. We inquired discreetly with the director of special ed about the possibility of switching OTs. He acknowledged that Cathy's experience was predominantly with much younger children, and her style doubtless suited them better. He joked that she patted even him on the head from time to time. But the bottom line was that there was no one else available.

The situation could have been humorous or trivial, but not when you've got a brain-injured kid with a dogged tendency to perseverate. Once Bart sank his teeth into somebody he disliked, like a pit bull, he'd never let go. Prior to the accident, I'd joked that Bart must have been a descendent of Marco Polo, since he had an Italian penchant for vendetta. (As far as I know Polo never made it as far as Korea.) Now his rigid inability to let go and move on was pronounced and maddening. A despised science teacher who had picked on him in ninth grade became the object of remorseless carping all over again. No amount of advice, discussion, or reasoning would slake his animosity, which was way out of proportion to any perceived offenses. We talked to the school psychologist as well as directly to Cathy Noonan, but she wasn't able to change a lifetime of practice to suit Bart. (She did try.) We advised Bart to speak with her directly about the head patting, after which she desisted. Bart complained bitterly about her every morning on the way to school. We'd try to divert him with replies like, "Well today's Monday, and you only have OT on Tuesday and Thursday." Though distractibility is generally a big problem with TBI, not so when it came to one of Bart's pet peeves. What a lousy, negative way to start the day for Bart and for anyone within earshot. Were we to point out that he was making too much of a fuss, it just sailed right over his head, or earned us an angry outburst for our trouble.

20

A Day at the Museum

The high school special ed department had scheduled a trip to the American Museum of Natural History as part of their science curriculum. Bart was invited to come, but only if chaperoned by a parent. I've always loved that museum. As a kid I'd lose myself in the vast Hall of North American Mammals, awestruck by the lifelike scenes of bison and grizzlies, antelope and cougars. So I jumped at the chance to skip work and go. Dayle and I both had some misgivings about the trip. It was a two-hour ride down to the city on a school bus and would make for a very long day. If Bart didn't nap en route, he might become overtired, which usually spelled trouble. There was also the matter of his medications. He'd need to take his meds at lunchtime but was not inclined to take them in front of peers. (At school there was the privacy of the nurses' office.) We were also concerned about his tolerance of busy, noisy environments. In the old days he'd have been the first to run wild making a racket; now he couldn't bear loud noises or chaotic places. A crying baby in a restaurant would set him to fussing. But he liked the science teacher, and he and I badly wanted to go, so off we went. I figured we'd muddle through somehow.

The ride down went quite well. One of the special ed aides from the science class came along. Bart was particularly fond of Joanne, so we settled down next to her. She was young and vivacious, and what's more, she wasn't JR. Truth be told, any aide charged with tagging after Bart everyday, reminding him where to go and when, would have earned Bart's undying enmity. He badly needed one (for one thing, he wasn't able to take class notes with his bum right hand, much less keep track of his homework assignments, which JR faithfully transcribed in his memory log) but he hated the public humiliation that an aide represented in his eyes. Under his hypercritical scrutiny, Mother Teresa would not have passed muster.

Arriving at the museum, Bart was getting pretty edgy, fidgeting throughout the tedious process of marshalling the kids, ticketing, and general waiting in line that was involved in shepherding a large school group into the museum. The next thing we knew, it was lunchtime. We'd brought bag lunches, so were expected to eat in special sections reserved for school groups. After a series of false starts (nobody seemed to know exactly where our designated lunch area was, just that it was somewhere in the basement), we were led to a large underground cul de sac and faced with a scene of bedlam. The place was really hopping—alive with screaming, laughing kids cramped cheek by jowl, swarming over cafeteria-style tables. This was where school groups who were not buying lunch in the cafeteria were consigned. The acoustics were so bad you could only be understood if you were within a few inches of someone's ear. I screamed in Bart's, "Ya wanna get out of here?" But he either didn't hear or understand. I made sure we sat at the pretty young aide's table. I knew he was overdue for his meds, and they couldn't be put off any longer. I tried to whisper but had to scream in her ear, asking if she'd mind handing him the meds, as he'd more likely tolerate them coming from her. Wouldn't you know, he managed to hear me speaking to her, and launched a major hissy fit. He threw the meds to the floor, wouldn't touch his lunch, and began muttering angrily to himself. Fortunately, I carried a spare dose, which she managed to get him to take later, after we had left that chaos.

But it was too little too late. As we began to traipse upstairs to the dinosaur exhibits, the highlight of the trip, Bart told me emphatically to stay away from him, muttering to himself nonstop about "the f---ing faggot." I backed off several steps, trying to give him some space, and he seemed to be cooling off as the tour guide began explaining the exhibits. I carefully moved to the opposite side of each exhibit, so he'd have the illusion of independence. But his concentration was fried by then, and eventually his gaze settled upon me. He seemed to snap, just like that, rushing at me, hissing that I'd better get the f--- away from him. I told him firmly but nicely that I had to keep him in sight; I'd promised the school—but he ran away, taking off as fast as he could, muttering loudly, that I'd better keep the f--- away from him. The hall was crowded with school groups and tourists, and with his blind side, he bumped into people a couple of times, like a wild beast, running for his life. He led me a frantic chase through three cavernous exhibit rooms, a couple times around each. Heart pounding, I didn't have a clue how I was going to capture him once I caught up to him, short of a football tackle.

I was heartsick and breathless when he finally stumbled into a group of kids from school. One of them was sitting on the floor against a wall, head in hands. Bart immediately asked, "Hey, what's up with you, Jeremy?" The boy looked up, a sickly look on his face, replying, "Big crowded places make me sick." Just like that, Bart was sitting next to Jeremy, commiserating, trying to get him to laugh. I caught my breath, kept a safe distance, and through eavesdropping guessed that Jeremy was a high-functioning autistic child who had trouble handling large groups of people. I was amazed by the sudden transformation in Bart's affect. As if a spell had been cast, instantly he was the funny, caring boy of old. Maybe the meds were kicking in. Who the hell knew?

At home that evening, reviewing the day's misadventures with Dayle over a bottle of wine, I had the sinking feeling of being in way over my head, like being pulled down as a kid by a riptide off Rockaway Beach. Though fully committed to seeing Bart whole again, I was unnerved and frightened by how far we still had to go. Ten months after the accident and he was still wildly irrational, plum out of his mind.

An old friend, Joe Vacarro, who's wrestled with post-traumatic stress syndrome since Vietnam, is wont to say, "Guys like us are never out of the forest." It did feel as if we were very deep in the forest, and if not totally lost, then far from familiar, well-trodden paths. Would the family ever find a way back to sunlit uplands? A congenital optimist, I've always felt deep in my gut that one can find a way through most anything. But with TBI, muddling through just isn't good enough. Careful planning and structure are required to have even a fighting chance of success. In recurring nightmares, sometimes Bart would be unreachable in the museum's cavernous halls, sometimes when I managed to catch him up, he was the pre-accident Bart, and Lord knows what else. I'd wake in a sweat, vaguely sensing what my mother was driving at when she pronounced the lugubrious judgment that "life is like a sentence, which we must serve."

21
The Conspiracy of Decency

School began to fall into a routine of sorts. The drive over contained the usual minidrama, with Bart railing against Cathy Noonan, JR, and anyone else who happened to be on his shitlist. Once at school, he would invariably be welcomed at the door by one or another of the coaches. Bart tried to follow along in classes but was unable to answer questions during discussion. He rapidly tired and was often sleepy during therapy sessions, but worked hardest in gym, where his physical therapist reported that he was making good progress. Gradually he began to walk with a more normal stride, left hand swinging in a regular rhythm, while his clenched right hand stubbornly refused. The coaches, as ever, were his biggest boosters. They encouraged Bart in gym class, and many of the kids followed their example. He even began to play a little five-on-five basketball, with the kids taking it easy on him. He only had wind for a couple of minutes.

Coach Defino approached me one day to propose that he work with Bart on basic basketball skills Fridays after school. He knew how much Bart loved the game and thought that with personal attention he could bring Bart along quickly. Who knew, maybe someday Bart could play in the town league? I loved the idea and insisted on paying for his time. After all, he was busy running camps and clinics, to say nothing of varsity teams—his time was valuable. Coach D thanked me but declined, saying he just wanted to do it—no charge. I dug in my heels; if he didn't want the money, he could put it away for his young kids. Shaking his head and still smiling he replied, "Listen, Joel, I've known you and Bart a long time. I want to do this for Bart, but I'm doing it my way or the highway." What can you say to that kind of offer? I agreed, overwhelmed by his kindness and generosity. He worked with Bart for an hour practically every Friday for the remainder of the school year, most of the following summer, and then again the next school year. Those sessions were the highlight of Bart's week. He complained a little after each that coach drilled him mercilessly, running many of the basic drills he had used with middle school and junior varsity teams, including endurance drills. Sessions always ended by playing some one-on-one. Bart began to show real improvement in his game, though of course he now played left-handed.

People seemed to just spring up whenever Bart needed them: John Dockery, Sensei Mike, Coach Tegeler and Coach Defino, Mrs. Z, Doug, the Rickards, the Kennedys, Jan Stivers, and on and on. Our friend Duffy, who lit a candle for Bart everyday for years, joking that he'd missed his chance to buy stock in a candle company, gave Bart weekly craniosacral therapy treatments that entire first year, then monthly for the next two. Like Coach D, he simply refused payment, saying only, "Bart's a great kid, and it's such a crushing injury. I just need to do something to help." Dayle and I began to marvel at the "conspiracy of decency," as we called it—good people going about their business quietly, trying to help out, making the world a little better place. Knock on any door, you'll find them, salt of the earth, tangible evidence of the divine spark in us all. Though not exactly breaking news, when I feel myself getting lost and overwhelmed in a desperate fight, it's comforting to remember.

Most Saturday nights Doug visited, usually stopping on the way to a date. The boys would watch a movie or maybe play a video game down in Bart's room. It was a bright spot. After Doug left, Bart would get on the phone and call around to all the usual suspects—Gary, Kyle, Rebecca, and a couple of others. They screened his calls, but if by chance he caught one of them off guard, each had ready excuses why they were unavailable. Saturday night was a big thing to Bart, and the Saturday night calling ritual went on for years, always with the same upshot. When he finally graduated high school two years after his friends, under his yearbook photo he wrote thanks to his "brothers" Kyle and Gary, an inscription that gave Dayle and me the creeps. It seems the harder a fact is to stomach, the more likely we are to dig deep and deny it. Bart simply could not accept that his former friends had abandoned him, despite all evidence to the contrary.

We were starting to play a bit of basketball out on the driveway, easy kids' games, like "around the world" and gradually, a little twenty-one—games that were not too strenuous and afforded plenty of chances to rest. When asked if he'd like to go out to shoot some hoops, Bart would invariably decline. But I know my boy, so I'd go out and begin to dribble around and shoot baskets. He'd be drawn like a cat to catnip. His reluctance was probably based on a couple of things. First, playing with dad was not his idea of a good time. More than that, Bart still recalled how well he used to play, often settling down to watch home videos of old middle or high school games. Now, his dribbling was barely under control, he avoided the right side altogether, and his shooting was quite erratic. Though his play suffered by comparison, it was good to see him play, and good for him to play. After a game one Saturday evening, John Kennedy, practically an uncle, took Bart to see *Jackass: The Movie* and then out to Hooters in Albany. The film and restaurant were both Bart's choices, and he had a great time.

At the end of October, we halved his dose of the antipsychotic drug Risperdal, hoping a lower dose would make him more alert. Bart was chronically tired, which is considered normal during recovery. He was also plagued with persistent memory trouble—remembering whether it was an A or B schedule day at school, or recalling and following one-step directions. His tolerance for JR was increasingly fragile, so Coach Phelps, fresh out of college, began subbing for her at lunch. It was a welcome break for both Bart and JR. The speech therapist constructed a visual schedule of the school week to help Bart navigate and orient better—with easy-to-read room numbers and photos of teachers. Weekly meetings with the school counselor, recorded in his memory log, continued to shine light on what was going on in his head. In typical teenage fashion, he rarely confided anything to his parents, but eagerly admitted to Dave R. that he was angry that he couldn't manage to recall parts of his life or recent events. Gym continued to be a highlight, and by Thanksgiving he was jogging six minutes at a time. We rejoiced in his ability to run at all, but Bart shrugged it off, mumbling that he used to run a sub-six minute mile.

Barty invented a game we played practically every time he rode in the car, whether a short hop to school or an hour-long ride to Albany to visit relatives. Whenever a new song came on the radio, with a wide grin on his face he'd pipe up, "All right, who can name this artist?" If we had no idea who the musical artist was, he'd gladly give us three choices. None of us could touch Bart at this contest—he seemed to remember the name of every singer or group, from 1960s classics through contemporary alternative rock and rap. It was a rare area where his long-term memory was still fully intact, and in a subject that really mattered to him no less. It was a real bright spot—a wonderful break from the long laundry list of things he had trouble remembering. Bart's natural playfulness, combined with the prospect of victory in competition, made the game irresistible to him, and he would return to it over and over again. The poor guy still found it practically impossible to have an interesting conversation, hamstrung by attention deficits, memory problems, and just plain inability to follow a train of thought. Yet, ever the extrovert, he desperately craved the give-and-take of social discourse, and this game was the next best thing. The only hitch was that the moment someone correctly guessed an artist, he would immediately change the station in search of another tune to examine. The net result was we no longer enjoyed listening to music in the car, since Bart was constantly switching stations midsong. It could drive us nuts. If he finally fatigued and drifted off for a few Zs, he'd soon wake up refreshed, hand reaching for the radio controls.

In early November the school district held its annual emergency evacuation drill. Bart rode home on the bus with all the other kids. Pam, his steady driver for ten years, was a card-carrying member of the conspiracy of decency. While he was in the hospital she had laminated a large handmade school bus–shaped card, inscribed with greetings from all the kids on Bart's bus. He kept it near his bed for years. An avid reader of the e-mailed Bart updates, she had written us and prayed for Bart daily and been a key organizer of the Bart dance. Like many people who found Bart a handful (she had referred him to school detention a dozen times), she adored him all the same. Anyone who is a bit of a rogue herself cannot resist Bart.

✦

To everyone's surprise, Bart was becoming an avid shopper. Saturday afternoons we'd drop him off at Marist College to spend the day with Brian. They'd hang out, shoot some hoops, and maybe take in a movie. But whatever else they did always included a visit to Poughkeepsie's Galleria mall. We would give Bart pocket money and he'd invariably return broke but with something to show from the mall—most often rap CDs. Entering the house, he'd hold up his trophy, and then happily show off what he'd bagged. Initially we figured it was harmless enough—if it afforded him a little pleasure, then it was well worth it. We became concerned when we noticed that whenever he had extra money from Christmas or birthday gifts, he'd come back Saturdays just as broke, with a bunch of stuff, mostly CDs and DVDs. He never saved part of the money for a later day but always blew it all in one spree.

What made it exasperating yet somehow absurdly funny was that Bart couldn't be sure of receiving the correct change from a purchase, since he was still struggling with math facts. But he didn't let that stand in his way. Once in a while we accompanied him to the mall, where he seemed like a man on a mission—until he emptied whatever money was in his pockets. It was a puzzle we never fully understood. Without other meaningful ways of expressing himself, at least he could buy things, partake in a socially significant transaction that was self-affirming. Buying cool stuff meant demonstrating that yes, he could do something important for himself. We were a little shocked, coming from the "hard work and thrift" school of parenting. Speaking with him was no use—he just shook it off, laughing, "Yeah, I just burn through money." Once he remarked something to the effect of, "What am I saving for, old age? Hell, I've already been nearly dead." That struck a chord in me. Though somewhat plausible given what he'd been through, I suspected that it was a rationalization for something more driven by emotional need than a sudden philosophical turn of mind.

This shopping mania was something entirely new. Bart had held several part-time jobs, knew the value of a dollar, and while not yet saving for a rainy day, was perfectly capable of saving for a car or other long-term goal. Famously generous with friends and family, especially his little sister, he was never a spendthrift. Like so many other newly acquired eccentricities, we hoped that in time this one would sort itself out. Meanwhile, when he came into a little extra money, like on his eighteenth birthday, and then later at his high school graduation, we split the cash into separate envelopes, agreeing to give him one envelope each successive week, hoping that would help him reestablish some self-control. Hope springs eternal in the human breast, but today he's still wrestling with the demon of compulsive spending, something common enough among survivors of TBI.

22
HBOT

Bart's progress was slow, painstaking, and punctuated with frequent maddening backslides. Minor breakthroughs were usually preceded by a ten-day period of debilitating tiredness and confusion. We were searching high and low for alternative means to accelerate healing. Dayle and I both had used alternatives to conventional medical care—massage, Chinese medicine, acupuncture, and healers. My interest in alternatives began at age fourteen when my mother was diagnosed with cervical cancer. After a long stint in hospital and a round of what was at the time an amazing new therapy, radiation, she returned home expecting to die. At that time mom and I both discovered Linus Pauling and vitamin C, consuming vast quantities of it over the decades. I became an enthusiastic supporter of the Linus Pauling Institute, quipping to friends, "There is no God but vitamin C, and Linus Pauling is his prophet." Dayle, a Reiki Master and herbal practitioner, shared my interest, so over the years we added many vitamins and minerals to our pantheon. Mom lived the better part of forty years after being given slim chance of lasting even one. It was not exactly scientific proof of anything, but it got me thinking outside the box when it came to health issues, especially since medical science was, and is, in its infancy. Moreover some medical doctors, like other professionals, are jealous of their trade secrets and hostile to any possible threats to income and status. Effective alternatives are viewed as meddlesome interference in a lucrative monopoly.

On the other hand, there are boatloads of hucksters and incompetents practicing alternative medicine, and it's damn tough to pick the oats from the manure. So Dayle and I cobbled together an unofficial medical panel of trusted experts—our beloved neurosurgeon Dr. Harter, Dayle's cousin Dr. Scott Groudine, and our close friend Dr. Michael Compaign, a functional medicine specialist. When through our own due diligence we found a promising alternative therapy, we'd ask each of them whether or not they thought the therapy might do any harm. Some of the most promising and exciting approaches failed this crucial test. Those that didn't make the cut most often relied on medications with potentially serious side effects.

Michael Compaign, ever eager to push the boundaries of conventional medicine, recommended a possible treatment that did pass the test, hyperbaric oxygen therapy (HBOT). HBOT had been around for centuries as a treatment for divers emerging too rapidly from the depths. (Those of us old enough may remember Lloyd Bridges in *Sea Hunt* rushing into a hyperbaric tank just in the nick of time to prevent deadly bends). Michael sees a lot of Lyme disease patients, referring some very advanced cases for HBOT therapy. The treatment reduces the brain damage associated with late-stage Lyme disease. He had never sent a TBI patient for the therapy but felt it couldn't hurt.

How HBOT works is only partially understood. The patient is placed in a diving bell that is gradually pressurized, then taken down to 1.5 atmospheric pressures, the equivalent of being under sixteen feet of water. The pressurized cabin is flooded with pure oxygen, which the patient breathes for an hour or more. Normally oxygen, which constitutes only 21 percent of the air we breathe, can enter the bloodstream only one way—it's picked up in the lungs and carried via red blood cells to the body's tissues. But breathing pure oxygen under pressure quickly overwhelms the carrying capacity of red blood cells, so blood plasma and other bodily fluids become saturated with oxygen—up to fifteen times the amount normally available. This is where the explanation becomes more conjectural. Excess oxygen helps injured sites heal by allowing them to revascularize—to regrow the network of tiny arterioles and capillaries supplying blood to the injured tissue. Apparently it is the new blood supply that does the serious work of healing—removing toxins and bringing in needed oxygen and other healing building blocks. That HBOT promotes healing is as well established as most other therapies in mainstream medicine. Burn centers routinely use HBOT, since it dramatically speeds recovery and reduces scarring. FDA-approved uses also include treating carbon monoxide poisoning, gas embolism, severe anemia, radiation burns, crushing injuries, smoke inhalation, and several other life-threatening conditions.

We were astounded to find that HBOT, which we had never even heard of, was part of the standard of treatment for stroke and TBI in Germany, Italy, and Japan. (I joked that it might be some kind of Axis powers' scheme to take over the world, from one of those grade-B movies, like *The Boys from Brazil.*) When asked, Dr. Harter replied that he knew just enough about it to think "it couldn't do any harm, and might even help." Dr. Scott was less sanguine, but conceded that it couldn't hurt. So, with our customary mixture of skepticism and high hopes, we set out to have Bart evaluated for HBOT.

That's when we met a most remarkable woman, Dr. Giuseppina Feingold. Originally from Perugia, Italy, she married a Jewish American doctor, adopting his religion and country. When Elisa, the oldest of their five children, was born with severe cerebral palsy, "Dr. Joe," as her friends call her, sought out the best minds in the field, only to be handed the same verdict time and again—the child's condition was so profound that she would be hopelessly disabled. Elisa would never be able to do the simplest things for herself, like sit up or speak. Dr. Joe left no stone unturned searching for therapies, eventually hearing about HBOT from relatives back in the old country. Traveling with baby Elisa to Italy, she undertook a long series of "dives." The results were so heartening that she returned to the United States determined to start her own clinic for Elisa and others similarly afflicted, mortgaging her home to buy a large hyperbaric chamber. Lucky for us, her clinic, Valley Health and Hyperbarics, was located a little more than an hour south, in Pawling, New York. The next closest HBOT facility was hours away on Long Island. (I'm not counting HBOT chambers at major hospitals, whose use is restricted to mainstream applications—for such conditions as burns, crushing injuries, and a few other FDA-approved uses.) In the United States, where medical care is very big business, using HBOT to treat TBI is considered experimental, outside the mainstream, and therefore is not covered by most insurance plans.

A diminutive bundle of energy, Dr. Joe balanced a career as an emergency room physician with running Valley Health and active involvement with her five lively kids. In its third year, the clinic offered HBOT and a variety of other alternative therapies to children with cerebral palsy and autism, as well as adults suffering from Lyme disease and strokes. She'd seen a couple of young people with TBI and felt Bart was a promising candidate. Her infectious warmth, enthusiasm, and determination were palpable. Doc Joe's greatest salesperson was

Elisa who, at age seven, was sitting up, tooling around in her own electronic wheelchair and chattering up a storm. She often bullied her way into the office to play computer games. Elisa had undergone several cycles of therapy. (A typical cycle runs forty dives.) All this from a child that conventional medicine considered a hopeless case. We were deeply moved. Over the next couple of years we were thrilled to observe her make a number of other remarkable advances. Dr. Joe later rejoiced, "My daughter is doing great. She's nine, fully conversational, speaks Italian, and says her prayers in Hebrew."

While she wouldn't promise any specific improvements, Dr. Joe anticipated significant gains in functioning and quality of life for Bart. So on November 24, 2002, a few days before Thanksgiving, Bart made his first two dives. With recovery time between sessions, the visit took all day. Dayle accompanied him on the first dive, and I went along for the second. The diving bell accommodated up to five people at a time. There is some fitting of hoses and such that goes on during the course of the dive, so we acted as Bart's aides, as well as companions. I found the tanks a bit claustrophobic, but at least they provided a TV screen just outside the portal window for diversion. We endured more than our fair share of SpongeBob and other kiddy stuff, as most fellow "passengers" were young kids with their parents.

The long stressful day was made tolerable by the good company of the other patients and even more so by Mary Ellen and Joanie, nurses who ran things at the clinic. As they say, "Shit runs downhill." Well, of course, everything runs downhill, including goodness. Dr. Joe hired the most caring, fun-loving nurses, with personalities matching her own. We became fast friends. A sunny disposition came in handy at Valley Health, as many young patients were struggling with profound cerebal palsy, severe autism, and other crippling diseases. Sometimes the immediate therapeutic goal for a child was as modest as becoming able to swallow whole food. Spending time with little ones fighting such grave fights, as well as with their parents, transformed the way I react to persons with disabilities. In past I might have avoided eye contact with such good folks, perhaps from fear, indifference, or a vague sense of unease. Now I see them differently and treat them as equals, as if a curtain has been lifted, revealing our common humanity.

We developed a routine of three dives per week: one midweek after school, two on Saturdays. After a mere three dives Bart seemed to pick up noticeably, becoming more talkative at home and school. His school memory log noted increased endurance and attention in classes, and that he finally made it through a shortened school day without a power nap. His appetite improved, and the school physical therapist reported that he was using his right hand more in gym. Dayle and I were fairly tingling with excitement, wondering what marvelous new improvement would come next. The very next day Bart had a major blowup at school with JR, refusing to acknowledge her the remainder of the day. The following day, in counseling with Dave R., he denied ever having outbursts. We were still unable to discern when he was in denial and when he just plain couldn't remember. But we gradually learned that for every step forward he took, there was likely to be a negative reaction of some kind, as if his brain was attempting to reestablish equilibrium.

After two weeks of dives, he insisted on shaving his head, something he had done often in the old days. I had mixed feelings about the new 'do. On the one hand, it was a return to familiar ways and also seemed like he was making a statement about being comfortable with his battle wounds. Still I felt uneasy, since it accentuated the huge scar running down the middle of his skull from hairline to hairline, then around to his left ear. Was he ready to accept this handsome scar as a sign of manly experience, as we had urged? We jokingly told Bart to reply when asked about it, "You should have seen the other guy." My instinct told me that he was not yet capable of that level of self-acceptance. Those suspicions were confirmed when I overheard someone ask him by phone if he still had any scars from the accident and he cheerfully and unhesitatingly replied, "Nope."

About this time we put Bart on an intensive program of vitamin supplementation, advocated by Dr. David Perlmutter in his book *BrainRecovery.com.* The program passed muster by our panel of experts (though none but Michael Compaign were enthusiastic) and involved a number of "brain foods," such as vitamin E, Coenzyme Q_{10}, alpha-lipoic acid and acetyl-L-carnitine. Starting a vitamin regimen at this time could be construed as introducing a confounding variable in terms of assessing the effects of HBOT, but we didn't give a hoot. Bart's progress was so far from a controlled experiment that one more variable couldn't hurt. Our experience would never be more than anecdotal at best. (For one thing we started giving Bart vitamin C at Helen Hayes as soon as he was able to swallow.)

✦

A few weeks after starting HBOT we visited Pavan, Siri, and her parents at the townhome they leased while Siri was attending the day hospital. We hadn't seen them since the end of summer and found Siri walking with the assistance of a walker and a spot from her father. She was all smiles as, lumps in our throats, we cheered her on; we'd never before seen her walk. What a trooper! Pavan explained that in the evenings after the day hospital, she worked with her father an additional two hours on walking and an hour on speaking. Her speech was a bit better, though obviously requiring great effort. If there is such a thing as a pure triumph of will then Siri would surely prevail. Utterly focused and determined, at barely twenty-four years of age, her courage and faith were inspiring and humbling. At her side now for almost eight months, her parents were the soul of gracious hospitality, serving us delicious homemade regional Indian delicacies.

It was like a homecoming for all of us, especially knowing that Rob and his wife would soon be returning to India with Siri to arrange for ayurvedic medical treatments. After observing Bart's initial progress with HBOT, they also arranged for treatments upon arriving in India (at one-tenth the price in the United States). Pavan would remain behind in the United States at his lucrative computer-consulting job. This beautiful young couple would endure the hardship of long separation on top of all they'd been through. Our hearts went out to them. Devout Hindus who dressed in their finest traditional garb for the Hindu holidays, Siri's parents seemed to embody the adage to "live humbly, and serve God." Saying good-bye to these kind, extraordinary people—probably forever—was bittersweet. Smiling, Pavan, a practiced yogi, stood in the parking lot barefoot in shirtsleeves, while we, bundled up like Eskimos, stomped our feet to keep from freezing. The contrast was both comical and yet somehow unnerving. We never saw them again, though as with other members of the fellowship, we keep in touch by e-mail, Christmas cards, and daily prayers. On the way home we stopped at HHH to visit with the nurses and staff of the brain unit. They were thrilled to see Bart, marveling at how tall he had grown. We topped that off with a stop for gelato at Sweet Lou's, where Bart was welcomed back as a hero.

23
Greece

We had been planning to visit Greece for several months, driven partly by fear of being trapped at home with Bart for the two-week-long Christmas break. He was so emotionally volatile that we counted it as a good day if he had only one outburst. Besides, at home there would be absolutely nothing for him to do except tag along with Dayle all day, which invariably drove him mad with boredom and frustration. His friends were nowhere to be found, so we took him with us to visit our friends and relatives every chance we got. But it was not middle-aged company that he craved. The HBOT dives were paying off nicely—JR wrote in the memory log that he remembered the names of kids in school and handled an English exam with ease, but as the fog lifted he seemed even more agitated. So we planned a two-week vacation in Greece with our old friend Elias Zappas, Cassidy and Bart's godfather. Elias's son Nick, a few years Bart's elder, would be visiting as well, an added bonus, since our kids adore him. We wanted to do something really big and celebratory to mark the one-year anniversary of the accident. Besides, what were we putting things off for? Till after we were all dead? Bart had a point there.

December 19, almost a year after the accident, we boarded a plane for Athens. Traveling with kids can be a trial. Waiting in Frankfurt's airport for our connecting flight, Bart threw a major fit my way. We were all tired and spacey. Thankfully, Elias met us at the Athens airport. Crammed into his small auto, he drove us in maniacal Greek fashion to his apartment, an easy stroll from the Acropolis. We spent only a couple of days in Athens, the highlight being a walk up to the Acropolis, with Elias showing the way. A graduate of

Athens College, steeped in Greek history, he made a wonderful, humorous guide. The only sour note was that on our first try, Bart found the ascent to the Acropolis too steep, so we turned back. The next day we decided to go early morning sans enfants which bothered the heck out of Cassidy. She didn't see why she should lose out just because Bart lacked stamina. Of course she was right, but there was no way we could leave him behind alone. Sometimes there is no perfectly satisfactory solution.

We spent most of our vacation on Corfu, the Zappas' ancestral island. The family had a home in Corfu town as well as a larger one on the beach a half hour north. Christmas and New Year's we spent doing what Greeks do best—eating, talking, and laughing, playing cards, and drinking. The beach house was always full of guests coming and going. Elias and his elderly aunt Eleni were superb cooks and made all our old favorites, topped with mounds of homemade tzatziki sauce. Christmas eve, around a blazing fire, Elias read the gospels in English, Greek, and ancient Greek. (The fireplace was not purely atmospheric; it also served as central heating for the five-bedroom house.) Greeks have a characteristic way of arguing loudly over next to nothing—say, how much garlic to crush into the tzatziki sauce. Bart, easily startled, was often alarmed at what he took to be violent arguments, which were no more than lively good-natured conversations à la Greek.

Greeks don't sleep. They go out to dinner at 10 or 11 p.m., then to a café until the wee hours. If they dine in, cards and merriment last until three or four each morning. We became devotees of biriba, a Greek card game similar to canasta. Bart somehow managed to keep up with this grueling schedule, though he didn't play cards, just watched and rooted. We encouraged him to take siestas, which he mostly declined, then held our breath expecting him to implode. One night we went to see *The Lord of the Rings: The Two Towers*, an interesting experience, replete with assigned theater seats. The movie was in English with Greek subtitles, which was only a problem when the characters spoke Elvish and we were unable to read the Greek. After catching the 11:30 p.m. show, we went out to a café for ice cream. Greeks don't sleep.

The highlight of the trip took place in magnificent St. Spyridon church in Corfu town, where Dayle was baptized by the bishop with what seemed like the whole town in attendance. In a nearby church the local priest also did a special healing mass for Bart, blessing him with the largest remnant of the true cross, a relic saved after the fall of Constantinople. Giving Bart the relic to kiss and blessing him with it, the priest declared that "now you can expect miracles, but you will have to work very hard." I thought what a wise man he was to cover all bases. Then he invited the whole family to kiss the cross. Later, back at Elias's place for more feasting, Bart remarked in vintage wise-guy fashion that his dad must be the only Jew to ever have kissed the true cross. "Uncle" Elias retorted that, on the contrary, in the early days, none but Jews had kissed it.

Dayle had been raised in an unchurched family and hungered for a spiritual home. As we had baptized the kids into the Eastern Orthodox faith years earlier so they would have a religious tradition, she felt drawn to join them in communion. For my part, I've felt for the longest time that one totem pole is as good as the next. Surely God can read our hearts without intercession of church or synagogue, priest or rabbi. Not that I'm hostile to clerics or the pious. I feel a deep connection with many of them, and some, like Father Zlatko Sudac or Father Rick Curry or my childhood rabbi Emanuel Rackman, are inspirations to me. I just don't feel the need to steep myself in ritual or join the One True Faith.

It would be hard to exaggerate Corfu's rugged beauty—mountains dappled by the silver-green of olive leaves, spectacular cliffs dropping to clear azure seas, and a charmingly picturesque ancient town, more Italianesque than Greek, with ancient churches on nearly every street corner. We were all wild about the place, captivated by its natural beauty and hospitable people. With so many friends to talk and joke around with, Bart had a great time with nary an angry word. We had the kids keep a log of the ways in which Greek life differs from American. They came up with thirty-four. Number one was that Greek breakfast consists of coffee and cigarettes.

Our last night in Corfu we stayed up until the wee hours as usual. Next morning, in the rush to get dressed and packed, Bart totally lost it, throwing a full-blown fit. Uncle Elias came rushing into our room where the fireworks were going on and loudly and forcibly put Bart in his place, explaining that being disrespectful to parents was absolutely unacceptable. Dayle and I knew it was due to exhaustion and the stress of parting, always a sore point for Bart. Interestingly, it was his last true outburst for several months. Of course, there was still a fair amount of door slamming, cursing, and angry muttering, but he always seemed to stop short of complete meltdown. When three months passed without a major blowup, we decided to take a chance and eliminate Bart's Risperdal altogether and hope for the best. No sooner was he off the stuff than his endurance increased and he was more mentally alert. The meds had seemed to dumb him down, and it was a pleasure to see him begin to come to his senses.

24

Coming Back to Life Again Like Spring

Striking while the iron was hot, we cajoled Bart into joining a local health club run by his former karate instructor, Sensei Mike. He desperately needed to get more exercise and we were hoping he'd strengthen his weak right side. Sensei had known Bart since he was a kindergartner and was eager to help, offering to be Bart's personal trainer at no additional cost. Maybe it was coincidence, but Sensei had been sitting right next to us in the stands the night Coach Tegeler held up the coin toss to welcome home Bart. As always, the best sermon is a good example. Since she was driving him anyway, Dayle joined too. We had stopped training in tae kwon do the day of the accident, and the chance to work out twice a week promised welcome physical release.

The second half of the school year saw a very full schedule of HBOT dives. We were hoping to complete the full round of forty by summer. Medical protocol called for taking a few months off before starting again after a full round. Almost immediately we began to notice encouraging signs. JR reported that his handwriting was becoming more legible. Bart's scrawl was still near impossible to read, but then his cursive before the accident had been nothing to write home about. The school speech therapist, Serena, whom he adored, wrote in the memory log that he was getting much sharper with words and phrases that had multiple meanings, as well as understanding metaphors and other subtle expressions.

Toward the end of January we drove up to Albany so that he could spend a little time with Ashlee of Mujigae. Cassidy and he hung out with her for a couple of hours at the mall. Afterward Cassidy told us that he hardly spoke a word to Ashlee. I guessed he just didn't yet feel up to the demands of free-wheeling conversation. He also had a tough time making his way through crowded places, frequently being surprised by people who seemed to simply pop up on his blind side. Muttering to himself about what assholes they were, he blamed the pedestrians, not realizing that it was his right-side neglect that was steering him wrong. Ashlee, a real trooper, was wonderful, teasing and joking almost as if he were his old self. It was touching and at the same time unsettling to see Bart happy just to be around her, yet unable to be himself or find his voice.

The next weekend we brought Cassidy along to HBOT so she could get a feel for what Bart was going through. On the second dive, she joined him in the chamber. He loved having her along, clearly preferring her company to ours. During the long break between dives we drove over to a nursing home to visit Joe Milano, whom we hadn't seen since he'd left Helen Hayes nine months earlier. We were not surprised to find his wife and daughter at his side. They had never seen Bart walking or heard him speak, and wept with joy at the sight and sound of him. Bart quipped, "I have that effect on women," a phrase he would use periodically in coming years. We all have a favorite "old chestnut" or two that we relish using when the opportunity presents itself, but with short-term memory loss, once Bart got hold of a favorite catchphrase, he'd ride it for all it was worth. We had corresponded regularly with Joe's wife Jan (she was not of the e-mail generation), and it was great seeing them again. Bart remembered them all warmly, which was reassuring. At the same time it was wrenching to see Joe, who had been so full of piss and vinegar, confined to a wheelchair, paralyzed hand in a sling, with a faraway look in his eyes. His stroke, compounded by a subsequent major heart attack, was just too difficult for him to overcome; therapies had been discontinued, and he had the manner of a man resigned but not at peace. We lost a dear member of the fellowship when he passed away a few months later.

About that time Dayle and I noticed with concern that Bart's right hand, long frozen in a clench, was beginning to shake. He would frequently place it in his pants pocket, or if riding in the car, press his hand against his thigh to conceal the problem. If questioned, he'd claim he was just tapping to the beat of the music. We inquired about it with Dr. Joe, who said there was nothing for it, but that shaking might actually be part of the healing process. After puzzling and worrying over it quietly for a year or more, it gradually went away as his hand became stronger. It seems an odd but undeniable fact that before things get better, they often get worse. We observed that disquieting rhythm time and again, much like the spike in temperature that comes before a fever finally breaks. Progress is most often ragged and uneven and accompanied by setbacks in unrelated areas. For instance on February 4, 2002, the school social worker Dave R. noted in the memory log that "Bart is doing well, affect bright, sense of humor apparent today." On the very same day, JR wrote that "spelling and organizing not very good today. Trouble remembering more than usual." Such is the world of TBI.

✦

The Super Bowl was that evening. Traditionally, a bunch of boys would go to Kyle's for the game. They would clown around, play at WWF wrestling in the back, generally have a loud, riotous time, and maybe even catch some of the game. One year they held the event at our house, and I was amazed at how little time the boys spent actually watching the big game, especially if it wasn't a close contest. Bart was still pretty out of it, but nonetheless wanted to watch the game with friends. Naturally he had a hard time reaching anyone by phone, but his persistence paid off and he finally reached Rebecca, who told him she was sorry, but she was studying for exams.

Clearly disappointed but undeterred, he hammered away at Kyle's cell and home numbers until he finally hit pay dirt, fairly begging to come over for the game. We dropped him off at the Thompson's before the pregame, where he received a big hugging welcome from a sheepish-looking Debra Thompson. I wondered about how he'd manage but tried to enjoy the rare private time at home, when early in the second half he called asking for us to come pick him up. It was quiet on the ride home, Bart saying only that "I dearly miss the Thompsons." When I asked if the regulars had been there, he dourly replied, "Gary was over for awhile, but left early." You didn't have to be a mind reader to figure that the visit had been less than satisfactory. The poor guy was in a no-win situation. He couldn't bring himself to give up the illusion that the old crew were still his friends. Nor was he socially nimble enough to make new ones.

Dayle and I rehashed this dilemma countless times, resulting in plenty of heat but little light. Friends would have to be relegated to the future, along with driving, dating, playing sports, and most everything else he valued. It must all be so very hard on him that we were puzzled how he could bear it. Dayle and I agreed that, as youngsters in his shoes, we'd have surrendered to anger or despair. I began to realize about this time how useful, even necessary, is the defense mechanism of denial. Believing one still has friends when one hasn't may be self-deception, but it serves a higher purpose if it results in the courage to get through the day. Squarely facing a terrible truth before one is ready may be so crushing to a teen's fragile self-esteem as to invite depression, always a threat. Suicide is the number two killer of teens, with TBI still holding the title. His world in shambles, the fiction of imaginary friends seemed like a small conceit. Some day he'd have to face facts and find the strength to make real new friends. We hoped and prayed that he'd gradually mature, meanwhile chipping away at his various deficits and building up his strengths. Eventually he'd rebuild self-esteem the old-fashioned way, based on real-life accomplishments. For now, denial was not so much a necessary evil as simply necessary. So we got used to nodding and smiling when he occasionally said things like, "Dad, don't ever wear that Guinea T-shirt when my friends are around."

Of course, Bart was not the only one counting on denial to get through the day. Dayle and I both required a daily fix, especially when it came to Bart's vision on his blind side. We'd been told by two prominent vision specialists—one a distinguished professor at SUNY's College of Optometry, the other a personal friend and low-vision specialist—that if Bart's hemianopia hadn't cleared up on its own within a year or so, it would be permanent. Even after searching the Internet fruitlessly for a contrary opinion, I flat out refused to accept the experts' judgment as final. We clung to hope that in time, through advances in science and technology, or even through the power of prayer and positive thinking, he would regain enough of his vision to lead an independent, normal life. Vision loss imposed a host of practical problems, such as difficulty reading—he couldn't see across an entire line of written text—it would "white out" before reaching the right side. Moving through crowded, chaotic places like malls, subways, and city streets was dicey. Playing ball was difficult and risky, with the ever-present chance of being blindsided. Most upsetting to Bart, driving safely was impossible. After all, there's precious little public transport available in car-loving Upstate New York.

It's hard to pin down exactly how denial works. Usually but not always adopted subconsciously, it seems to be a stance in which one refuses to face facts, because to do so is too painful. We certainly respected these experts' opinions; else we wouldn't have sought them. They based their prognosis on the best available knowledge. Jim Cayea, low-vision expert, friend, and Mujigae parent, urged us to give Bart the bitter medicine sooner rather than later—arguing that it was kinder than letting him harbor false hopes, sure to be shattered in the long run. I replied, with a bit too much feeling that as the economist Keynes liked to point out, "In the long run we're all dead." The authentic question is what attitude to adopt in the interim. There would be time enough for facing facts. If they proved utterly immutable, finally battering us into submission, then we'd surrender. For now, we'd hold out hope to Bart and ourselves, with the understanding of course that there were no absolute guarantees. We would choose denial for as long as we could stomach it. Turns out we were eventually right about his vision, though only very partially.

25
School Daze

Daily notations in Bart's memory log by JR, Serena the speech therapist, and others were for the most part helpful and informative. For instance JR pointed out that Bart could not see the birdies when playing badminton in gym, so was unable to hit them. She sensibly recommended painting them a bright color. But Dave R.'s counseling notes continued to be the best window into Bart's frame of mind and hidden feelings. This was especially the case after March 3, when he went off antipsychotic medications for good. Soon after, Dave reported that it was increasingly hard to keep Bart on task due to inappropriate joking and remarks. Partly in jest, Bart accused the nurse of being a racist who hated blacks and Asians. Ever since Cassidy's arrival, Bart has strongly identified with people of color. In an overwhelmingly white school, he was friends with every last African American or Asian. If perchance the nurse had been hard-pressed and a bit persnickety with him one morning, he interpreted that in a paranoid way. This marked the beginning of his paranoid period, which we sometimes jokingly referred to as the "Tourette's phase," since he often piped up with outrageous language. We were usually able to get him to tone it down by asking, "Is that any way to talk in front of your little sister?" Deeply ingrained protectiveness toward Cassidy went only so far as he became progressively more disinhibited. After the family saw the movie *Dickie Roberts: Former Child Star*, Bart happily adopted its slogan of "nuckin' futs" as his own. I found myself using it quite a lot, often interchangeably with the now ubiquitous "wa-haaa!"

Mid-March, a scant week before his eighteenth birthday, we went to county court to be declared Bart's legal guardians. (We threw no big birthday party this year; we kept it low key, as there was really nobody to invite aside from a few relatives.) Court was a pretty straightforward proceeding, made poignant by the presence of far more severely disabled adult children there for similar purposes. Though chronologically eighteen, Bart was mentally and emotionally more like a ten-year-old. We told the judge that we hoped to return to court sometime in the future in order to rescind the guardianship. The judge, who was more than kind, said that he admired our devotion and pluck but hoped that we would not push Bart too hard, and have the wisdom to know and accept when Bart had reached his limits. This carping on final limitations annoyed me no end. We lived and fought one day at a time. Who the hell knew where any of us would be at the end of the line?

Dave R. wrote that Bart wasn't sure whether or not his memory was improving and that he complained of becoming bored when memory failed. In English class, they often read short stories and then were expected to answer questions. By the end of the story Bart had forgotten most of what came before. When that happened he either got angry or bored. Dave reported that Bart couldn't recognize, without prompting, the changes in his life resulting from the accident and so was unable to set realistic goals. When discussing career plans for after school, Bart suggested that he might like to be an announcer for sports or wrestling.

Physical healing continued to outstrip mental and emotional progress. On March 24, to our amazement and delight, Bart completed the one-mile run in 11 minutes, 58 seconds. The mile run is a pretty big deal. A semiannual ritual at the school, it's mandated by New York State, and gym classes train for it for weeks, running progressively longer distances. We would never have guessed that he could run that far. Apparently, an unknown Good Samaritan had run alongside urging him on. Since he couldn't recall which boy that was, we never had a chance to thank him. When we gushed excitement at the news, Bart shrugged it off, saying dourly, "I was the last kid to finish." Dayle shot back, "Well a year ago you'd have been rolling around the track. How would that compare with running a sub-twelve-minute mile?" He smiled coyly, agreeing that running the mile beat pushing a wheelchair. Though I suppose he couldn't help comparing his time with past performances, we felt it important to keep him focused on his progress, something made difficult because of spotty memory. When we complimented him on how well he handled a fork or chopsticks with his right hand, he'd look at you as if you were "nuckin' futs." Though vividly recalling his pre-injury dexterity—he could use chopsticks to pick up a single grain of rice with ease—he forgot that until very recently, he couldn't hold chopsticks at all. He had the same sort of reaction whenever we remarked on how well he was coping with commonplace things like walking stairs or typing.

✦

On June 2, 2001, the YMCA celebrated 150 years in America with simultaneous fun runs in thousands of communities across the country. Our branch was doing its bit, staging a walk-run on the local rail trail. The board members were busy that morning hanging banners and setting up a registration table and refreshment stand. The weather was iffy, gray with light rain threatening, so turnout was sparse. Bart and Cassidy were raring to go as we officially kicked off the run. Intended as a fun family event, there were no prizes awarded to top finishers; instead every racer received a commemorative T-shirt. One serious runner showed up and led the small pack down the four-mile course, with Bart and Cassidy in hot pursuit. They finished in the same order, our kids in a dead heat for second place. At age eleven Cassidy was still just gullible enough to believe it was pure coincidence. Bart had been stuck in a rotten teen phase lately, even being miserable to Cassidy, but not today. Today they were laughing, romping around like a pair of pups, bursting with health and high spirits.

I admonished them more than once during that awkward time, when Bart was sometimes beastly even to his little sister, that no matter how they tortured each other, they must always close ranks, shoulder to shoulder, against the world. They fidgeted and squirmed as I lectured, "You're a unique minority: full-blooded Koreans raised Greek Orthodox, with a Jewish father and name. In the entire world, no one is exactly like you. So protect and defend each other always; never let each other down." Bart was so reactive in typical teenage knee-jerk fashion that there was no way of knowing whether I was getting through. Cassidy probably didn't get it either, but I was operating on the premise that if you brainwash early and often, the message may just stick.

✦

The admonition to know thyself, inscribed thousands of years ago on Apollo's temple at Delphi, has always been recognized as essential to living the best kind of life. Bart apparently does not recall that YMCA race, which is a crying shame. There is an eeriness to memory loss. If we don't recall our own past, precious moments shared with loved ones, the pain of adolescence, the struggles, triumphs, and heartbreak of coming of age, then how do we navigate life's passageways? On a purely practical level, since the most reliable guide to the future is the past, how would Bart find his way if his past was lost?

✦

In April Bart admitted to Dave R. how angry he was about not graduating along with his friends and also acknowledged being angry and hurt that certain people no longer associated with him. A couple of sessions later he shared his fear of independence—how would he ever be able to support himself? By May he was regaining some confidence in his ability to socialize with peers. One day in the cafeteria, he stealthily snatched a pudding off a student's tray and scarfed it down, roaring with laughter at pulling off the little prank. The kids informed JR that this sort of thing was vintage Bart. Now he often sat at the girls' table and had them all cracking up, playing king of the lunch table. This clique of girls had known him since kindergarten and was very sweet and supportive, at least in the cafeteria, if not outside of school.

Dave R. asked Bart if he'd be willing to meet with another boy from the district who had suffered a TBI. After some hesitation and anxiety, he agreed. The meeting went okay, but the two boys never struck up a real relationship. Apparently Bart found the kid a little too weird. (Talk about the pot calling the kettle black.) Fundamentally, Bart didn't yet have the social skills to build a genuine friendship and clung to the belief that he already had "normal" friends. Later, when Dave insisted on talking about realistic career goals that didn't require good memory, Bart could only come up with one—tollbooth collector. Dave noted frequently that Bart continued to joke around as his main way to connect with people.

Occasionally we developed a dialogue with Dave R. via the memory log. On May 27, he wrote, "Bart was very fidgety this session. He was unable to recognize when it happened and did not know why we was experiencing this 'restlessness.' He was generally animated and joking. He discussed his Korean background and spoke about being adopted. Bart is looking forward to school ending." To which Dayle replied, "Dave—Thanks for the heads up on Bart's restlessness. I noticed it myself as of a week ago Thursday. There seems to be a ten-day period where B goes through restlessness and is followed consistently with a breakthrough of sorts. So I expect by around Sunday or Monday he'll achieve something new and improved."

With the end of school at hand, Bart's simmering resentment of Cathy Noonan boiled over. June 12th entries in his memory log included the following hastily scrawled note: "Bart got upset today when working on the outline of a puzzle. He stated, 'I can't do this. I quit.' When I said, 'Bart, you can do this; just try,' he said, 'Shut up. Just shut up.' He then completed the puzzle outline—then threw the pieces up in the air and onto the floor. He then stated, 'I don't like working with you because you are old.' There was silence for 2–3 minutes and then Bart apologized and wanted to shake hands. We then completed the session with a different activity. Cathy Noonan, OTR/L"

Beneath that note, JR added: "I came into the room about 5 minutes before the end of the OT session. I could tell by the look on Bart's face, especially his eyes, that something had happened. We went to lunch where he was very quiet and didn't eat most of his lunch. I asked Tom Tegeler if he would shoot some baskets with him for about 10 minutes, which he did and Bart seemed a little bit better after that. By the end of science he was feeling much better."

The next day, Dave R.'s final heads-up for the year reported that he had discussed the OT incident and that Bart was able to express his frustration and anger. Bart was happy and relieved that he had "finally told Cathy N. off." He also shared how he still struggled with the limitations of his blind side. Dave said that Bart was glad school was ending, and he was pleased with the progress he was making.

So the Cathy Noonan saga ended not with a whimper but with a bang. It could have been worse. Bart's explanation to her had been somewhat incoherent—after all, it wasn't her age that rubbed him wrong but rather her manner and approach. Still, without cursing her out or being violent or otherwise outrageous, he had made it plain that he no longer wished to work with her. We respected his wishes and sought OT services outside the school district. Luckily, St. Luke's, a nearby hospital, provided outpatient services. The OTs there appreciated Bart's riotous sense of humor, which contrasted with their typical elderly patients, and he quickly became a favorite. With the prospect of clowning around and flirting with pretty young occupational therapy assistants, he went happily to his weekly sessions and worked hard to please. Lucky again, our health insurance covered most of the costs.

The end of school was notable for a number of special events. Bart received the Triple C award (for character, courage, and commitment) from the New York State attorney general's office, which goes to an inspiring special education student at each high school. He was genuinely proud and honored to be publicly recognized at the annual awards event. In the school yearbook, Bart was named "most memorable" by the graduating class—ironic, since most of the class had worked hard at forgetting him. His good buddy Doug won "most outrageous," an honor that Bart would surely have given him a run for in years past.

Coach Defino and Bart had been doing some batting practice to add a little variety to their Friday afternoon basketball routine. I was a little incredulous, but Coach Defino assured me that Bart could hit a ball. It wasn't clear how he managed to judge a ball without depth perception and being blind to the right, but somehow he compensated for the losses and actually hit pretty well on slow-pitch machines. So we went off to the batting cages for the first time since the accident—an exciting and hopeful prospect.

When we least expected it, Bart would surprise and delight us, doing things that should have been near impossible. Oddly, he rarely understood what the fuss was about. We started to play catch, with Dayle and Cassidy sometimes joining. A pitcher at the middle school, Cassidy threw so hard she was dangerous to catch, but Bart somehow managed. All of his basic baseball skills were coming back to some degree, which we attributed partly to HBOT, since by now he'd nearly completed the full forty dives. With his right pinky still completely useless, he gripped the ball with only four fingers, causing his throws to slice off to the right unexpectedly. He gripped a bat or cup or glass the same way, pinky standing straight out, which we made light of, saying it gave him a very distinguished, aristocratic air. He knew we were kidding; as always, better to laugh than wring one's hands. Even with his "aristocratic" grip, he made four out of five throws accurately. He also caught pretty much anything in his vicinity, but couldn't snag a ball thrown out of his reach. The simultaneous effort of walking or running to the right spot while catching was a little too complex and difficult. So while he wasn't ready for prime time, at least the family could all get out together and have some fun. It was great.

Bart developed a self-defeating pattern. Previously a center fielder, he'd rush to the outfield and try to lob the ball to home plate. At that distance his accuracy as well as ability to judge a fly ball was considerably diminished. He'd soon become frustrated, discouraged, and want to knock off. The only chance of getting him to play catch at a manageable distance was to complain that I'd thrown my arm out and needed to take it easy. He was usually obliging, but not always. It was the same in basketball. He'd rush to shoot three-pointers though he still hadn't the upper body strength; or persist in trying to cross over while dribbling, even though he hadn't enough control on his right side to succeed. Not interested in building basic skills slowly and steadily, he remembered doing more advanced techniques with ease. It was as if he recalled how to play fluidly, but didn't know how to approach playing within his current limitations.

✦

The last week of June my brother, David, and his wife, Hope, came to the New York City area to attend a bat mitzvah. We packed up the kids and drove down to visit with them and some other relatives. David is a truly amazing person. His wife and both his children suffer from recurrent life-threatening bouts of Crohn's disease, while he and Hope both struggle with cancer. Lord knows most men would despair, take refuge in a bottle, or simply chuck their problems and run for the hills. But David is a real mensch, keeping his sense of humor and zest for life, in the teeth of unremitting heartache. How he keeps his balance is beyond me, but his example has been an inspiration always. Once he confided that he seeks daily doses of simple pleasures, good things at one's fingertips—especially music (he'd been in a rock band for years), his dog, flowers, and some fine booze. Words to live by.

On top of all that, he's crazy about Bart, who in some ways is a kindred spirit—both lovable rogues. David has a wild side, which of course endears him to Bart. We had a fun time catching up, with David and Bart getting pretty ribald. David asked our uncle Michel Schwartz, a brilliant artist, to draw a pornographic cartoon on a napkin, which Bart still treasures. On parting, David promised to take Bart clubbing if we visited him in Florida. Though generally shaky, Bart's memory is fine if he's highly motivated, and he's always eagerly prodding, "When are we gonna visit Uncle David?"

26
The Living Is Easy

Summer officially begins with Camp Mujigae. Not up to the rigors of dorm life (the older kids stay up practically all night), Bart slept at nearby Aunt Cathy's. But he handled work as a junior counselor with the younger kids, who attend half-day sessions. Evenings he hung out with "Mujigae babes" Ashlee and Kaili, as well as the guys he had grown up with, who by now were senior counselors. He managed to keep up with most of the doings—bowling, carnival, the dance. After a socially arid year at school, camp was like an oasis of love and acceptance. It was always sad when Mujigae ended, but that year especially I found myself wishing that somehow it could go on, that Bart could drink longer and deeper of its healing waters. Though it's relatively easy to be loving and supportive for one week out of each year, it wasn't clear that even these "brothers and sisters in Mujigae" would stay the course had they faced the realities of Bart's condition every day, year-round. How many outbursts would they witness or bear the brunt of, how many perseverations would they sit through before they too drifted into the woodwork? Still, beggars can't be choosers, and we were all happy and grateful for Mujigae and the boost it gave to Bart's spirits. He had come a long way since the previous year when, a couple of months after discharge from Helen Hayes, he had been practically hand-led around the campus in a dreamlike state.

✦

With end of school year it was time for an eighteen-month checkup with Dr. Harter. Had it really been a year and a half since the accident? Time had lost its customary rhythms, as we fumblingly learned to live day by day. We had been down to Westchester Med only once since Bart's discharge, for a six-month checkup. Since then he had made huge strides. His gait was near normal, and six months of Sensei Mike's bird-dogging had packed on some muscle. As always Dr. Harter was the soul of kindness, giving Bart a long hug coming and going. His beaming face showed how pleased he was with Bart, who promptly challenged him to an arm wrestle. Dayle and I were aghast, since, like a pianist, Harter's hands were his prized instruments. But he brushed aside our concerns as he readied himself to take on Bart, who easily won, with Dr. Harter quipping, "You could have at least made it look hard."

While Dayle and Bart walked back to the reception area, I lagged behind to ask Harter one last question, something that had been gnawing at me for months: Did he think Bart would ever be able to live an independent life? Without missing a beat, he replied, "Well yes, he'll be an independent guy, so long as you continue to advocate for him." Then as an afterthought, he added, "Of course so long as you can bear five or six years of hell." I've replayed that conversation in my head hundreds of times, usually for reassurance and confirmation of our faith that Bart would eventually be independent; other times, to mentally mark the calendar, figuring how much hard time remained to be served.

Harter explained that accepted wisdom held that one year was about all the time one had to make a good recovery from TBI or stroke, but his experience was that significant improvement went on for at least six years, and even after that some improvement was likely. Well, I figured that I could bear six years of hell standing on my head, if that's what it took. As we had on the six-month visit, after leaving the doc we popped over to the NICU and pediatric ICU to visit with and thank the nurses. They marveled to see Bart walking and talking, and posed with him for goofy photos.

✦

I remember phoning my aged mother once at her Florida hospice on New Year's Eve. When she inquired about our plans for the evening, I replied that we were staying close to home, just in case there were blackouts or other problems after midnight. It was the much-ballyhooed Y2K. Relieved, she said, "Well Judi's staying home too, so that just leaves David to find out about." Amused, I kidded, "Ma, I'm the *kleiner Sohn*, and I'm over fifty. When are you gonna stop worrying about us?" Laughing, she replied, "Soon. Very soon." Mom passed away some months after. I've thought about her often, how she would have gladly born any hardship for our sake.

27
The Best Medicine

Glad to be free of JR, Cathy Noonan, some other least favored teachers, and the general hassle of school, Bart continued to perseverate on them with boggling regularity. Pointing out to him that those people were "so yesterday" didn't make a dent. Sometimes we'd joke or try singing, "Always look on the bright side of life," or "You've gotta accentuate the positive, eliminate the negative, and latch on to the affirmative." Music was the best way to reach Bart, and he knew both songs well. My father would have said, "*Gornisht helften,*" meaning absolutely nothing on God's green earth helps. That's the way it was with Bart's perseveration. If someone innocently asked him, "How was school this year?" they would be treated to a full-blown diatribe. The compulsion driving him was so powerful that it wiped out everything good from his mind, at least for the moment, when the question was posed and a response required. We'd have to pipe up, reminding him of Friday afternoons with Coach D, and of the great progress he'd made during the year. Amazingly he was running a nine-and-a-half-minute mile, shooting hoops, tossing around a softball, even hitting again. What the hell! But nothing could break perseveration's iron grip, so sighing inwardly we learned to live with it. Like a summer shower, sudden and disruptive, it was quickly over. Unlike a shower it might recur, five, ten, or more times on a summer's day.

Summer school was minimal, amounting to twice a week each of speech therapy and occupational therapy. The district had hired an OT summer intern, a tall young fellow named Jessie who mostly played basketball with Bart during their sessions. Bart adored the guy, pointing out every time on the way to school. "You know Jessie can dunk!" That was all the credentials he needed. Speech continued with Serena, whom he had grown to love. She had a knack for bringing out his best, and he really worked hard for her. After observing one of their sessions, our TBI coordinator, Josephine Todaro, remarked enthusiastically that Serena was engaging in far more than speech therapy—she was bringing to bear a host of related cognitive therapies. Not easily impressed, Josephine called Serena a real keeper. Coach D generously continued to meet with Bart Friday afternoons, working on both basketball and softball skills. Sensei Mike was still putting Bart through circuit training at the gym twice a week, rounding out Bart's schedule. Not exactly a demanding academic program, but we thought he could use some R & R after a tough school stretch in which he'd worked hard at keeping up in class and managed to pass all courses.

Only nine months earlier, more learned heads than ours were doubtful of that outcome, urging against even placing him in a school setting. The day hospital at Helen Hayes had been so emphatic they had insisted we sign a release acknowledging that we were enrolling him in school against their recommendation. So much for the experts! Better to aim high and nobly fail than to go quietly into oblivion. We felt vindicated, though by no means did we feel as though we were out of the woods. Regular setbacks, persistent memory lapses, crazy outbursts, and perseverations kept us from crowing too loudly or getting cocky. It was obvious that we still had a long hard row to hoe, but felt we were making headway. Even Bart would have acknowledged that much.

It would be a mistake to conclude, in light of his too frequent perseverations, that Bart was generally melancholic or pessimistic. Born a sunny, fun-loving rascal, his basic temperament remained upbeat. The persistently negative, carping perseverations were like lint on a cashmere sweater, standing out in stark contrast to the background because they didn't belong. Like lint, though maddeningly hard to remove, they never entirely obscure the sweater's basic color or texture. He was still Barty boy, ready to play, if not always able.

The cognitive therapy program at Poughkeepsie's Saint Francis Hospital had been recommended by Dr. Harter, so in late July Bart reported there for a series of evaluations. We were startled when the director of the program, Dr. Smoller, came in with a large folder filled with Bart's medical records and test results, saying quite matter-of-factly that there was a possibility of restoring his vision through a program of visual stimulation including video games such as Tetris and flight simulations. We picked up the games on the way home, and Bart has been an avid and accomplished Tetris player even since.

We learned there are two kinds of hemianopia. One is caused by organic damage to the area of the brain involved in processing visual images. A stroke or TBI often destroys brain tissue in that way. Another type of hemianopia often associated with TBI results from a more generalized injury known as neglect—a bizarre condition in which a person becomes literally unaware of one side of their body. People with right-side neglect often bump into things because they don't notice their right side and so can't judge where the center of their body is as they move around. It's as if their right side doesn't exist, including their right-side vision. Bart showed nearly all classic signs of right-side neglect. When he struggled awkwardly with a slice of pizza, if I suggested, "Why not use both your hands?" he'd react as if he'd just discovered he had a right hand. If he were lucky and suffered from neglect rather than organic damage to the visual cortex, then his right field of vision might be bullied back into service through a long course of visual stimulations. It was pretty heady stuff, but we remained low-key with Bart, not wanting to get his hopes up too high. Of course, we cockeyed optimists were secretly sure this was it—the big break we'd hoped and prayed for.

In his spare time, and he had loads, Bart went to the movies. He saw practically every movie out there, with the exception of animated G-rated ones, usually within days of their release—including mainstream and even some small independent films showing in the artsy theaters. Bart has always loved the movies, and besides, it was something to do. Marist College companions were not available in summer, so we were Bart's constant buddies. I went off to work most days, but Dayle and Bart were together around the clock. Often enough, they got on each other's nerves. She relished the chance to read a book while Bart was at OT or other therapies. For the first time since he was a little boy he accompanied her grocery shopping. It got him out of the house, where he'd have gone stir-crazy. His energy was gradually increasing, and with it his restlessness. For the next couple of years I never drove to town on an errand without Bart asking if he could ride along. Poor guy—he didn't really want my company, just something, anything, to do.

We all enjoyed the movies, especially comedies. After seeing them at the theater, we'd frequently rent or buy them for home viewing. I don't know if laughter is the best medicine, but it beats most anything else. Bart loved the *Scary Movie* series. First *Crank Yankers* and then *Chappelle's Show* became TV favorites, though he often got fidgety during the stand-up comic segment of the latter, since many jokes sailed right over his head. But he loved the skits no end. He must have watched the "Mad Real World" and "Clayton Bigsby" segments a hundred times, his booming voice and loud belly laughter reverberating through the house. Always a social animal, he'd greet me at the door returning from a long day at work with, "Come on down to my room and watch Chappelle." (He had the DVDs, which he practically wore out.)

Our comedy immersion was more than an indulgence of Bart's predilection. Laughter not only lightened the load, Dayle and I honestly believed that it promoted healing. Reading Norman Cousins's *Anatomy of an Illness* years earlier, we'd been struck by Cousins's success in fighting off a normally fatal condition with only laughter and vitamin C. In the 1960s after being declared a goner by medicine's best minds, he'd taken a stab at saving his own life by booking a hotel room, renting the collected works of the Marx brothers, Laurel and Hardy, Abbott and Costello, and other classics of comedy, and trying to laugh himself well. (A daily dose of twenty-five grams of intravenous vitamin C probably didn't hurt either.)

I had doubts about laughter as a treatment for TBI, but it clearly met the test of "does no harm" (we didn't bother consulting our medical panel on this one) and at least promised us all lots of laughs. So we jumped at every chance to enjoy live theater, movies, and TV shows—anything that promised to be funny. We usually skipped sophisticated comedy, but found to our surprise and delight that Bart loved *Something's Gotta Give* and *As Good as It Gets*, both starring Jack Nicholson, his longtime favorite actor. *As Good as It Gets* became a perennial favorite. Even with his spotty memory, he knew most of it by heart. A line from the film, "Go sell crazy someplace else; we're all stocked up here," appears as the quote under his picture in his high school senior yearbook.

Bart hadn't had a seizure for over a year, and the last one had been very mild. Antiseizure medications have the well-known side effect of slowing down thought processes and making one drowsy. Bart's energy level and thinking were still below par. So we asked his neurologist about discontinuing the antiseizure drug Keppra. In order to assess the likelihood of having seizures first, he would have to undergo overnight brain monitoring at a sleep lab. In preparation for those tests, Bart had to stop taking the meds for ten days. During that prep period he became much more animated and aware, more recognizably his old self. The test results indicated a 90 percent chance that he would never have another seizure. With even a 10 percent chance of recurrence, the doctor favored a cautious approach, saying it was probably prudent to continue the medication, but that ultimately it was a judgment call. Dayle and I agonized for days, but in light of the mildness of his earlier seizures and the 9 in 10 chance of living life without another one, we opted to drop the drugs. By then Serena had already written asking if Bart had gone off his meds—his personality and affect were much brighter, more full of piss and vinegar. Thankfully, he's stayed free of both meds and seizures ever since.

About this time the therapists at St. Luke's occupational therapy outpatient clinic asked Bart to write in a daily log, homework to exercise both hand and mind. Newly drug-free, Bart's first entry was, "Hi! My name is Bartholomew. I'm adopted for [*sic*] Seoul, South Korea. My little sister is from North Korea. She is a communist." While not exactly Shakespearean, it was sounding a lot like our Barty boy. Several weeks later he scribbled, "Hello, first off, I would like to apologize for not keeping on this. I am a lazy S.O.B. But, going on I saw (for the second time) *The Matrix Revolutions.* It was good. I think my dad thought it was good too. Bart G." Self-deprecating humor and insight had always been hallmarks of his personality, and glimmers of both were beginning to shine through the fog. Though always a class clown, Bart's deeply felt poetry had been judged good enough by teachers to be published in school literary magazines. It seemed that some of that depth of feeling and insight was still there, bubbling up toward the surface of consciousness. Katie, the terrific OT at Helen Hayes, had emphatically insisted that knowledge, math facts and all, was still in there, and that if we drilled long and deep enough it would reemerge. Between the prospect of regaining his sight through vision therapy and signs of increasing mental clarity, we were all feeling pretty good when summer drew to a close. While vacationing in Maine during the last week of summer, a family tradition, to everyone's amazement Bart was able to join us for an afternoon outing of sea kayaking. He really felt great about himself, and I couldn't have been happier if we'd circumnavigated the globe.

28
Super Senior

The second year back in school marked a watershed. Lots of things were different. The class of 2003 had graduated, his classmates since kindergarten gone. Their absence was in many ways a blessing, since it meant fewer awkward, painful chance encounters. Bart had always been friendly with kids in grades ahead and behind him, especially former teammates, so there were plenty of kids to josh around with, but with less intense feelings all around.

Scholastically there was another sea change—from now on he would split his time evenly between academic classes at high school and job coaching at the county vocational center, the Ulster Board of Cooperative Educational Services (BOCES) Career and Technical Center in Port Ewen, some twenty minutes away. Along with other vo-tec kids, most of whom were perfectly "normal," he'd hop on a bus from the high school around 11:00 a.m. heading for BOCES, with JR in hot pursuit. Within days he came up with another favorite cheer that he'd belt out at unlikely times, a wide grin on his face. "Ulster County BOOOCEZ!" A sighting of a BOCES bus or facility of any kind would be met gleefully with that cheer, poking fun at himself and all vo-tec kids. It instantly joined his repertoire of favorites, alongside "wa-haaa," "booyah," and "nuckin' futs."

Timing is everything. Now we could document that Bart was completely off medications, so the CSE, after some goading, agreed to let him try a regular class. What a terrific boost for Bart. He was going back into a classroom with "normal" kids! Pass-fail and based entirely on class discussion, "Health Issues" was an ideal way for him to test the waters. To cap it off, the class was taught by Coach Ciliberto, who, like all coaches, had a tender spot for Bart. Our joy for him was mixed with worry, gratitude with nervousness. Would he be able to measure up? In addition, he was taking U.S. history and math in the special ed department. In the loss column, school social worker Dave R., Bart's good buddy and confidante, had been transferred to the middle school. Bart felt stuck with a new counselor, Lisa W., whom he didn't particularly like. Sorely missing his safety valve, a friend to whom he had confided frustrations and peeves and with whom he could let his hair down, he complained bitterly about having "too many damn women therapists." Dayle and I lost a trusty pipeline of inside information on Bart's frame of mind. Lisa W.'s remarks in the memory log were usually to the effect of, "Met with Bart for twenty minutes today"—not very illuminating. It would take nearly the entire school year for her to gain his trust.

BOCES's career explorations program was tailored to special ed students not expecting to get an academic diploma, but high-functioning enough to hold down a steady job with a little help from a job coach. It involved month-long internships at various stores—CVS, Staples, Rite Aid, RadioShack, and the like. Most jobs revolved around stocking shelves. Bart's evaluations were uniformly excellent, with some store managers noting that his only weak area was memory. (No kidding!) The job coach, Janet McGill, adored him; he became a real teacher's pet. She reported enthusiastically that he worked hard, had a terrific attitude, and was an inspiration to other kids, often helping those having trouble or bucking them up with a joke. Her note in his memory log reads, "He has a lot of friends and seems happy to be here." To hear him tell it, the jobs were nothing special—boring really, and the kids were "all retards." Both accounts were true in their own ways. Bart was always one to make the best of a situation, to "love the one you're with," to clown around and socialize with ease. At the same time, he never once invited any BOCES kids over to our place, or visited theirs. Still dreaming of cruisin' with his buds, he wasn't interested in cultivating new friendships beyond the level of mere school acquaintances.

Mid-October, along with the Kennedys, we drove down to Philadelphia to visit our Mujigae friends the Rickards who had come up in a rainstorm to visit Bart at Helen Hayes. Their grown daughter, Jenny, had sewn a friendship quilt with patches inscribed by Bart's friends from school, from Mujigae, and all around—a true work of love. Their son, Dave, hosted Bart, Cassidy, and her best friend, Lauren Kennedy, as well as Sam Wallace's two boys for a sleepover, staying up to the wee hours. The next day, while the boys were playing "knockout" on the basketball hoop out back and the adults watched from inside, Sam Wallace remarked on how well Bart was playing. (He'd had a year of private lessons with Coach D.)

Sam asked matter-of-factly if we thought Bart would like to work as a counselor at his sports camp next summer, immediately following Mujigae. Bart had attended as a camper for several years. Dayle and I were flabbergasted. How would Bart handle taking responsibility for other kids, when he needed an aide at school to keep him on track and Marist companions to shepherd him around weekends? Yet if Sam Wallace thought he could manage, the idea could not be lightly dismissed.

Sam is a marvelous man who spent his early life as an orphan begging for food on Seoul street corners, suffering privations that resulted in a three-quarter loss of hearing. Although considered unadoptable due to his age and failing health, he was lucky enough to be adopted into a Philadelphia family of educators and has continued in the family business. Though international adoption is commonplace now, in 1956 the Wallaces were pioneers. He seems to have inherited their spirit, going into the brand-new field of special education, sure that he possessed unique insights into the circumstances of disabled persons. In addition to teaching in a private school, Wallace became a master of the Korean martial art Tang Soo Do, founding the Amkor Karate School in Upper Darby. His devoted students hardly notice his hearing impairment, though they learn that if they wish to be heard, they must avoid speaking on his left side.

Sam especially enjoys teaching disabled children, claiming they tend to make excellent students, dedicated and persistent, qualities he prizes. He has patiently reinterpreted the basic moves, forms, and self-defense techniques of his martial art to make them accessible to students with cerebral palsy and other crippling diseases, and he runs a weekly training session for them that is just as demanding as any of his other classes. A couple of these students have reached the rank of 1st Gup, or red belt, just one rank shy of black belt. So when Sam Wallace, who had a pretty good idea of Bart's condition, said he thought Bart would do fine at camp, that "he'd keep an eye on him," I didn't see how we could refuse. When Sam asked Bart, with a glint in his eyes he replied, "Sure," and was off again with his friends.

We left Philadelphia feeling ever so grateful to Sam, who must be chairman of the board of the conspiracy of decency, but also wondering how on earth Bart could ever rise to such a challenge. Bart had enjoyed the quality time with his "Mujigae bros 'n ho's" and was genuinely flattered that Master Wallace, whom he admired as someone who "could kick just about anybody's ass," trusted him to be a counselor at his sports camp. He knew firsthand that Master Wallace was not easy and would expect a lot. Throughout the rest of the school year we used that recognition as leverage to get Bart to push himself, something Sam doubtless counted on. We also had a selfish motive—the prospect of two whole weeks off.

The Philly trip apparently gave Bart a big boost in confidence. Monday morning as she left the house to drive him to school Dayle was astonished to see Bart sitting behind the wheel of our car, windows rolled down, rap music blaring, and a big smile on his face. He had backed out of the garage, turned the car to face the street, and appeared ready to rock and roll. Heart pounding, she stammered out an explanation of why he wasn't ready to drive—his vision needed to improve (and lots of others things too like his memory, judgment, and impulse control) but he wasn't having any of it. She finally got him to relinquish the driver's seat by pointing out that he'd never taken his driving test, so had no license. Even his driver's permit had expired. Somehow that struck a chord, so muttering under his breath about what a bitch she was, he relented.

I got an emergency page from Dayle, panicked over the morning's close call. We put out an SOS to Josephine Todaro to intervene. Drawing on over twenty years experience advocating for youngsters with TBI, Josephine had developed a close rapport with Bart. That evening after a long talk with him out the back porch, he seemed to get it—that he might accidentally injure someone if he drove before he was ready. When would he be ready? That was hard to say. Thereafter we hid the keys to both cars, a pretty extreme measure in a neck of the woods where most folks leave car keys dangling in the ignition. This new menace, that Bart might suddenly take off with a car, put such a fright into Dayle that it left her permanently nursing an extra little edge of worry. I caught hell a few times for carelessly tossing car keys into the wicker basket by the front door instead of hiding them.

Bart continued to do well at school and in his job internships, though he tended to become a little agitated and disoriented when it came time to switch to a new job assignment. He complained about the long ride to the Kingston worksites (forty minutes by school bus) and persistently asked why he couldn't do internships right here in town. You have no idea what persistence means until you've lived with someone suffering compromised short-term memory. After a lot of pushing and pulling, with his job coach an enthusiastic ally, we managed to get BOCES to enlist some local New Paltz businesses to join the program and employ Bart. He seemed much happier and bugged us to patronize the local RadioShack and Rite Aid to demonstrate gratitude for their help. Gratitude was always one of his finest qualities.

During twice weekly sessions at Saint Francis's cognitive rehab program, he learned to scan a page of print to the end of each line, enabling him to read more fluidly. He was usually enthusiastic about going, since the neuropsych, Dr. Ingrid Duerme, was an attractive young woman. He worked hard for her, but never did regain his blind-side vision, a stinging disappointment to the cockeyed optimists. It turned out he had both types of hemianopia—right-side neglect and organic damage to the occipital lobe. For me, it was back to nightly Internet searches for some remedy to this disabling condition. Untroubled, Bart had forgotten the program director's original encouraging remarks and was thrilled to be doubling, then tripling his Tetris scores. Competing with him on our home computer, betting fifty cents a game, I lost a bundle. I never could get the hang of Tetris, which involves arranging falling geometric pieces so that they make a solid base. As the game progresses, the player has less time and space to maneuver pieces. It requires fine eye-hand coordination, which is why it's recommended by the rehab clinic. The fact is I had never enjoyed computer or video games—they always made me tense. Bart loved them, so playing games for homework was a cinch.

Dr. Duerme conspired with speech therapist Serena at the high school to figure ways to get Bart interested in using simple assistive technology in order to compensate for poor memory—things like a pager with a silent alert to remind him of lunchtime or when to catch the BOCES bus. They were hoping to make him more self-sufficient, less dependent on JR and others, but Bart stubbornly refused to carry or use any device that marked him as different or special. Ironically, his refusal had the unintended consequence of ensuring that

JR was always tagging along, annoying the heck out of him. Sometimes he'd blow her off with assurances that "I know what I'm doing," then forget to go to class and end up hanging around kibitzing with Mrs. Z or Coach Phelps in the lunchroom. When JR would finally come to fetch him, she would not be warmly received.

This year the Marist companions were a tag team, Dan and Mike, who alternated Sundays. Doug, now attending the local community college along with Kyle and Gary, continued to visit, sometimes even going out with Bart to the diner for a bite, but much less frequently, perhaps once a month. Sometimes he'd cancel at the last minute, a big letdown for Bart, who was keyed up all day by the prospect of seeing him.

Christmas break was quiet; we stayed close to home. One day during his Saturday night phone calling ritual, he happened to reach Gary, who along with Doug took Bart out to the movies. It was the first contact with Gary since graduation last June. Behaviorists know that intermittent reinforcement is more powerful than uniform reinforcement. A complete fluke that never recurred, that night at the movies with old friends only served to reinforce and prolong Bart's age-old longing. December 29, the second anniversary of the accident, was spent at Aunt Cathy's in Albany with a movie and dinner, and then we celebrated a quiet New Year's Eve at home with the Kennedys. Splitting into teams to play Trivial Pursuit, a game Bart excelled at, especially in the categories of sports and music, we'd choose teams by families, by sexes, and haphazardly, but any way you sliced it, it was hilarious.

We also made an overnight trip to New York City to see a show and take in the sights. New York is a walking city, and Bart had a tough time negotiating holiday crowds, especially at places like Rockefeller Center and Times Square. He stepped on my feet or biffed the backs of my shoes four or five times each block, politely apologizing every time, as is his habit. My dogs were plenty sore that evening. Thereafter the number of run-ins with Bart's feet served as a rough index to how well his spatial orientation was progressing. We'd make a family trip to the Big Apple every six months or so, and each trip I'd swear that next time I'd wear an old pair of iron-toed work boots. Of course, six months later I forgotten that oath.

The results of the first series of HBOT dives had been so encouraging that we started a second round in the new year. Twice weekly drives down to

Mahopac were tough on everyone, doubly so because Bart usually emerged agitated and testy from treatment.

After winter break, Bart began balking at working with me on his homework. I'd been assisting him in one way or another all along, sometimes reading an assignment out loud, other times just helping him stay on track, but no more. He was emphatic about doing it on his own. We figured this was a positive development and were glad to oblige. I was frankly relieved, since doing homework at the dinner table with him was a delicate matter, like working with nitroglycerine; it could blow up at the slightest false move. Bart was determined to go it alone, and though the spirit was willing, his injured brain would not oblige, and he struggled awfully trying to organize longer homework assignments like essays, papers, and other projects. We hired a local teacher as tutor on Sundays. Bart never blew his stack at him—that was a privilege reserved for close family members.

Sometimes, it's not what you know; it's who you know. The coaches were all trying to help push Bart along and so cooked up the idea of Bart doing his job training as a gym teacher, a career to which he had previously aspired. With the help of BOCES and the entire school district, Bart was assigned to shadow Coach Veder at Lenape Elementary School. A graduate himself, Bart felt quite comfortable at Lenape, where he was a well-known figure. He loved the short three-minute bus ride over as well. After a couple days of observing, he was given responsibility for leading warm-ups as well as assisting in refereeing games of all sorts.

He loved the work, but in the beginning Coach Veder was less enthusiastic. Bart couldn't remember the proper sequence of warm-up exercises, skipping some and doing others twice. This would elicit loud raucous objections from the kids. A written cheat sheet was developed, and eventually, Serena, Josephine Todaro, and even the district's assistive technology expert were all enlisted to help him keep it straight. Bart didn't just call out reps to the kids, but instead got down on the floor and led by example. When it came to running in place or doing sit-ups for thirty seconds, the kids had to call time out or Bart would just keep on truckin'. Startled, he might stop the next endurance warm-up way too soon, say after only fifteen seconds. This exasperated the coach, but the kids didn't mind—they enjoyed yelling out corrections. Someone found him a stopwatch. Things became a little better ordered, though it remained a collaborative effort between Bart and his young charges. He rarely complained about his coaching work, but occasionally grumbled that the kids were "bitchy" when he forgot part of the routine. Then we'd remind him that his Lenape experience was perfect training for Master Wallace's summer sports camp, and he'd brighten right up. Bart was psyched about his summer gig—a chance to be away from home, hang out with the "Korean Mafia," and even get paid. It was heady stuff for him, and we used it as a great big carrot.

Even with some speed bumps, he continued to enjoy the work tremendously, did some quality work coaching basketball, and even took a particularly klutzy boy under his wing, offering encouragement, advice, and support. Reading about that in the memory log was a rare thrill for Dayle and me. It was classic Bart, sticking up for the underdog—a glimmer of his old robust self. Everyone was impressed, including the coach. BOCES allowed him to work at Lenape for several consecutive job assignments. After all, he got a hell of a lot more out of working with kids than from stocking shelves.

Word of his success at Lenape got around, and the YMCA offered him an opportunity to put in a few hours each week as an assistant counselor in their after-school program. They knew him because he had worked there prior to the accident. They even paid him a couple of bucks, which really excited Bart. Somehow, in spite of shaky memory and physical limitations, he still knew how to relate to kids, and his fun-loving gift for winning their trust and friendship, though dimmer, still shined.

29
Three Times a Junior

After he successfully tested the waters in the fall with the pass-fail course "Health Issues," spring was now the time to see if Bart could really jump in and swim. The CSE agreed to allow him to take a regular academic course, "Participation in Government." Universally called PIG by the kids, it is a requirement for graduation, generally taken in senior year. In my time we called it civics. A huge step up compared to special ed, it involves a good deal of reading and writing, as well as lots of fieldwork—visits to local government bodies, with follow-up written reports. With all that, PIG is considered one of the easiest required courses, so seemed like a good place to start.

Seizing on the fact that PIG was a course for seniors, Bart came to us with what seemed a harmless request. His report cards continued to list him as a junior, which bothered him no end. Couldn't he be categorized as a senior? Then he would appear as such in the yearbook, rather than as a junior for the third consecutive year. Three times in a row, for crying out loud! This seemed to me like a small thing, quite reasonable really, but upon inquiring we ran smack into a bureaucratic wall. It seemed only kids expecting to graduate that year could be listed as seniors. I pointed out to the guidance department that it was a sad but undeniable fact that many of those seniors never actually graduate, but drop out, or fail to complete all requirements, and just fade away. Sorry, we were told, there's nothing for it. Since Bart was acknowledged to be continuing in school next year, he couldn't be classified as a senior. The matter didn't seem like a big deal to me, but being a kid, no less a "super senior" (meaning someone who stays in high school after his original class has graduated), I understood Bartman's wish to have the dignity of being dubbed an official senior. But while I felt for him, this hardly seemed an issue worth going to the wall over.

At periodic conferences, CSE hearings, and team meetings (the team was the set of teachers and therapists working with Bart at any particular time) we wrestled over what Bart should be doing next year. Everyone agreed that he needed at least another year of school in order to have even a fighting chance of graduating. State regulations permitted special ed students to remain in school until the year of their twenty-first birthday, so with Bart turning nineteen we had in principle another two years in which to line up our ducks. As a practical matter, though, it was becoming ever harder to keep Bart interested in going to school. He was already joking darkly about "my eight years in high school," saying he had bested John Belushi's character in *Animal House*, who had wasted only seven years in college before being expelled. With Cassidy moving up to high school next year, a prospect Bart dreaded, there was an even greater sense of urgency. We were running out of time.

✦

Of all the eccentricities springing from his brain injury, one of the most enduring has been Bart's way of relating most everything to movies. We've all met people, especially young fellows, who habitually reference scenes from *The Godfather* to make a point. Bart took that a giant leap further, often struggling to find a movie scene to illustrate the most mundane ideas. *The Godfather, Scarface*, and *As Good as It Gets* were the most common source material, but every movie he'd ever seen—and he'd seen plenty—became grist for his mill. This seemed to express a deep-seated need, since he often agonized about coming up with just the right movie scene, even when it added nothing to what had already been said. It was as if movies had become his first language, the language in which he was most comfortable. The brain is a strange and marvelous thing.

✦

On February 20, the new school social worker wrote in his log, "Bart says to write, 'He's a good kid.' Great sense of humor! Lisa Watkins." Finally after six months, he was warming up to her. Once again we began to get glimmers of helpful insight from her log entries. The year slipped by, one day at a time, highlighted by Friday after-school workouts with Coach D, Saturday HBOTs, and Sunday morning tutoring followed by visits with Dan or Mike at Marist College. Of course, our friend Duffy continued to give Bart craniosacral therapy, and every other day of the week featured some type of session—OT at St. Luke's, cognitive therapy at Saint Francis, and so on.

Evenings were hardest. Everyone was tired, including Bart, but he was also restless. We spent many edgy nights walking on eggshells, hoping to get through without an outburst. Practically anything could set him off. The most common spark was asking him to repeat himself. His speech was slurred, especially when he was exhausted. If you had the bad luck to miss what he said and asked, "Sorry, what was that?" he'd stare at you in wild-eyed disgust, then storm off to his room, slamming doors in his wake. Dayle and I both learned ways to dodge asking that loaded question, often just guessing at what he'd said, taking a stab at a reply. But if you guessed wrong—look out. Many evenings went from hilarious laughter one moment to sullen storms the next. I can't even guess how many times he invited me to his room to watch *Crank Yankers* or *Chappelle's Show*, only to unceremoniously show me the door after I mistook something he said. I'd head straight for the wine rack, shaking my head, sadly musing over how many people he'd driven away by these sorts of shenanigans. No way of ever knowing.

◆

The 2004 presidential primary season was shaping up with a full field of Democratic hopefuls. Each student in PIG was required to write a ten-page research report on a favorite candidate, followed by an oral presentation. Bart gladly picked Reverend Al Sharpton, who possessed two qualities that made him irresistible to Bart: he was African American and frequently outrageous. With a humorous, sarcastic, mocking, in-your-face manner, Reverend Al was Bart's kind of guy. If that weren't enough, Sharpton's platform, the most liberal of all candidates, suited Bart. A tried and true man of the people, Bart always identified with the underdog. His tutor worked overtime, helping him research articles, cut and paste photos, and practice his oral presentation.

The night before class presentations were due, he favored us with a run-through of his speech, which was predictably funny and surprisingly good. It was grand and moving to see him taking an interest in anything that got the gray matter working, and we were sad when Sharpton dropped out of the race, since with his withdrawal Bart's interest in the election abruptly ended. Not that Dayle and I were Sharpton supporters—hardly. We both typify the old saw that "any young man not a socialist has no heart, and any old man not a conservative has no brains." But Bart had such a painfully limited conversational repertoire, mostly just music and movies, that conversing about politics was a welcome, if temporary, expansion of his small world.

For his nineteenth birthday, Bart and I met James and Jane Chang in New York City for a Knicks game—Michael Jordan's last ever at Madison Square Garden. The game was exciting, Michael put on a big push at the end, with the Knicks still squeaking to victory. It doesn't get much better than that. We ate family-style Korean barbeque in nearby "little Seoul." The Changs were great friends, Jane walking arm in arm with Bart around the neighborhood, chatting and laughing like in the old days. Being with loving friends that day especially meant a lot to him. I was grateful and relieved they had been able to join us, since I couldn't think of anyone else to invite. Knicks tickets, a gift from my employer, John Dockery, had become a birthday tradition with Bart, and I hated to let him down, or worse, be reduced to taking Dayle and Cassidy to the game as hostages. (Neither of them followed basketball). In the old days, Kyle and Gary had been our guests.

The Knicks game was a highlight, but as usual, was followed by a string of setbacks. JR reported that Bart was short-tempered in gym, uncharacteristically going straight to the weight room instead of playing basketball. None of us could figure out why. After all, our boy used to wear a T-shirt emblazoned "Basketball Is Life." He always loathed working out with weights—now all of a sudden he was choosing that over basketball? After a little digging with the coaches, we learned that he was in a freshman and sophomore gym class. The boys were unfamiliar with Bart's recent history, so weren't cutting him any slack on the boards. He couldn't manage to keep up with the speed and roughness of play, and so retreated into the relative safety of the weight room, where Coach Matter, a huge Bart booster, gave him personal attention. This was distressing, but there was nothing for it. Meanwhile Matter, the wrestling coach, worked Bart hard, which was fine, especially since he refused to attend Sensei Mike's gym after his nineteenth birthday. Quitting Sensei's was his birthday gift to himself.

A few days later he became flustered and confused in PIG, needed a lot of redirection, had trouble even following simple directions. Then he reported for work at the Lenape School cafeteria instead of the gymnasium. When he finally got to the right place, warm-ups were particularly disorganized and he skipped a couple of exercises and tried to do some more than once. The kids were quick to correct him, which he didn't particularly appreciate. It was a tough day. We became accustomed to his off days. If a day was particularly lousy, we'd just grin and bear it, hoping that the next would be better. Most often, it was. But every so often a day was too hard.

Sometimes we just had to get away. After Bart turned in, usually around 9:00 p.m. school nights, Dayle and I would steal into town and walk around the sprawling two-hundred-acre college campus. Sidewalks plowed clean and well lit year round, it was a safe place to walk even in the heart of winter. The campus was filled with happy memories of earlier days—its frosty lake, prepped for ice skating and hockey, the scene of many father and son fishing trips. The old quad had been the site of art and music appreciation lessons when Bart was a preschooler, as well as the location of the raucous middle school "moving up" ceremony years later. Cassidy had performed in dance recitals at Studley Theatre. Fidgety Bart had always been a perfect gentleman, waiting patiently for his snow angel to perform, afterwards clapping, stomping, and cheering wildly.

Though filled with sweet memories, the campus was now haunted by nagging images of what might have been. Pesky undergrads were always out and about, rushing, laughing, lounging, and smooching, in all their youthful vigor and glory. I was unsettled by the spectacle of what these kids took for granted—everything Bart was missing. Swept up by feelings of wistful longing and sadness, I resented these young people for the thoughtless indulgence of their precious gifts. At the same time I was repulsed by my own petty feelings. Was I turning into some kind of creature of the night, a vampire who hates youth, vitality, and life itself? It was all mixed with a heavy dose of pity for Bart, who had suffered much, yet was not near the end of his trials. Pity for Bart, blended with self-pity, made for a sickly, sickening brew. These dark, creepy feelings unnerved me, and I vowed to avoid campus, so that I wouldn't feed the beast.

Then a few weeks later, I'd forget, we'd leash the dog and be off to the college again for some quiet time, and dreadful feelings would well right up, which though not exactly jealousy were akin to envy. Each time I'd be surprised by my reaction, since Dayle and I had always enjoyed the company of young people. But now somehow Bart's life and our lives seemed to suffer by comparison to these joyous youngsters. I was sad and ashamed of harboring such base and unworthy feelings. Even counting my blessings, a habitual antidote for heartache, couldn't drive them away. Adding to the general gloom, Dayle pointed out that any one of these kids, bursting with energy and life, could be laid low by a small thing. Life is so damn fragile. Wrestling with these feelings was a recurrent low point, one I never completely resolved, though mercifully the feelings slowly faded over time as Bart continued his recovery.

✦

Easter break meant movies most every day for Bart. One day we drove down to Helen Hayes to visit the nurses and therapists. Lisa, a speech therapist in the day hospital, far and away our favorite person in that disappointing program, was amazed at how well Bart spoke. When she asked him how school was going, he responded, "Okay I guess. I'm in sort of a transitional program, going from special to regular classes." Her face lit up as she repeated admiringly, "Transitional program, eh?" We hadn't connected with her on previous visits, so she had last seen him when he left the program almost two years prior. Delighted and frankly somewhat astonished at how far he had come, she told me, "Whatever he's been doing, keep it up. He's amazing." When we popped over to visit Sweet Lou's, we were met by the melancholy spectacle of a closed and shuttered storefront. The pipes had burst one frigid winter night, flooding the store then freezing and ruining all the ice-cream making equipment. Sadly, Lou hadn't been able to recover, and we never saw him or his store again. It was a loss for all, especially Bart who idolized Lou.

"God gives you only what you can handle." I'm afraid that aphorism belongs with "Things always happen for the best" and other wishful thinking. Meredith's family was dealt too ample a dose of heartache. Their oldest son, Nick, a promising architecture student devoted to Meredith, suffered a TBI while snowboarding and wound up in the trache room at Helen Hayes. When we visited, he was decked out in Scoobie's former bed. Our hearts went out to the O'Briens who had two kids with TBI, and their youngest son, Arnold, shipping off to Iraq with the Marine Corps. We left reeling with flashbacks and near overcome with pity and sorrow for these fine people.

Easter was celebrated in Summit, New Jersey, at our friends the Kotopoulos's, with all the trimmings, including a roasted lamb and pig. Late Sunday afternoon the young people played touch football, with Bart able to join in.

After I dove through a hedge of bushes to complete a touchdown, everyone agreed that I was getting a little too old for that sort of thing and would have to hang up my spikes. I was the only player on the field over thirty. The Kotopouloses were struck by how well Bart was doing, their son Nick (every Greek family has at least one) remarking that Bart seemed almost like his old self. They had spent a fine time discussing the football games on TV, and Bart was lively and well informed. While he was definitely improving cognitively, you needed to speak with Bart for only a few minutes before coming abruptly to a discontinuity, where the "mirror of the mind" had been shattered. A few days later, after visiting New York City, Bart reported to Serena, "There's another Ollie's Restaurant; this one's in Poughkeepsie," when the restaurant was actually on the upper west side of Manhattan, near Columbia University. That sort of confused, fuzzy thinking, often merging facts from disparate experiences, was still a regular feature of his mind.

As the school year wound to a close, PIG students were required to keep a log of their community service hours. Coaching at Lenape, which was unpaid, qualified as community service, so Bart kept a daily account. On May 17, 2004, he wrote in legible block letters, "Today we played kickball in gym. The kids were good. This [*sic*] one or two kids, who were African Americans joked around with me. Good game overall." And a few days later, "Today we played capture the flag. The children played very well. No bickering of any sorts. On a scale of 1-10 they gave a 9.5. Good class altogether."

A week before school ended, Bart dictated the following letter to Dayle, then handed one copy to JR and another to the school principal:

> To My Aide, JR:
>
> I wanted to write this letter to you so that you, Mr. Dan Siler Wexler, Ms. Theresa Pabon, Ms. Mary Kay Canino, and Ms. Lisa Watkins know exactly how I feel about our continuing relationship. First off I want to state that I don't want to be seen with you when my little sister and her friends come to the high school in September. Second of all, I feel that you are too controlling, and I'm not your kid. Being seen with your presence is very deteriorating factor to my self-esteem. Also, your presence reminds me of how I was when I first came back to the high school.

> I've been controlling myself not to get angry and yell at you like I did with Cathy Noonan. I'm very frustrated that no one understands my side of the story, except my parents. I have been driving up the wall since Christmas '03 to get me a new aide. [*sic*]
>
> In closing, you're a nice person and a great aide, but you need to work with someone who has more special needs than myself.
>
> Bart Goldstein

The letter caused a bit of a fuss. JR was so upset that Dayle and I both apologized for any offense given and tried to help her see it wasn't personal. Bart's time with JR was finished—he needed a male school aide going forward, someone he could look to as a role model.

Making the rounds at end of school year, catching up with all the coaches and many of Bart's teachers, present and past, I ran into Serena, Bart's wonderful speech therapist. She was enthusiastic about how far he'd come this year. I opined that someday, years down the road, he'd be able to live an independent life. She replied, with a nervous laugh, that if what I meant was he could have his own place, she agreed but added that then he'd always need someone to look in on him, review his checkbook, make sure his bills were paid, and so on. I could read in her eyes that she considered my expectations hopelessly unrealistic. For my part, I felt that high hopes and expectations lead to the best possible outcomes. Was I certain that Bart would eventually be independent? No way! Only time would tell, and as of this writing, the issue is still not settled. So Serena and I politely agreed to disagree.

I dearly hope that Bart is someday completely independent. I think it's possible and pray for it every day. Dr. Harter seemed to agree it was possible. But no one knows, nor can anyone predict exactly what steps are necessary to reach that goal, or if it will ever be reached. All we can do is take one step at a time, searching, probing, if need be digging for the next firm foothold, like climbers on a windswept mountain ridge, approaching unseen obstacles, turning around some, tackling others directly. En route there may be false summits; large arêtes that when finally surmounted reveal yet larger ones, the true summit out of sight, lost in clouds. Like a climber, drawn by the real yet elusive goal of the summit, at any given moment all one can do is grapple with the patch of rock, snow, and ice at hand—one step at a time.

30
Anger Management

Bart was always the funniest, most generous, most grateful and affectionate member of the family. In these defining ways his emerging self was remarkably like his old, to the great relief of all. Sometimes he was unsure about that, often asking in the months after returning home, "Am I still funny?" Of course, he had changed in important ways. He was always hot tempered, a regular firecracker. On a couple of occasions when Dayle and I drew a line in the sand to forbid some adolescent excess, he blew his stack so loudly and dramatically that it took our breath away. Coming from a long line of hot-tempered dads, I was impressed yet dismayed by the depth of his outrage. But then Bart always felt everything deeply, even how his socks felt or how his shirt labels rubbed his back or a thousand other small things. I used to joke on family trips, when debating where to stop for lunch, that just once before I died I wished to hear Bart say, "Whatever you like, Dad, I'm easy." Like a Labrador retriever—the best dog in the world, but not for the faint of heart—Bart required a strong hand, or for sure he'd run deer.

During recovery anger became such a regular feature of Bart's life that we all took it for granted. Sometimes amounting to little more than irritated, nervous muttering, it could escalate in a heartbeat to enraged, off-the-wall outbursts replete with screaming, cursing, and door-slamming. Gradually it seemed to focus squarely on me. Cassidy, thank God, remained beyond his ballistic range. Dayle caught hell frequently enough, but I really seemed to get under his skin, sometimes just by being around. I didn't have to say or do a thing but was a lightening rod, a big target painted square across my back.

This became one of the toughest, most puzzling and heartbreaking parts of the whole long struggle. A parent's worst nightmare—living with an angry, resentful adolescent all over again, only this time one demonstrably not in his right mind. The hostility ebbed and flowed according to how engaged or happy he was generally, but could flare up anytime, unexpected and unprovoked. Many years earlier, my sister's adorable toy poodle, Cupcake, in his dotage, developed what is referred to as a terror bite. The sweet old boy had never hurt a fly, but now suddenly might without warning snap viciously at your hand if you absentmindedly went to pet his head. It was positively unnerving. So it was with Bart. Most days, most times, he was all right, but there was the ever-present possibility of that changing in a flash and going terribly wrong. Chess masters say that the threat is worse than the execution. Living under that threat took such a toll on my nerves that I resorted to prescription medication to help control the anxiety. Evenings I drank, mostly red wine, my long-time favorite, which had now become indispensable. This went on for years, bringing to mind the ancient Greek saying, "Those whom the gods wish to destroy they first make mad." There were times I wasn't sure whether Bart was getting better or I was going nuts.

Once he lost it, there was nothing for it but to let the surging anger run its course. I tried everything else—sweet reason, yelling back, threats, you name it. Though never allowing myself to get really angry—even the yelling was role-playing—I was truly shaken with pain that mixed fear, pity, sorrow, and confusion. The nearest thing I can relate it to is being kicked hard in the stomach, something I have experienced a few times sparring in tae kwon do. It takes your breath away; your heart is in your ears. No amount of deep belly breaths can manage to reestablish a sense of well-being. You ache from the solar plexus to the lower gut, still sore, tender, tentative, and shaken long after.

Time and again I wracked my brain, trying to understand his seemingly implacable anger. Lord knows he had good reason to be angry generally—he'd been dealt a very tough hand, one which in some ways got tougher over time, as the full impact of his losses dawned. But why focus his fury on me? The few times I've asked him what he was so mad about, his replies shed no light. He just told me that I bugged the hell out of him in too many ways to name. Prior to the accident, I'd never have tolerated such behavior. But now I was constrained on two counts. First, I'd promised God that if Bart lived, I'd never be angry with the boy again. Dayle and I were also keenly aware that he was at risk for depression, which in a teenager is dangerous business. He had lost practically everything he valued—friends, independence, playing sports, driving a car, his accustomed place in the community. If he felt rejected by his parents, virtually his last safe harbor in a crumbling world, what might that do to him? We sought advice from professional counselors, not wishing to enable this awful behavior. They advised reintroducing his antipsychotic meds (they called it titrating his medications—a method of determining the smallest amount he required to have an effect) or just weathering the storms until he was rational enough to undergo counseling. The latter seemed the safest and best route for Bart. For one thing, eliminating the meds had improved his alertness and cognition immediately and dramatically. We'd just have to learn to live with verbal abuse and acting out behavior that we'd never even dreamed of before. Parents of emotionally disturbed children or children with mental illness know the churning, aching, demoralizing sense of helplessness.

✦

When Bart was barely two years old, I launched Crimson Air Services, a specialty courier and airfreight company. Nearing forty, I yearned for adventure. A bit long in the tooth for mountaineering, which had been my youthful passion, I figured entrepreneurship would be just the thing—plenty of risk and adventure, but of a more age-appropriate kind. So I left a well-paying position with an established firm to fly my own ship. I became hooked on the business—excited, committed, and engaged in that special way of brand-new business owners. More than a little carried away, I hung a sign in my office quoting John Paul Jones: "I wish to have no connection with any ship that does not sail fast, for I intend to go in harm's way." While I was busy enjoying my midlife crisis, Bart and Dayle paid the unintended consequences of my working eighty or more hours a week, making frequent business trips, or working so late at the office that I didn't even bother coming home. Borrowing a friend's video camera, Dayle and I recorded a tape titled "To Bart from Dad" in which I read *Goodnight Moon* and other bedtime favorites, sang lullabies, and generally assured Bart that I'd be back in a few days. The tape, which was meant to reassure Bart, had just the opposite effect—he became angry and refused to watch it after the first couple of times. Young kids are creatures of habit, reassured by bedtime rituals—the same song, the same story, time and again. Attempting to capture those rituals in film, I neglected the obvious—that while some things are conveyed well in video, parenting isn't one of them. Bart, who was angry about my abandonment of the family, showed it in some pretty obvious ways. Once, returning bushed from a long few days on the road, I tried to put Bart to sleep, going through the real-life ritual, when he snapped churlishly, "Go back to work, Daddy." That stung me into guilty awareness of the price Bart was paying for my fun and games, so I started to take him to work with me, even visiting clients and vendors with him in tow. We had some fun times, but any way you sliced it, it was still baloney as far as Bart was concerned. He bore eight years of Crimson Air Services, before, with the business in trouble, my partner and I finally sold it off. Within months, enjoying the luxury of plenty of quality time with dad, Bart remarked, in his usual expansive way, "Boy am I glad you sold Crimson, Dad." I was less thrilled. The acronym for Crimson Air Services was CAS, and Cassidy had been named for the company. Still mourning its loss, I half-jokingly suggested to Dayle that we change Cassidy's name now the company was gone.

Might those earlier entrepreneurial misadventures still haunt my relationship with Bart more than a decade later? Maybe. We'll probably never know the source of his hostility, but it has meant a nagging, searing, sadness for me. Doubtless, it's been no picnic for him either. Dayle thinks the root of it all is the "father-son thing." I'm not sure exactly what that means, but there seems to be a fair amount of it around, especially between fathers and their teenage sons. Maybe it's a later version of oedipal competition for Mother. Whereas Mother represents unconditional love and nurturing, Father represents the demands of the world—to achieve, to make one's way, to be competent. Bart has steadily become painfully aware of his own losses, shortcomings, and consequent dependency. Perhaps in Bart's eyes somehow I represent an unspoken rebuke. God knows I would give anything to see him happy; he certainly deserves that. But our relationship has been haunted and bittersweet ever since the accident. When he's loving and expansive, he's the very best—still the funniest, most generous and affectionate member of the family. But then suddenly he's a holy terror. I'm afraid I may never understand or resolve this misery.

With the routine wear and tear of the ongoing struggle, punctuated by crises that seemed to crop up every couple of weeks, this father-son thing drove me to bouts of high anxiety and sadness.

31
The Olympic Games

The following is a letter Dayle wrote and sent out via e-mail to the Camp Mujigae community early July 2004:

> "PAEAN TO MUJIGAE"
> (Another Bart update)
>
> Greetings to our Mujigae Family,
>
> We wanted to take this opportunity to thank all the members of the Mujigae Committee who have continually "busted their humps" year round to make Mujigae happen once again this year. On the surface, to an untrained eye the camp seems to run effortlessly and tirelessly. Those of us who've worked on the "inside" know differently. Those who are in total communion with and commitment to Mujigae understand its value to our children. We wanted to share a story in the life of just one camper, whom most of you know and some of you don't know, Bart Goldstein. To let you know how we as his parents understand what Mujigae has done for him, and how he himself comprehends its role.
>
> Two and a half years ago, Bart at sixteen and a half years old was in a tragic automobile accident, which most of Mujigae was made aware of through Marlene and John Kennedy's periodic updates. The accident left Bart with traumatic brain injury (TBI), including cognitive, physical, visual, and auditory deficits . . . though no spiritual ones. It

has been through your prayers and love that Bart has found his inner strength to continue moving forward to restore his life.

When Bart was approximately three years old he voiced his dislike of his handsome Asian face. He wanted to "fit in" to the Caucasian world that he'd known since his arrival home at age five months. We were the lucky parents! We were the ones who were told at this tender age, just how [much] Bart's self-esteem was wrapped up in his adoption and Korean culture. We knew, at that moment, we needed to begin to seek out ways to have Bart grow up feeling good about who he was, long before the dreaded teen years would hit.

In our search, we joined and were fully active in a local support group. We participated in helping to create our own local Korean Heritage Day (from which Bart still sports a T-shirt).

I remember when Bart was five years old, Marlene and John had returned from a day of observing Camp Mujigae and phoned us enthusiastically about it. Our two families couldn't wait to enroll our children the following year. Bart's attended Camp Mujigae ever since.

When Bart was released from four months in the hospital, it was only six weeks to Mujigae 2002. Many of you remember how he was three camps ago—not even able to keep up any sort of rational conversation, with his deficits much more noticeable than they are now. However, Bart was able to tag along and participate in a Discovery Group for three hours, for only one day. (He didn't have the physical stamina to do more.) He also had the opportunity to be hugged and valued by his longtime friends and feel the rush of loving faces at his "home" in Mujigae. Mujigae propelled a subsequent breakthrough in his healing.

At Mujigae 2003, Bart was able to work as a counselor in Discovery, albeit alongside a leading counselor, and strong parent leader, and CIT (counselor in training). He was able to work the two mornings and was totally whipped by the end of the three hours. We would retire to sleep at a relative's home the rest of the day and visit Mujigae for an hour or two in the evening, then leave. Bart made another huge leaping breakthrough in his healing after camp ended.

Prior to Bart's accident, for several years he would go directly from Camp Mujigae with the Rickards, a Mujigae family from the Philly area.

He'd spend a week or more continuing to bask in the glow of Mujigae. While down there, he'd also go to Master Sam Wallace's sports camp, where he'd play whatever sport was going on at that time. Tish Rickards, her son and Bart's pal, David, and her married-with-children daughter, Jenny, took an eight- to ten-hour-roundtrip drive in the pouring rain to visit Bart for a few hours while Bart was at Helen Hayes Hospital.

One year, Master Sam Wallace, a Korean adoptee who was around forty years old at that time, attended camp through the efforts of John Kennedy. Sam, being a master in Tang Soo Doh, had never been to or seen a camp like Mujigae. He was moved beyond words and developed a close bond with David Kennedy, and the following year with Bart.

When Sam heard about Bart's accident, he was devastated. Sam is hearing impaired, having lost three-fourths of his hearing as a child on the streets of Korea. He's also a special ed teacher during the rest of the year and fully understands Bart's condition.

This past year, we went down to Philly with the Kennedys to visit the Rickards, who are also very close friends with Sam Wallace. Sam couldn't believe how well Bart was doing and had told us that Bart could work as a counselor at his camp in 2004. We were stunned by his generous offer. But would Bart, in fact, be ready and able to do it? It seemed like a huge stretch at the time.

At Mujigae 2004, Bart attended counselor training on Wednesday evening and worked as a co-junior counselor in Discovery, with a very strong leading counselor, Alicia Coulson, who is studying to become a special ed teacher. Aimee Gottesman was CIT, and a parent leader wasn't necessary. Bart's known Alicia and Aimee for many years at camp. He hardly napped at all in the afternoons and couldn't wait to see his girlfriends from camp, Kaili Stanley and Ashlee Danford. (Kaili and Ashlee had visited Bart on his seventeenth birthday at Helen Hayes Hospital.) Bart participated in all evening activities this year and hung out with his longtime Mujigae buddies, Chris DeMarco, Peter Delmonico, Chris Coulson, James and Jane Chang.

Bart's buddies, girlfriends, and other people whom he's known these past fifteen years at camp treated him completely normally. For the first time in two and a half years he felt normal and, more importantly, included within his own peer group. (Bart's friends here at home are a disappointment. They've distanced themselves from him and left him adrift. Bart's current friends at home are middle-aged Caucasian people.)

What's different about Mujigae friends is that they view Bart as part of themselves. They understand viscerally, sympathetically at a moment what Bart is going through and identify. They are there for him, no matter what condition he's in, they accept him fully and lovingly. That experience is immeasurably affirming for Bart.

Toward the end of camp when asked if this was the best Mujigae ever, Bart replied incredulously, "No way. Being a camper was ten times better!"

In closing, you'll all be happy to know that Bart left Mujigae this year with the Rickards to spend two full weeks with them while attending Sam Wallace's camp, working as a counselor. Upon his return we'll be engaging him in more alternative therapies as well as taking him to the Olympics in Greece, where his godfather, who lives in Athens, will be hosting our family.

Oh, and in case you're wondering, Bart's made another huge leaping breakthrough during camp this year.

So THANK YOU, MUJIGAE! We love you, and GOD BLESS YOU ALL!!!

Your Mujigae friends and family members,
Dayle Groudine and Joel Goldstein

Immediately following his sojourn in Philadelphia, Bart was pitched headlong into a whole new alternative therapy at Dr. Joe's, just as he was completing his second set of forty HBOT dives. Mary Bolles, mother of an autistic son, had originally developed sensory learning therapy as a treatment for autistic children. Her approach combined intense simultaneous stimulation of auditory, visual, and vestibular senses. Imagine lying on a gurney moving gently up, down, and around in a programmed sequence, wearing headphones playing specially selected music and sounds, all the while in a completely darkened room, watching a specially colored, pulsating laser light show on the ceiling.

It makes for pretty intense sensory input. Somehow that stimulation improves integration of the senses, understanding, and the ability to learn. The therapy easily passed our "does no harm" test. Frankly, it reminded me a little of a ride at Disney World, only in slow motion.

Sensory learning was a logistical nightmare: sessions had to be taken on twelve consecutive days. Every day, including weekends, Dayle and Bart made the hour-plus drive down to Mahopac, with me standing in for Dayle on Sundays. Following that was an additional eighteen days of twice-daily sessions done at home in a darkened room with a special box that emitted sequenced colored lights. Thirty days of therapy in all. Why or how any of this works was beyond me, but Dr. Joe was excited about it, and we were hopeful it could somehow help. Hell, maybe we'd get lucky and it might even lessen Bart's hemianopia, a result Dr. Joe thought possible though not terribly likely.

In less than a week we were leaving for Greece and the 2004 Summer Olympic Games, and the light contraption would have to come along so Bart could complete the final ten days of therapy. We expected a hassle getting it through customs in the post-9/11 era, as the device looked distinctly like a detonator. Armed with documentation from its manufacturer and from Dr. Joe, we hoped to sweet-talk our way through successive customs checks in the States, France, and Greece.

Attending the Olympic Games, in Greece no less, was a dream we had nourished for many years, ever since Athens was named host city for the 2004 games a decade earlier. Tickets to everyone's favorite sporting events were purchased months in advance: soccer, basketball, softball, track and field, beach volleyball, even a little wrestling, boxing, and table tennis. We were psyched. There was a lot of buzz about possible terrorism at the games, so loads of people stayed away. Those of us who went felt we were among the privileged, expecting a once-in-a-lifetime experience. We were not disappointed. Elias Zappas and his brother George hosted us again, this time in their adjoining apartments in Athens. Elias's son Nick joined us, as well as some other relatives in town for the Olympics. Packed cheek-by-jowl into their small apartments, some sleeping on sofas or inflatable mattresses, we were excited and happy, the cramped conditions only adding to a festive atmosphere.

Summer in Athens is hot, so most evenings we'd sit outside on their spacious top-floor veranda enjoying the sea breeze and watching the sun set over the Acropolis. After dark, the Parthenon was lit as if by torches from inside—a sight so beautiful that it was mesmerizing, drawing one's glance back to it over and over again, as if one couldn't believe one's eyes. We knew we weren't in Kansas anymore. With so many adults available, Bart was able to go off to events sans parents. One morning he went with Nick Zappas and Cassidy to rhythmic gymnastics and another evening he and Nick went to boxing. It was great for him to be out and about in Athens on his own. He was not quite ready to go solo; he couldn't remember the way from the subway stop to the Zappas's apartment building some five blocks away. After a week or so he gradually got the hang of that too and would rush to lead the way.

The thing about the Olympic Games is that you get no idea what they're really like by watching TV. American television focuses on personalities, with features like "Up Close and Personal" highlighting individual stars or up-and-comers. It doesn't even begin to give a sense of the spirit of the games. The day after the opening ceremonies, which we watched on TV like everybody else because they were too expensive see in person, we took a train to the brand-new soccer stadium to watch an early round women's matchup, Nigeria versus Japan, followed by a men's duel of Mexico versus Korea. The first thing we noticed is that most everyone ignored assigned seats in favor of sitting with their team's rooting section, with fans numbering in the thousands. Novices, we dutifully found our assigned seats, more or less directly behind the Japanese rooting section. They don't just play the national anthems; the teams march carrying huge flags sprawling across the field. Thousands of voices joyously sing out their anthems as fans stand together, a moving enough spectacle, and one I've never witnessed before, even at Yankee pennant games. Cheering sections, more enthusiastic than at any Yankee game, chant, sing and, and, yes, dance throughout the entire match, accompanied by traditional musicians. The Japanese had drum bands, the Mexicans mariachi bands, the Korean traditional farmer's dance drummers.

We thought the Japanese were insanely, painfully loud, but after they vacated, only to be replaced during the next game by Korean fans, we learned the true meaning of loud. At first the chanting was so deafening that it was like standing next to a jet engine, all sound and fury, but then section leaders emerged to organize and lead the frenzied masses. We recognized many of the Korean cheers, ranging from folk songs like Arirang to Beethoven's "Ode to Joy," back to just plain chanting, "Corree! Corree! Corree!" The cheering never slacked off, not even during halftime. There were dueling bands—a mariachi band would play accompanied by wildly cheering Mexicans, to be answered by crazed Korean farmer's dance drummers, then back to the mariachi, and around again. When there was a shot on goal the whole place went berserk for several minutes. Swept along, we were gradually pulled closer to the Koreans, who in this contest were definitely our "home team." The teams were evenly matched and after a scoreless game, the Koreans finally made a goal in the last five minutes to win 1-0. As in the previous women's match, the teams presented themselves to their fans, most climbing right up into the stands to join their countrymen.

Korean fans, crazed with victory, joining hands, danced out of the stadium, then danced around its circumference. It was as if Yankee fans danced a hora around Yankee Stadium. We watched the spectacle with amazement and delight from the safety of the upper tiers, hearing many visitors expressing admiration for the Koreans who "really know how to celebrate." Hell, we'd danced the same farmer's dances many times at Camp Mujigae, but not with this sort of wild abandon. Exhausted, we drifted with the crowds to the subway for the ride back to town when we began to notice something totally unexpected—hundreds of Koreans were wearing sombreros while Mexicans sported Korean farmer's outfits. It seems they had spontaneously swapped outfits on their way back to Athens town for more partying. High spirits and goodwill among heretofore competitors extended to absolutely everyone else, and we marveled at the Olympic spirit that somehow transformed madly competitive nationalists into friendly, happy rivals. During the train ride we played a game trying to guess people's nationalities, as at each stop new groups would join us from other venues, speaking strange languages and wearing exotic costumes. Even to a New Yorker accustomed to a mélange of peoples, it truly felt as if all of humanity was together in friendship and solidarity under the Olympic banner. Everyone knows that the Greeks invented the original Olympics and that while those were in session wars were suspended in their honor. We experienced a bit of that special spirit of reverence at the games, something that does not come across just watching them on television.

There were other highlights. We yielded our tickets to the basketball quarterfinals so our hosts, Elias and George, could take off with our kids to watch Greece face Argentina in a much-ballyhooed matchup. The young

Greek team had already beaten the disappointing U.S. "dream team." Leaving the apartment the kids were glowing with excitement, Cassidy looking adorable draped in a large Greek flag. Meanwhile we strolled around Athens that night, catching most of the game on TV, since every shop and taverna in the city had it blaring. The whole country was watching as Argentina edged out a slim victory in the final minutes. Later that night the kids told us the chanting and cheering were "nuckin' futs" amid a virtual sea of frantically waving Greek flags.

By contrast, we spent the evening quietly picking our way through Athens's ancient agora, or city square, where Socrates had prodded his fellow citizens and stone pillars still stood where the original stoics had speculated on the nature of things. I'd been fascinated by the ancient Greeks since being forced to read an abridged version of *The Iliad* in P.S. 39. But somehow they always seemed larger than life, too heroic and astounding to be real, almost like the peoples of Tolkien's Middle-earth. But when you walk in their footprints and sit in the judges' seats in the Theatre of Dionysus, where Aeschylus and Sophocles competed head-to-head, you feel their presence and understand they were real men and women, all the more astounding.

Bart was doing so wonderfully that we decided to try a quick trip to Italy without him. Cassidy, a little too young and shy to stay behind, joined us for a three-day second honeymoon on romantic Lake Como. Thirty years earlier we'd eloped for a weekend at Bear Mountain Inn, just north of New York City. Upon returning from Italy and a beautiful restful time, we found that Bart had thrown a full-bore, over-the-top fit the previous night. They had all been out very late, and while fumbling with the keys to the door, he had snapped, soundly cursing out Nick. Uncle Elias, jumping down his throat à la Greek, had put him in his place, sending him to his bed for the rest of the day. Before leaving for our little trip we had reminded everyone to make sure that Bart napped and didn't get too overtired, but I suppose it was inevitable that he'd stress out eventually. It was the sole outburst on the trip, and nobody dwelled on it. The Greeks are that way—they scream and rant, get it out of their system, then get on with life. Bart has the makings of a good Greek, except for the perseveration. Most nights at some point we'd stroll to the Zappas' favorite café and sit for hours nursing beers. Bart got a big kick out of the fact that at age nineteen he was "legal" in Greece, and he invariably ordered a tall one.

One day the family made a trip to the beach at Piraeus. Plato's *Republic* begins with Socrates walking back to town from Piraeus, but we took the trolley. Arriving at what had been advertised as the family beach, we were surprised to find quite a few topless bathers. Walking along the shore we couldn't help notice a sprinkling of entirely nude sunbathers. Dayle and I had been to nude beaches in Rockaway Park growing up, but this was quite an eye-opener for the kids. I repeatedly reminded Bart that what makes the whole thing "work" is that one doesn't stare, but pretends nothing is out of the ordinary. Of course looking out the side of your eyes is fine, even recommended. Bart loved the beach. Cassidy was more ambivalent, complaining that she'd "been scarred for life" by the sight of some topless old women. I bit my tongue, explaining that the old gals were once beautiful young women, why should they have to cover up now? Later we lazily strolled up the hills toward the center city, stopping several times for iced coffee, treats, and souvenirs. As always the Greeks were friendly and hospitable, especially when they learned we were Americans. They seemed to all have relatives in the United States. On days like this the family really felt almost normal, as though we could catch glimpses of those sunlit uplands we only dreamed about.

Our last event at the games was the track and field finals. Under the magic glow of the Olympic torch, ninety thousand spectators filed into the great stadium that evening. With several events running concurrently, the scene resembled nothing so much as a three-ring circus. The crowd was so pumped that it repeatedly broke into "waves" between events—by way of participating in and helping to build excitement. Ninety thousand fans doing the wave is so overpowering, so hysterical, that it feels as if one is literally lifted into the air by the wave as it comes thundering across the stands. I've done the wave at Yankee Stadium and at Madison Square Garden, but those were like mild breezes compared to the Olympic typhoon. Medal winners took their victory laps, wrapped in national flags, and we cheered until we were too hoarse for words. Walking to concession stands circling the stadium, we ran into several medal winners, still sporting olive wreaths, and stopped to congratulate each, making for an unforgettable evening.

This time Bart led the way on the strenuous hike up the Acropolis. Elias made a brilliant guide, regaling us with tales, some funny, some poignant, about the history of the storied place. After Athens fell to the Nazis in 1941, they straightaway furled an ugly swastika flag in triumph atop the Acropolis, symbolically staking claim to Hellas and its ancient heritage. But the flag guard on duty, rather than raise the Swastika flag, wrapped himself in the Greek flag and jumped off the Acropolis to his death. A month later two young patriots scaled the steep northern walls under cover of darkness. Next morning the rising sun revealed the blue and white Greek flag defiantly greeting the entire city and world. They are still revered today as national heroes.

Our triumph on the sacred mount was far less dramatic, but nonetheless keenly heartfelt by Dayle and me and the other adults who remembered turning back eighteen months earlier in deference to Bart's frailty. I'm not sure if Bart recalled his earlier attempt, but now he laughingly raced ahead, stopping to take and posing for tons of pictures, a sight for sore eyes. The next Christmas we sent out customized cards, the cover showing Cassidy and Bart smiling atop the Acropolis, with Athens and the sea at their feet. Sometimes, as the poet says, "life is like a flag unfurled."

32
The Big Chill

Summer began in the glow of Mujigae and then raced on to success at Master Wallace's camp, sensory learning therapy, and finally the Olympic Games. Bart handled everything that was thrown at him. Though hopeful about the new school year, we remained prey to chronic, nagging worries. How would Bartman adjust to big changes in the works? Would he be able to control his impulses, frustrations, and anger? His short-term memory was still quite shaky, and he could be distracted by the slightest thing. Could he muster the cognitive skills, especially focus and concentration, to make the next giant leap? I had to remind myself, practically every evening, that worrying is pointless, even corrosive, since it saps energy—just take it one day at a time, try to cover all bases, then hope and pray for the best.

That fall when our kids went back to school, they were both attending the same one for the first time ever. Bart's near peers had moved on, but "Cassidy and her little friends," whom Bart had coached in the town soccer league years earlier, were now in high school with him, a prospect that appalled both our kids. We made Cassidy promise to acknowledge Bart at school; he'd been ignored by too many friends already, and we wouldn't tolerate the same from her. She complied, and as far as we could tell (and we were at school everyday, dropping Bart off and picking him up), her friends went out of their way to make him feel welcome. He'd been counselor to some of them at the local Y day camp, had refereed others in the youth basketball league, and was still regarded as a great guy.

Her friends accepting Bart so naturally made it easier for Cassidy to do likewise. Early that fall, at the homecoming dance, a worried-looking Vinnie B. came over to Cassidy, whom he was sweet on, complaining that Bart had taken him aside in the gym, threatening, "You'd better treat my sister nice, or I'm gonna mess you up." Later that night at home, listening to Cassidy's heartfelt complaints about Bart's meddling, I bit my lip to keep from laughing and told her honestly that I hadn't put him up to anything, but didn't have a problem with what he'd said and done. Like it or not, Bart was still her big brother and his heart was in the right place.

His snow angel was increasingly chilly around Bart. When forced together by geometry of circumstance, such as around the dinner table, she avoided eye contact, speaking to him only when he persisted in trying to engage her in conversation, and then her replies were listless and monosyllabic. Cassidy was the quiet child; after all, the role of rambunctious extrovert had already been filled. Trying to pry feelings out of her was impossible—she just wouldn't talk about them, but continued to withdraw into her own private world. Dayle and I guessed that she was wrestling with issues common to survivors. At some barely conscious level she must be relieved it was Bart and not she who was injured, and doubtless felt guilt and shame for that. Fear was gnawing at her—fear of sudden catastrophe, fear of loss of control over her life, fear of death itself. An obsessively neat and organized child, here she was cheek by jowl with wild, violent, unmanageable events. Bart's bouts of fury, though never directed at her, did little to reassure. She also had every right to feel more than a little neglected. By painful necessity, Bart's needs came first. During the years following Bart's accident, she gradually determined to become rich and successful. After all, if you're rich and successful, nothing tragic can touch you, right?

Holed up in her bedroom, Cassidy rarely joined the family in common activities. Thank God for our beloved Yankees, else she would never even watch TV, a supremely important pastime to Bart, who had way too much time on his hands. Of course the Bart she knew and loved, the big brother who taught her to be funny, to play sports, her advocate against all comers, was gone. In his stead was an unpredictably volatile, often weird stranger. Our assurances to her that the old Bart was still inside trapped, struggling to emerge, seemed hollow. To a thirteen-year-old, any way you sliced it, it was still baloney. His transformation was frightening, incomprehensible, overwhelming.

Gradually her estrangement worsened. Ironically, Bart's continued healing made things harder. As he became more alert to his condition and surroundings, he became acutely aware of Cassidy's changed attitude, railing against it, often complaining that she was a hermit up there in her room, or that she "didn't care about the family." Eventually we found a counselor for Bart who came to our home each week for an hour or two. We bullied Cassidy into meeting with her as well by presenting an ultimatum—she either had to speak with the counselor or speak with us—her choice. At first she met with Melinda one-on-one and eventually together with Bart. After several sessions Melinda told us that most of Cassidy's issues were a result of entering adolescence, not specific to Bart. Of course, Bart still saw her as his baby sister, a role she was rapidly outgrowing in many ways. Where, for instance, he had originally taught her to burn CDs on their computer, now she found herself awkwardly reteaching him to do the same. If the process involved too many steps, she posted neat, handwritten directions on the screen. He was no longer an able protector, though he didn't easily concede the point, clinging desperately to that defining role.

Besides Cassidy attending the same school, which was huge to Bart, the biggest difference this year was that JR was gone. In her place was a tall, gangly fellow known to the kids as Coach Moore. David Moore had graduated from the high school several years earlier through the vo-tec program. Still in his midtwenties with an easygoing manner, he lived in town with his folks and could almost be mistaken for a high school super senior. Though his job description was school aide, he also coached the modified basketball and junior varsity football teams. His mentors, Coach D and Coach Tegeler, gave him carte blanche to stop by the gym and shoot hoops with Bart whenever they had a few spare minutes, a privilege they often enjoyed. From Bart's point of view, as long as he was stuck with a school aide, they didn't come any cooler than Dave Moore. A coach no less! For the first time in two years, on the drive to school Dayle wasn't regaled daily with diatribes about JR, who had assumed the place of honor after Cathy Noonan was drummed off Bart's team. Though no longer part of his daily life, Bart would occasionally rant about both Cathy and JR for good measure, lest anyone think he had forgiven, forgotten, or become too normal.

Academically, Bart was enrolled exclusively in mainstream classes—an English class for seniors, "writer's workshop," and, at BOCES, computer art and graphics. Dave Moore, proud of his own BOCES training, forbid Bart to sound off with his deprecating "Ulster County BOOCEEZ" cheer on the bus ride over to the vo-tec center. Bart really missed doing it, so made up for it by more frequent razzing during the car ride to and from school. In order to help with the increased course work, Bart's schedule included a daily block in the resource room. Staffed by the special ed department, the resource room was a kind of guided study hall where teachers assist students with projects or studying for tests, or provide other interventions as needed. Though manned by special ed teachers, it was really designed to support kids struggling with mainstream courses. Still carrying a reduced course load, Bart spent the remainder of his day in gym and therapies. High school kids participate in gym only in alternating quarters, but with the coaches' blessing, Bart enrolled in physical education every quarter without fail.

And, oh yes—he was finally a senior! He would be moving on after this year, no matter what. That entitled Bart to sit for senior pictures—including the class of 2005 group picture—be sized for cap and gown, and enjoy all other privileges reserved for seniors. This class was the last group of kids with which he had any appreciable contact while coming up through school. They had been freshmen when he had been injured as a junior. Grinning, Bart would flash his school ID marked "senior," happily quipping that his "nine years of high school" were finally drawing to a close. What came after graduation remained an open question, but ready or not, he was "blowing this joint." Since he was short a couple of Regents exams required for a Regents diploma, he'd have to settle for an IEP (Individual Educational Plan) diploma, a less prestigious sheepskin. Bart didn't mind much, so long as he was getting out.

He spent lots of time in the resource room with Allan Podell, a master teacher who mentored him through what seemed like an endless string of papers in writer's workshop. There was one due most every week—a Herculean schedule for Bart, who still declined any assistance at home with schoolwork. The assignments began simply enough—a few paragraphs comparing the Mets and Yankees—but built eventually to full-length research reports. Bart chose international adoption as the subject for his major paper, combining research with personal experience in a very moving and effective presentation. Podell, a real trooper, put in long hours with Bart, even helping out on weekends at crunch time. Keeping teenagers motivated and on task, let alone learning-disabled ones, is tricky business, and Podell had the right mixture of fun-loving personality and backbone to command respect.

A month or so into the school year, the sensory learning therapy finally began to kick in. Dr. Joe told us that Bart's right-side hearing was much improved and now nearly balanced with his left. We had already noticed some subtle changes—his stride was more natural, and balance improved. General cognition seemed to ratchet up a notch or two across the board, but still no improvement to his field of vision. That damned hemianopia had skunked us again! Meanwhile, Bart continued to ask matter-of-factly, "When do you think I'm gonna be able to drive, Dad?" He usually posed the question when sitting next to me in his customary shotgun position, admiring passing cars, speculating on which ones he might like to get—maybe a nice used Honda Civic. Uncomfortable as hell, I'd hedge about the timeline. Who the hell knew when? When his vision improved—but when would that be? I had agonizing doubts about the merits of denial as a coping mechanism, but my stubborn optimism would not allow me to throw in the towel.

School was far more demanding now. Bart's first full-length paper came back with a large red C+ scrawled across the top, along with the remark, "Very good. You can revise it for higher grade if you wish."

Dayle wrote the following note on September 29, 2004:

> For Mr. Zimmer. Bart worked extremely hard on this paper, with Mr. Podell as his primary tutor. Given that Bart is brain injured, this paper is a miraculous achievement for him, and I personally don't know how Bart can improve upon it. The paper was given a C+ and yet says, "Very Good." I don't understand how "very good" translates to a C+ for a severely learning-disabled person. Let the grade stand as is if you will. (Any further revisions I'd have to do and that wouldn't reflect his work.) Mrs. G.

Dayle and I had never, ever gone to bat over our kids' grades for several reasons: we felt that grades were not that important, that they were probably roughly correct, and finally, that learning to deal with difficult, arbitrary, sometimes unfair authority figures like teachers and bosses was, alas, part of growing up. So the kids got advice from us if they asked, but they did not get bailed out. Dayle must have been deeply conflicted, really flailing about, to finally break down and throw herself before the court in that way. Bart had done his very best and was disappointed with the C+. He had wanted to do better, still had some competitive pride, and felt frustrated by his inability to write, a task that previously had come easy.

Sometimes there is nothing more to be done. We couldn't expect a teacher to inflate grades in deference to Bart's disability. Hell, if Bart had wanted easy grades, he could have stayed in special ed. This was the big time, the Olympic Games, and somehow he'd have to measure up. If, God forbid, he couldn't, then there was no use fooling him and ourselves. We arranged for additional tutoring so that he'd have every possible support, encouraged him, and prayed daily for him to continue to heal and find a way to rise to the level of the work. I was reminded of words from an old Negro spiritual, "You've got to walk that lonesome valley; you've got to walk it by yourself. There's no one here can walk it for you. You've got to walk it by yourself."

A week or so later we received word from the school psychologist that a visiting OT was in the district, covering for Cathy Noonan during an extended illness. Bart hadn't received occupational therapy in school for a year now, and the school asked if we would like him to meet with the new guy, reputed to be expert in TBI? An expert in TBI? Would we ever! Arrangements were made for Bart to see Ralph LaCasio twice a week. After the very first session, Dayle ran into Ralph while picking Bart up from school. He told her without fanfare that he believed Bart's short-term memory could improve significantly with proper therapy. He'd worked with comparably injured youngsters and thought Bart might even be able to train for a career as an occupational therapist someday. This was pretty heady stuff, since most days Bart couldn't for the life of him remember if it was an A or B day in school or what time the bus left for BOCES. Studying for exams was painfully time-consuming and frustrating. I called Ralph later that day by phone, since Dayle's report seemed too good to be true, so I figured she must have somehow gotten it wrong. With Bart hovering impatiently after school, it's easy to get things mixed up, rather like trying to concentrate with a horsefly buzzing your face. But Dayle had heard right. Ralph explained that he'd seen good success with a couple of other TBIers, both of whom had gone on to have careers in OT. His background was absolutely first rate: he'd concentrated on brain injury for years, supervised a large staff of OTs, and had even cofounded an OT program at a nearby junior college. He promised to help Bart get into the program if he was interested. For now, the plan was to focus exclusively on short-term memory, which, even more than hemianopia, was standing in the way of Bart living a normal life. Ralph claimed his approach would help Bart's brain form new neural pathways, effectively working around injured areas to regain lost functions.

Like a track coach, Ralph would drill, push, and bully Bart to his limits, and Bart would get stronger, faster, and smarter. I warned Ralph to make sure he had first established a personal relationship before pushing the envelope too far. Bart would gladly burst his heart for a friend, but wouldn't do diddly-squat for an impersonal taskmaster. Fortunately Ralph had the gift of gab and was an old-timer from Boston, and he and Bart soon developed a warm friendship based on Yankee-Red Sox rivalry. For the next six weeks, Ralph worked with Bart, writing after his last scheduled visit in the memory log: "Bart is doing well with six-digit number recall STM [short-term memory] forward and backward while doing a fine motor task." Intrigued, I called and asked what exactly that jargon meant. Though we never actually met, Ralph and I spoke by phone regularly and developed a warm rapport. Direct to the point of bluntness, with a good sense of humor and irony, and a fine mixture of world-weariness and idealism, he was my kind of guy. Ralph explained that he'd had Bart working on putting washers and nuts onto bolts of various sizes while simultaneously memorizing random six-digit numbers, reciting them forward and backward. The task simulated the kind of real-world multitasking he might face in school or on a job. This drill struck me as rather difficult, even for someone without impaired memory. Six digits backward? Ralph agreed. "We're getting close to the lower range of so-called normal memory. I'm pretty sure he can be pushed further along."

Then he said good-bye, wishing us good luck with Bart, of whom he had grown quite fond. His temporary assignment with the school district was over so he was heading back to the Albany area, where his practice was based. He didn't know anyone else in our neck of woods who took an approach similar to his. The school district offered to have Cathy Noonan work with Bart again, even to have her "cross-train" with Ralph, but Bart wouldn't hear of it. He'd built a good relationship with Ralph and could even see some tangible improvements, but he wasn't interested in "going back to that old bitch." Actually, Noonan was very far from a bitch. Not for nothing had she chosen a career helping kids. Dayle felt connected with Cathy, especially after she tragically lost her adult son to brain cancer. Like most teens, Bart never really saw his teachers or therapists as human beings, much less vulnerable persons fighting their own hard fights. As suddenly as he had come, Ralph was gone, though not irrevocably. We managed to cobble together occasional sessions with him, though between the hurdles of distance and cost, it was pretty hit-and-miss, mostly miss.

Ralph was a real eye-opener. Remembering random six-digits backward? Hell, I have a tough time managing that. Dayle and I speculated late at night, during our few stolen movements alone, about how well Bart would be doing if, instead of six short weeks, he'd worked with Ralph all along. Bart had endured hundreds of OT sessions with half a dozen therapists from Katie at Helen Hayes to the young gals at St. Luke's, but no one had directly assaulted the central problem of impaired memory head-on except Ralph. Dayle reminded me of the old joke about cardiologists, not all of whom are created equal—"Some patients get Dr. DeBakey, and some patients get Dr. Shake 'n Bake." To be fair, these other folks were well meaning and effective as far as they went. But their experience and perspective were limited.

Though it was tantalizing to speculate on how far Bart might have come had Ralph turned up a couple of years sooner, it was pointless to dwell on what might have been. Ralph provided the jolt we needed to continue pressing for further solutions outside the box. It seems a truism, but even the best-trained, most-skilled, and well-intentioned professionals in the world can suffer a kind of tunnel vision, sticking to familiar, well-trodden paths that pioneers once blazed.

33
Vision Restoration Therapy

Scanning a newsletter from Los Angeles–based Centre for Neuro Skills, I was gradually dozing off when a headline halfway down the page jumped out at me: "Restoration of Vision Loss After Stroke and Brain Injury." I read the scant paragraph with rising excitement. It mentioned a company in Florida and studies done in Germany. Besides hemianopia, there are several other common vision problems associated with TBI and stroke, and it wasn't clear from the article which types of vision loss were supposedly being restored. Too restless to sleep, I searched the Internet for further information without much success and waited for morning, haunted by images of Bart's vision loss. My stomach tensed every time we played basketball and he awkwardly fumbled to his right for the ball, every time he called, "Shotgun!" as he jumped in the car's passenger seat, every time he bumped into a household object like a vacuum cleaner or air filter, which were daily occurrences. Could this be the big break we'd been hoping and praying for?

A series of calls the next morning to NovaVision in Florida seemed to confirm that vision restoration therapy (VRT) had been successful in patients with hemianopia. Next a quick call to my brother, David, about possible accommodations in the Miami area, since the program was offered exclusively through the auspices of the University of Miami medical center. Why Miami? I wondered, guessing the explanation might have something to do with an ample supply of stroke victims. As always, the devil is in the details, so we'd have to fill out an extensive medical questionnaire and submit medical records to establish whether Bart was a suitable candidate. While waiting a couple of weeks for their verdict, I forcibly wrestled down my raging optimism and read what little I could find about NovaVision and VRT, most of it published by NovaVision. They claimed 66 percent of patients with hemianopia experienced increases in field of vision after six months of therapy, though the average increase was only about 5 to 10 percent. I tried to imagine what a 5 to 10 percent increase would look like by placing cardboard blinders on my glasses, first covering a full 50 percent to the right of each lens, then covering only 40 percent. The extra 10 percent made a noticeable difference in ease of getting around. As luck would have it, NovaVision was preparing to roll out another pilot program at Columbia University Medical Center in New York City, 1,200 miles closer than Miami.

Mid-December 2004, nearly three years since the accident, Bart, Dayle, and I drove down to Columbia University's brain mapping laboratory for an evaluation by one of its directors, a top gun named Dr. Randolph Marshall. The hospital was a city within a city, a vast, sprawling complex of pavilions that seem to stretch for miles. The Neurological Institute of New York had its own building, the size of a typical rural hospital. Doc Marshall was a pleasant surprise: a world-class scientist, he was nonetheless down-to-earth, charming, warm, and humble—cut from the same mold as Dr. Harter. After spending the better part of the day running tests, he was already a card-carrying Bart booster, marveling at his sense of humor and zest for life.

While the results were sent off to NovaVision for final confirmation, Doc Marshall told us that Bart seemed to be a very promising candidate. "Randy," as he kindly allowed us to call him, was really quite excited, since Columbia theretofore had a grand total of three patients enrolled in the VRT study, all elderly stroke victims. Bart was their first-ever youngster with TBI, and that was a big deal, since the scientists at the brain lab believed that young brains might respond even better than old.

Dr. Marshall explained that VRT was so brand spanking new that he wasn't sure it really worked as advertised. Proponents claimed that after a damaged area in the brain lost the capacity to see, adjacent neurons could be stimulated into taking on the visual function. Brain cells that had never previously been involved in processing sight could adapt and learn to do so, a phenomenon known as neural plasticity. If it turned out that brains could repair themselves by rewiring around damaged areas, that would be an important, even revolutionary, discovery.

Improved visual fields had been well documented in German patients. (NovaVision was a German firm.) But it was not clear whether those increases were actually due to neurons adopting new functions in the brain or simply a result of improved visual scanning skills learned during the course of therapy. Was the increased vision due to learned skills in the eye, or really due to neural plasticity in the brain? Scientists hoped these studies would answer that question. Some of what Randy explained sailed right over our heads. Bart seemed bored with all the medical talk, though he was particularly interested in Dr. Marshall's pretty young graduate assistant, who did most of the testing and training.

VRT handily passed the "does no harm" test and apparently had a two-thirds chance of restoring some of Bart's vision, although the how and why of it was still poorly understood. If Bart could see 10 percent more, whether by neural plasticity, visual scanning, or sticking a feather up you know where, I was ready to try. But there was a serious question mark about Bart's suitability that had nothing to do with vision. The therapy involved twice-daily sessions, lasting twenty minutes each, during which a patient must focus completely and concentrate on the task. Even a momentary shift in attention jeopardizes the results. Bart, like most severe TBIers, was fidgety and easily distracted, hardly the most promising profile for VRT. A method of testing attention had been developed in order to screen out elderly stoke victims who might also suffer from senility or Alzheimer's, and who would thus be incapable of attending to the exercises. A score of 90 or better was required in order to perform VRT in a satisfactory way, and Bart's best score was only 88. Randy believed that with practice, he might be able to make the grade. Why, just in the course of one long day's practice, his scores had improved from the mid-70s to 88. Did we want to go ahead and try? Randy made it abundantly clear that there were no guarantees. I laughed, replying that people who give guarantees are usually trying to sell something like used cars.

During our lunch break, we walked around campus, searching for a place to grab a bite. Finishing our meal, we happened upon a small chapel just outside the cafeteria, and Dayle wanted to go in and light a candle. The place was dark, chilly, seemingly falling into genteel neglect. A service was in progress, with a handful of people listening to a sermon. The priest spoke of Jesus curing a blind man, giving the gift of sight to one who had never before seen. We didn't stay long due to the chill, but Dayle felt the bible passage an auspicious sign. After she and Bart took communion, as we traipsed down the dank stone stairs back into the hospital, Dayle turned suddenly to Bart asking if he understood what the priest was really talking about. Bart smiled and said, "Yeah, me. I'm gonna get my sight back." For me, the bible story, though not necessarily a sign of anything, was a welcome reminder of the power of faith—faith, hope, love, and the brain-mapping lab to boot; how could we lose?

A couple of weeks later a large crate arrived at our house containing VRT equipment: a specially designed laptop computer, along with the apparatus to align ones head and eyes during training. While focusing on a center point on the computer screen, you had to click the mouse whenever you saw a light dot anywhere else on the screen. The dots appear randomly, but mostly just on the border between sighted and blind fields. Gradually, with practice, the border can be pushed back, bringing new areas into the sighted field. VRT sessions are no fun. When the program was demonstrated at Columbia, Dayle and I both remarked that it obviously had not been designed with kids in mind. The only time the program gave user feedback was when you missed a light dot—then it made an annoying buzzing sound that indicated you'd missed. When you successfully caught the dot in time, nothing whatsoever happened. There was no scoring, so you never knew if your performance was improving during a session, or from one session to the next. VRT was so ungamelike that it provided absolutely no positive feedback. Motivation to keep plugging would have to come from within.

Doc Marshall asked whether we would mind if a TV crew from NBC followed Bart's progress. I was reluctant, remembering my old mother's admonition to never bring undue attention to oneself. Bart, the TV addict, was excited by the idea, so Dayle and I finally agreed, hoping that all the attention and hoopla might help him get through the long grueling course of therapy. A crew showed up every couple of months at Columbia or at our house, and that would invariably buck up Bart's interest.

34
A Christmas Story

Christmas 2004 was going to be special. Plans called for flying down to Fort Lauderdale to welcome home Alana, our niece's newly adopted baby. David and Hope's first grandchild, she was arriving home from an adoption in northern Florida. Corinne and her kid brother, Zoie, had been on hand nineteen years earlier for Bart's arrival at JFK, and we felt flying down to welcome Corinne's child into the family somehow completed the circle. Bart and Cass were a little surprised, even disappointed, to learn that Alana was not Korean, but soon got up a head of steam about going to Florida to add another adopted kid to the family. Bart joked that "the adopted kids are gonna take over." He was especially worked up about the trip, since Uncle David had promised to take him to a topless bar. The previous spring, a friend of the family had taken Bart to celebrate his nineteenth birthday at the Blue Moon Caberet just outside of town, and the visit proved to be a highlight. He invariably retold the story (minus the X-rated details, thankfully) every time we drove by the place. Bart was hoping Uncle David, well known for his artistic temperament, flamboyant wardrobe, and generally unconventional ways, would outdo the Blue Moon.

We were a merry crew driving up to Albany on Christmas Eve. A new baby, especially an adopted one, touched each of us deeply. For Dayle and me it brought back tender memories of our own kids' arrivals. On their anniversaries we celebrate each child's homecoming as "arrival day"—a handmade family affair. After watching videos of Bart or Cassidy's arrival at JFK, we usually go out to a big dinner, then back home for New York–style cheesecake, a family favorite. Sometimes we are joined by friends with adopted kids. The adoption circle is also a fellowship of sorts, albeit a sprawling, amorphous one.

With a 7:00 a.m. departure, we had decided to camp out in a hotel near the airport, ready to roll out of bed and fly first thing. We showed up at US Airways' check-in counter before 5:30 a.m. only to find a huge throng of Christmas Day travelers who were up and at 'em even earlier. Hanging around, we began to catch wind of wholesale delays, two hours or more, all over Florida. We were already tired and hungry, and the rumors put us all in a grumpy mood. For Dayle, who was ensconced in a wheelchair, it didn't take much. The prior evening, leaving Christmas Eve services, she slipped on a patch of black ice in the church parking lot, landing square on her knee, where she had previously torn a meniscus. She was hurting.

When we finally reached the front of the line, the flight board was indicating our flight was delayed and the check-in clerk warned us to expect it to be at least two hours. So we headed over to a café for a leisurely breakfast; after all, there was no rush. Imagine our shock when we arrived at the departure gate to find it besieged by a mob of disgruntled travelers. Seems every US Airways gate was similarly encircled—all flights, arriving as well as departing, were delayed. I was puzzled, since the weather seemed pretty fair, but, resigned to a long haul, parked myself in line and waited for some news. As I listened to the check-in clerks scrambling to help other customers, I sensed that something didn't smell right. Why all the delays? Someone suggested snow in Pittsburgh, the hub city for many flights. A young man with a PDA proved that wrong by checking the weather channel.

When we eventually got to the head of the line, I asked the woman attendant calmly but firmly what was really going on. She was ashamed to admit, practically whispering in my ear, that a wildcat labor action was in the works—people were calling in sick all over the country. The Pittsburgh flight, which was slated to take us on to Ft. Lauderdale, was grounded because two flight attendants had called in sick. I joked that we'd be glad to fly without peanuts but was beginning to worry in earnest. After explaining the purpose of our flight, pointing out the kids and how we couldn't miss our niece's arrival, the clerk looked me directly in the eyes and said with obvious feeling, "Don't worry, Mr. Goldstein, whatever it takes, I'll get you there. I'm adopted myself. I was the second of unexpected twins before the days of ultrasound. Thank

God my parents agreed to keep my sister and me together." I breathed a little easier. There had to be a way to get to the Ft. Lauderdale airport, one of the biggest destinations on the East Coast. But as cancellations mounted, I agreed as a contingency to accept a flight to Miami or West Palm Beach, then eventually anywhere in Florida. To my astonishment, she couldn't get us to any of those places, even if I drove first to New York City or Boston, three hours away. Meanwhile cancellations were cascading across the flight board and the country. Dayle wheeled over and suggested a bit of triage—Bart and I would go, since two seats would be easier to find than four. I agreed. There were two seats to Pittsburgh, two seats to Indianapolis, two seats to Baltimore, but no connecting flights to Florida. US Airways eventually cancelled over two hundred flights that morning due to sick-outs, just as all one thousand Comair flights were simultaneously grounded. The stranding of people and luggage, especially at US Airways' Philadelphia hub would drag on for days. Finally after almost three hours brainstorming, punctuated by a few false leads and near misses, the clerk tearfully threw up her hands and admitted defeat. We literally couldn't get there from here! I found myself consoling her; she had become so wrapped up in our family drama.

Shaking my head in disbelief, I called my brother, who had already booked us a motel suite and planned a big dinner for that evening, along with my sister's family. I had to repeat myself twice. David, not easily shaken, was well and truly stunned. "You can't get here? What about another airport?" I assured him that as an old airfreight man I had exhausted every single possibility. Hanging up, I turned wearily to the family, who looked bored out of their gourds, and said cheerily, "Let's go eat Chinese." "And see a movie," Bart chimed in. After all, we still had our health, and weren't going anywhere—so we may as well make something of the rest of the day. Bart and I even sang a little "Deck the harrs with boughs of horry," from the Chinese restaurant scene in *A Christmas Story*. It was almost 2:30 in the afternoon, after nine mind-numbing hours at the airport.

Driving home late that evening after seeing *Meet the Fockers,* we were all dog-tired. I was even feeling a little punchy, so I resorted to rolling down the window to help keep awake on the near deserted thruway. The kids were so bushed they didn't seem to notice the frigid air whistling in—nobody stirred. At home Bart, as usual, was first in the shower, emerging with a wild look on his face, rushing at me, screaming, "What the f--- are you looking at?" He caught me so completely off guard, I couldn't stammer out a response. He proceeded to storm through the house, upstairs and down, slamming doors and screaming like a wild banshee. I was blitzed, head pounding, brains addled, and finding myself yelling back at him, telling him to shut the f--- up and go down to his room. He ran downstairs, screaming and cursing, slamming his door, over and over, while hurling a stream of obscenities.

We held our breaths, listening and waiting for it to pass, but the tirade came in waves, which would crescendo, then trail off, only to ignite again, all the while accompanied by the thud thud thudding of a slamming door. This went on for nearly half an hour, and we were becoming genuinely alarmed. Was this some kind of seizure-type event? What kind of madness would drive somebody to slam a door for thirty minutes? In desperation, I phoned Bart's counselor Melinda, apologizing for calling her at home on Christmas Day. After listening to a brief recounting of the day's events, she advised that his brain was overloaded, or flooded, and there was nothing for it. He would eventually spend himself, then fall into deep sleep during which his brain should recover. I'd hardly hung up the phone when the racket trailed off and there was silence below. A few minutes later I quietly peeked in, finding him sprawled across the bed, still in his bathrobe. The doorframe was broken beyond repair.

Our confidence in Bart's ability to make his way in the world also took a heavy beating. This was the mother of all outbursts, compared with which previous episodes were mere farts in a blizzard. Recently we'd begun looking into colleges that specialized in accommodating learning-disabled students. How on earth could Bart cope, if when he felt exhausted and stressed, commonplace occurances in dorm life, he was liable to go bananas? It had been three years since the accident; was it ever going to ease up? Three more years of hard time according to Dr. Harter's prediction, but even that wasn't written in stone. Heaven help us.

Tired, weary, and heartsick, Dayle scribbled a note for Melinda asking that she focus on anger management with Bart and block out additional time for Cassidy, who was terribly put off by the spectacle of her brother flipping out. That evening was a low point, but we still faced a long hard Christmas break, especially Dayle, who wracked her brains to come up with activities to occupy her constant companion. For my part, I was glad to escape to work, though evenings often involved exquisite feats of eggshell walking.

35
Unsung Heroes

Spring semester was at hand, Bart's last in high school. He chose a senior elective course, film studies, which turned out to be an all-time favorite. The students watched movies in class and for homework to boot! Of course there were essays to write, but with hard work and a little boost from Mr. Podell, he managed. Serena reported that his understanding of complex humor involving multiple-meaning words was coming back big-time. He could understand jokes like, "How do you stop an elephant from charging? Take away his credit card." With those kinds of subtleties no longer eluding him, conversing with Bart gradually took on a more nearly normal feel. Not quite normal enough, since no one in his film class was willing to work with him outside of class on peer critiques, so Cassidy stood in as the closest thing to a peer.

Our kids seemed to be getting along a little better, a huge relief to Dayle and me since we frequently worried and fussed over their tattered relationship. Cassidy was a bit more herself around him, though not nearly enough to satisfy party-hardy Barty. Melinda had been encouraging Bart to write down his most deeply felt worries and concerns, so he'd remember to bring them up during their weekly sessions. In his memory log he wrote in huge block letters:

Things to Talk with Melinda: [*sic*]

1. Cassidy reclusive
2. Working on eye exercises for driving
3. No Cathy Noonan

The list was the best guide we had to what was eating him, especially since he'd grown to trust Melinda and eagerly looked forward to her visits.

As always, Cassidy topped his list of concerns, and though he sorely wished things were "like the good old days," he seemed to have lost the knack of talking with her. Sometimes he plain tried too hard, became disinhibited, hurling a few inappropriate phrases, maybe even an "f-bomb,"—a sure turn-off to Cassidy, who never cursed, even if she stubbed her toe or banged her funny bone. Other times, he'd try slipping back into the time-honored role of big brother, giving sage advice, but end up clowning around, or offering guidance more suited to his peers. He'd warn her to steer clear of drugs, or to keep away from the unsavory dropouts hanging out in downtown New Paltz, advice his goody-two-shoes sister hardly needed or appreciated. Desperate to relate to her, he couldn't seem to find common ground. His cognitive deficits made it tough for him to think on his feet, and her silence and reticence made it harder on them both. Their alienation, after being so very close, was heartrending, but there was no obvious fix. We hoped Melinda could open a dialogue between them, and that gradually Bart's return to normal would allow them to reconnect. Meanwhile we did everything we could think of to keep their connection alive, from fun family outings to quietly saying grace before dinner—whatever it took to prevent their hearts from turning cold. That would be too cruel to bear.

The second item on the list of things to discuss with Melinda was about doing eye exercises so that he could drive again, which was the whole point of VRT as far as Bart was concerned. For the first month he worked faithfully, a near miracle since it involved plodding through four ten-minute sessions daily. Sporting a patch over one eye at a time, his shaved head bearing a huge scar, he resembled a figure straight out of *Treasure Island*. With his shaky short-term memory, forgetting to do the sessions was a chronic problem, yet he didn't take kindly to even gentle reminders. Emotionally Bart was very much the reactive teenager, much as he had been at age fourteen or fifteen. We devised a system that used large index cards numbered one through four to indicate the number of sessions remaining. He'd flip a card at start of each session, starting with four, and eventually finish them all. Gradually he developed a routine: shower first thing then, still dripping wet, knock off a session before breakfast. With any luck he'd do another after eating and only have two more to worry about upon returning from school. After a month or so we began to notice subtle changes having nothing to do with vision. He seemed to be more focused, less easily distracted. Bart remarked that he was finding it easier to follow along in class. When we returned to Columbia for a checkup, Dr. Marshall confirmed that increased focus and concentration were oft-noted side effects of VRT, very welcome news. After finishing his examination, he announced with obvious pleasure and excitement that Bart had regained almost 5 percent more of his visual field, mostly in the lower half of the field. He felt that would help him read as well as better navigate around objects. Everyone left that day tired but happy and hopeful.

The novelty and excitement soon wore off, but not the drudgery that gradually, inexorably, sapped Bart's motivation. He began to skip a session here and there, often cheating by flipping two cards at a time. We reminded him and encouraged him up to a point, mostly getting hassled for our trouble. Unfortunately, the initial spurt of vision field enhancement was about all he ever got. Though he continued the sessions for almost seven months, additional improvements were quite marginal; making for a grand total of 5 or 6 percent increased visual field. Even that little bit significantly improved his reading and walking about, but would not enable him to drive, for him a searing disappointment. As weeks and months dragged by without additional dramatic improvement and he realized that driving was not in the offing, his enthusiasm sputtered and finally died. We were worried sick about his slacking. After all, there might be a few more degrees of vision waiting to be bullied back by conscientious application of the therapy.

Sometimes the oblique stroke is best. John Dockery, one of Bart's heroes, called with words of encouragement, and even sent an 8 × 10 signed photo of himself still in Jets uniform, inscribed with words of encouragement, friendship, and solidarity. The framed photo still hangs on Bart's wall in a place of honor. Dockery's timely intervention bucked Bart up for a couple of weeks. Next we turned to a friend whom we had met through Dockery, Brother Rick Curry. Dayle had originally urged me to seek Brother Rick's prayers years earlier, and I called again, explaining our quandary. Though bravely fronting, Bart was inwardly terrified by the whole driving thing, and by a future that seemed more filled with menace than hope. Rick promised that, along with his brother Jesuits, he would pray that Bart find courage at this difficult time.

The first thing that strikes one about Brother Rick is his sparkling eyes, harbingers of his warm, welcoming, infectious sense of humor. Like many an Irishman, he's a born storyteller, with a knack for poking fun at himself and skewering the foibles of others. An accomplished thespian, he acted on stage and in television, and taught theater at Saint Joseph's University and New York University before founding his own acting school and repertory theater. He was blessed with many gifts, and his highly regarded books *The Secrets of Jesuit Soupmaking* and *The Secrets of Jesuit Breadmaking* attest to his expertise in the kitchen. His love of cooking eventually led to the founding of the Belson Bakery in Belfast, Maine, purveyors of Brother Curry's bread and Brother Curry's miraculous dog biscuits. Such a multifaceted, energetic, and resourceful individual was bound to make his mark. Oh, did I mention that Rick was born without a right hand and forearm? According to him, that was his greatest gift, which led him to a life of service to handicapped persons, helping them find ways to lead independent and fulfilling lives.

Raised in a religious family and educated in parochial schools, Rick was taught never to use his handicap as an excuse. Learning to ride a bike, roller skate, and play baseball, he grew up feeling that he was just like other kids who happened to have two arms. Yankee fans will remember Jim Abbott, who, born with only one arm, pitched a no-hitter against the Cleveland Indians. Rick Curry preceded him by a couple of decades, but unlike Abbott, found his true gifts off the playing field. Joining the Jesuits at age eighteen, he was drawn by their devotion to education and went on after seminary to earn a string of degrees in theater. While teaching and completing PhD studies at New York University, he learned that fellow students were earning their keep by working in commercials on the side. When he showed up for a scheduled audition for a mouthwash commercial, he was literally laughed out the door by a thoughtless receptionist convinced he had been sent up as a gag. That was the first time he ever ran smack into discrimination against persons with disabilities. Rick was hurt and angry but put those feelings to good use, founding the National Theatre Workshop of the Handicapped (NTWH) in lower Manhattan shortly after, in 1977. Since then thousands of disabled persons have studied acting, music, dance, art, and writing. NTWH expanded its programs to include a summer workshop, fine arts gallery, bakery, and baking school in Belfast, Maine, all run for and by handicapped persons. Always alert to feeding the need, Rick more recently launched the Wounded Warriors Writers' Program, a writer's workshop for disabled veterans returning from Afghanistan and Iraq. Participants learn to tell their stories through dramatic monologues written for stage or screen.

At my wit's end, I turned again to Rick, and, as always, he responded generously. Brother Rick is far from a stereotypical somber cleric. He's full of piss and vinegar, ever ready with a quick-witted riposte. He loves to tell the story of a documentary filmmaker who while shooting at the workshop showed some pretty obvious discomfort working around disabled people. Rick, by way of "putting the little bald fellow at ease," told him, "Listen, I'd much rather have one arm than be bald, so relax." I'm pretty sure he meant it too. At any event, after we called Rick, Bart seemed to settle back into the VRT routine, and remained steady to the end.

The last item on Bart's list for Melinda, "No Cathy Noonan," referred to the possibility of Cathy taking up where Ralph LaCasio had left off. Though that issue had already been put to rest, Bart was always paranoid about the threat that poor Cathy Noonan might come back into his life, ready to swat him in the head.

What follows is a letter to the editor that appeared in the *New Paltz Times* on February 2, 2005, under the title "Unsung Heroes":

> Prior to the summer of 2002 we had never given much thought to special education, except perhaps to grouse occasionally about its high cost in the school budget. But an automobile accident the previous Christmas left our son Bart with learning deficits and pitched us headlong into the world of New Paltz schools' special ed department. What we discovered there impressed and moved us. Sterling quality administrators Theresa Pabon and then Stephanie Forsyth, and director Dan Seyler-Wetzel, manage to delicately balance the needs of students with the district's limited resources. Surely a daunting, thankless challenge that would probably leave King Solomon weary and cross-eyed. Yet they approach their mission with professionalism, caring, and commitment, leading a cadre of teachers, therapists, social workers, and aides who do a superlative job in the trenches. Few aspects of New Paltz schools match the standard of excellence that these underappreciated

workers achieve in special ed, day in, year out. Their students are not elected to the National Honor Society, [and do not] appear in featured bios in the *New Paltz Times.* We, who know that all God's children are equally precious in his eyes, want to thank everyone involved with the special ed department. You are unsung heroes. A few demand special mention: Allan Podell, master teacher, inspiration to students and teachers alike; Jeannine Ridgeway, who aided Bart through his tough return to school; Serena Wunderlich, speech therapist par excellence; Mary Kay Canino, school psychologist and overall guardian angel.

The high school's general administration, led by Barbara Clinton and Dennis DiBari, has been uniformly warm and supportive. Three deserve special mention: Maureen Zdroski and Patty Matter, who furnish much-needed steadiness and tough love. And Pam Parker, the bus driver.

Last but not least the coaches: Matter, Ciliberto, Defino, Tegeler, Phelps, Acosta, Barberio, Moore. New Paltz is blessed with a rare breed of coaches who understand their true vocation is teaching youngsters how to run a straight race, not merely to win. The TLC they lavished upon Bart, more than anything else, made his three-year slog to graduation bearable. In a wider culture that debases athletics through the headlong pursuit of winning by any means, these men are a national treasure. Special thanks to Coach D for all the extra time, and to Coach Tegeler for coming off the field just prior to the coin toss to welcome Bart home.

All these good people and many others—special educators, regular teachers, staff, and coaches—made Bart's remarkable comeback possible. Moved by professionalism, duty, and love, they have been a godsend to him and our family, and surely to countless others. We salute them all and gladly acknowledge our debt of gratitude.

The Goldstein Family

That letter turned out to be a bombshell, sending shockwaves through the school district. Duty-bound to publicly acknowledge our gratitude, we had expected the letter to pass pretty much unnoticed. Previous epistles to the editor written from time to time about civic matters—endorsing a candidate for school board or concerning the YMCA—had gone unnoticed, presumably unread, but not this time. There were phone calls and letters of appreciation from the superintendent, the director of special ed, and the school principal. Copies of the letter were distributed to teachers and posted around the school building. Hearty handshakes and backslapping came from all the usual suspects—coaches, special ed teachers, and the like. The fuss caught us off guard; we were frankly a little embarrassed. After all, the letter simply acknowledged the obvious. When I said as much to one of the teachers, he replied, "Yeah, sure, but we never see things like that in print. It's always bitch, bitch, bitch." It was sobering to realize that these everyday heroes are so unappreciated that they go ape when publicly given the kudos they deserve. It was awkward to receive their thanks when we were the ones who owed thanks. These fine people crave the recognition they've earned but are apparently denied by a culture that worships celebrities. Dayle and I decided to throw a dinner for the coaches, by way of unmistakably showing thanks and also giving Bart a chance to say farewell to this special group of people.

We booked a room in a local gin-mill on an evening of the coaches' choosing (they picked the week between winter and spring sports) and had a sumptuous dinner, with short speeches and anecdotes roasting each guest. A grand time was had by all.

We realized that, at least in our community, coaches play a huge part at the heart and soul of the high school. Their influence is pervasive and benevolent. For one thing, they're the only faculty that has every single child in their classes, for each of the full four years. Coach D once confided to me, "What does a gym teacher really teach? Sure there are the games and they're important, no doubt. But I think of my job as teaching kids how to get along, how to cope, how to live right."

36

One Day in the Life of HBOT

"Love's Austere and Lonely Offices."

—Robert Hayden

We were gearing up for a third round of HBOT—another forty dives. Bart's short-term memory and general cognition had improved after his time with Ralph LaCasio but were still nothing to write home about, and we were looking for another breakthrough. Dayle had accompanied Bart on the first three so it was my turn to go with him for dives number four and five. Saturday was a cloudy, threatening-rain kind of day, almost exactly three years after Bart's discharge from HHH. He'd come a long way but his tolerance for me was still quite limited, and HBOT meant spending a very long day together. We shoved off at 8:00 a.m. for the hour-plus drive down to Mahopac. Medical protocol called for a minimum of two hours between dives, and since the first was at 9:30 in the morning the second dive was not scheduled until 2:00 p.m.

The long layover between dives was always a dicey time. Bart was restless and bored just hanging around. We had developed comforting traditions that helped kill the time. We'd stop at the Greek diner where Bart wolfed down meals on principle while I tried to eat a long, leisurely lunch. Then we'd stop at the wine store, where I'd buy a bottle of Chianti. Next it was over to the Jefferson Valley Mall, where we'd agree to split up for an hour. Bart would cruise his regular haunts—shopping for CDs, DVDs, and T-shirts. He enjoyed visiting malls since he could experience a degree of independence, though always just a cell phone call away. Jefferson Valley Mall is relatively small, with decidedly lower-end merchandise, and he'd invariably ring me up after twenty minutes or so, asking, "When we gonna blow this joint?" As usual we'd rendezvous at the food court, he'd show me his purchases—mostly rap CDs and crappy T-shirts—his all-time favorite was one blazoned with "Sperm Donor." He'd let me buy him a drink at the food court, although he'd already downed one or two Cokes on his own. His manner today was somewhat chilly, impatient, and slightly agitated. I was worried he'd had too much caffeine, which he habitually craved. He was not thrilled to be chillin' with Dad. But we managed to get through the mall rituals without a flare-up, and I was grateful to be driving back to the clinic for another seventy-five minute respite. As usual, we arrived back a half hour early, since Bart was always glad to schmooze the staff, especially Joanie and Mary Ellen. He seemed more on edge than usual, possibly a reaction to the new series of oxygen treatments, possibly just annoyed at being stuck with Daddy for the day—on a Saturday no less. Bart was keenly aware of Saturday night. He remembered fondly evenings spent with friends, capped with *Saturday Night Live,* his all-time favorite show. He'd get on his cell phone and call Gary and Kyle and Doug, repeatedly leaving messages. Once in a great while, perhaps every month or two, he'd actually catch one of the boys on a call, and, embarrassed, they would scramble for an excuse to dodge seeing him. But he persevered, or more strictly speaking, perseverated.

The second dive finished around 3:15 p.m., and in a mad rush to get on the road, Bart brushed by me, asking if we were going to a movie. I began to go over the choices with him—we could either see a movie in Mahopac and then eat out afterward, or drive halfway home to Fishkill, eat dinner first, and then catch a movie. He cut me off, snapping, "Drive to Fishkill. I'm not two, ya know." We drove the half hour to Fishkill in a stony silence broken only by blaring rap music. As I often did at these times, I prayed for peace and harmony in the family. He cracked his knuckles repeatedly on the drive. Bart cracked the knuckles of each hand without an assist from the other hand, a knack he'd only recently regained in his right hand after a series of dives. Regaining that ability, lost for three years, made Bart a true believer in the benefits of HBOT.

At the Fishkill theater, as usual, he had a last-minute change of mind, so we hurriedly bought tickets to a different movie than the one we had meant to see. Still an hour before show time, we drove to a nearby Wendy's for a bite. I could sense his simmering agitation, so I said as little as possible, hoping to slip through dinner and quietly into the movies. Bart adores movies, always has. His memory for movies, actors, scenes, and even lines from scenes was uncanny and seemed hardly diminished by TBI. I often wondered how he could remember the exact lines of a movie he'd recently seen, but not remember the names of the kids in his classes. Just a peculiarity of his injury, I suppose. Perhaps film engages a whole range of sensations—auditory, visual, and emotional—all at once in a way that somehow sticks. I never could figure it, though I often said, not entirely in jest, that if they could set algebra to film, Bart could be a mathematician.

At Wendy's, out of the blue, a dark look of disgust crossed Bart's face and he stammered, "I have other friends you know—not just you and Mom." After a moment of stunned silence—I didn't know what to say—he continued emphatically, "As a matter of fact, I don't want to go to movies with you at all, you faggot." I had lost my appetite and thought it best to just wait and see what would happen. Sometimes his outbursts blew over. As we got back in the car, I asked him if there was something I did that annoyed him. I was willing to change, but he'd have to help me understand. He seemed somewhat calmer and replied flatly, "There's just so much you do that annoys me, I can't begin to explain." I asked for an example, but he couldn't come up with one, and I didn't press. Moved equally by compassion and worry, I said, "Your life's gonna get better. James Chang will be with us for the summer, and you'll be hanging out together. Then it's off to college." Shaking his head he whispered with deep conviction, "Yeah, I gotta get out of fuckin' New Paltz." As we drove back toward the movies, he said that it was okay to go to the movies, but not to sit together. "Fine," I replied sadly, feeling so very sorry for my boy, and a little sorry for myself.

The next morning, in a laughing, near manic tone Bart quipped to Dayle, "You know, I gotta get out of this town. I have no friends here." The fog was continuing to lift, and his sense of loss coming into sharper focus. In the course of three complete cycles of therapy, we made eighty-eight trips like this to HBOT, some were single dives, others double.

✦

A couple of weeks after that HBOT trip, with his own money Bart mixed a CD on iTunes for his mother and me. The gesture was typical Bart; generous to a fault, always ready to share the last of his food or his last dime. After his hilarious sense of humor, generosity was his best quality. Alone in the car next day on the way up to the YMCA, I chanced to play the CD and was completely blown away. The music was mostly unfamiliar—new music, alternative rock. The mix amounted to Bart's musical confession. Song after song filled with hurt, sadness, terrible longing, and loss, yet somehow still defiant, and sometimes hopeful. The songs resonated with an element of introspection and even self-criticism that I thought may have been lost to Bart. It was a relief to see he still had real heart. Although the mix spoke of his pain and loneliness, it also evidenced spirit and hopefulness, even if oftentimes confused and defiant. The lead cut was predictable and vintage Bart—Pink Floyd's "The Wall" with its blatant denunciation of school authorities. The song fairly spits out teen rebellion—no school, no education, no thought control.

Most of the other songs opened a window to Bart's hidden frame of mind. While Bart never spoke with us about his deepest feelings, the songs testified eloquently, deeply, sometimes darkly to his inner struggle. One in particular seemed almost like his theme song—"Hold On" by the band Good Charlotte. The lyrics sing sorrowfully of isolation, desertion, and loneliness. Yet the chorus calls for us to hold on through the pain, to keep searching, keep moving forward and not surrender to despair.

Another song, "Breaking the Habit" by Linkin Park, expressed Bart's feeling of loss of control over his own life. It speaks of confusion, of being saddled with struggles not of one's choosing. The songwriter cries out, asking how he ever got in this mess, and vows to somehow break the cycle.

The theme of dreaming recurred in several of the songs, most notably "So Far Away" by Staind. The lyrics speak with dread about being trapped in a nightmare. The chorus tells of the struggle for acceptance, for forgiveness and peace. It urges one to relinquish the past, accept and live in the moment, carry on day by day.

The CD has become a perennial all-time favorite of Dayle's and mine, always at hand in the family car. I've heard it hundreds of times, often with Bart alongside in the passenger seat. We'd both laugh when it came to track number twelve, an awful rap song Bart inserted as a practical joke that I would always skip. With that much raw feeling on display, Bart was sure to take refuge in a little gag.

37
College Bound

> "Security is mostly a superstition. Life is either a daring adventure, or nothing." —Helen Keller

By the early 1980s adoptions from Korea were running at an all-time high, with prospective parents overwhelmingly requesting baby girls. There was even a name for this marked preference: the China doll syndrome. Since Dayle and I hoped to eventually have both girls and boys, we figured it was just common sense to request the gender less in demand. Besides, bucking the trend appealed to our contrarian streak. At the very least, we hoped it would speed up an already tedious and time-consuming process. As director of Love the Children, Mary Graves had a reputation as a quirky yet benevolent dictator that resulted in a good bit of nail-biting among hopeful adoptive parents. She was so pleased by our stated preference for a boy that she promised to get us "the pick of the litter." Not a very flattering metaphor, but we were glad to have her enthusiastically onboard. While wading through the process, we joined a support group of young families, some with newly adopted kids, others still awaiting a match. We learned valuable lessons about navigating INS regulations, social worker home visits, infant care, and perhaps most importantly, dealing with Mary Graves. After Bart's homecoming we continued to attend group meetings for a year or so, enjoying our status as grizzled veterans, retelling old war stories, and enlightening anxious "newbies" waiting for that all-important match.

Dressed in a bib-style turtle costume, seven-month-old Bart cut a handsome figure at the group's Halloween party. Walking quite well, holding hands, he was a strapping bundle of energy and boyish good looks. A robust, almost rakish manner contrasted with the rest of the sweet babies and toddlers on stage, nearly all of whom were girls. You could have dressed him in a tutu and he still would never be mistaken for a baby girl. Dayle loved to call him "Butchky boy," meaning husky boy. Several parents came over, asking if they could hold him, and were delighted to find him friendly, outgoing, and affectionate. Three different couples confided to us that they had originally asked for girls, but after spending time with Bart at a couple of meetings, they had reconsidered and switched their request. When asked why, they confided to never realizing that Korean boys could be so robust and rugged, thinking they somehow must be scrawny. One couple actually asked would we mind if they named their son Bart. Why should we mind? How chagrined were we when a couple of years later a new cartoon TV show launched featuring a wiseass kid named Bart? After lovingly playing the name game for years before finally deciding on Bart, Dayle was plenty pissed that his beautiful name was being maligned. I wasn't worried. After all, how long could a stupid cartoon show last anyway? It would be hyperbolic to claim that Bart single-handedly broke the logjam, but soon after, a torrent of boys began flowing into our little support group and then rippled out to the wider Love the Children community throughout the Northeast. In the years immediately following his arrival, the ratio of arriving Korean babies nearly reached gender equality. Bart often has a striking effect on people.

✦

As he was serious about attending college in the fall, the district's CSE thought it prudent to have Bart undergo a full neuropsych exam to determine whether his plans were remotely appropriate or feasible. These exams are quite comprehensive, taking the better part of nine hours. He'd been assessed prior to discharge from Helen Hayes, then again a year or so later at the insistence of the no-fault insurance company. When I picked Bart up in Poughkeepsie after the tests, the doctor and I spent a few minutes chatting, and we arranged for a sit-down meeting with the entire family a few weeks later to review the formal findings. This was the first time Bart had the stamina to take the exam at one stretch. The results of both previous assessments had painted portraits of a severely challenged youngster, functioning at an IQ of barely 70, with scores for factual knowledge, verbal and mathematical reasoning, and general understanding in the lowest 2 or 3 percentiles of his age group. Dr. Louis Calabro, dean of local neuropsychologists, was genuinely surprised and delighted to find that Bart's overall IQ had climbed to 86, with a verbal IQ of 91. (Ninety is the lower boundary of the so-called normal range of IQ.) Beyond the numbers, he was even more impressed by Bart's charm, humor, and knack for putting everyone at ease, rare traits indeed for a TBIer. The warm feelings were mutual. Calabro was confined to a wheelchair, and Bart likes most anyone who has faced great adversity.

Calabro confided to me that in light of the severity of Bart's injuries, he was making a remarkable recovery. According to the insurance doctor's report, written more than a year after the accident, at that time he had still been in very bad shape. Somehow he'd made marvelous progress these last two years. I remarked that we had begun the first cycle of HBOT shortly after the insurance exam and were now engaged in a third round. He expressed a positive attitude toward HBOT, so I took him for someone with an open mind, which was a pleasant surprise.

Calabro led off the formal meeting two weeks later with the good news. Astonishingly, Bart no longer suffered from attention deficit disorder (ADD), a condition afflicting nearly all survivors of severe TBI. While of course we knew Bart was easily distracted, somehow it never occurred to us that he was technically categorized as suffering from ADD. When examined two years earlier by the insurance doc, Bart had been positive on eight out of nine tests for ADD. Now he was positive for only one, which was considered within normal range. When he went on to say that the one positive test was for perseveration, I couldn't help nervously giggling aloud. In twenty years of practice he couldn't recall anyone injured as severely as Bart who was no longer suffering from ADD a mere three years after trauma. Dayle and I conjectured that his long course of VRT, in addition to HBOT, may have contributed to this surprising but happy outcome.

Not all the results were as upbeat. Bart's short-term memory was still moderately impaired and liable to be an ongoing weakness, rendering college much more problematic, though not out of the question. To have a fighting chance at success, he'd need a comprehensive range of accommodations—

class note-takers and recordings, review sessions and tutors, extra time for tests, and so on. If he wanted it badly enough, and we could find a college willing to accommodate, Bart might be able to make the grade. But the doctor made it very plain that Bart would find it far more difficult and frustrating than other students. Leaving the meeting Bart seemed pretty agitated. Nobody likes having their dirty laundry set out to dry in public. Calabro had gone over Bart's limitations in meticulous, excruciating detail, along with the special accommodations they necessitated, and I think Bart found it all pretty hard to take. Cassidy seemed blitzed; Dayle and I were thoroughly drained.

✦

College was a very long shot, but Bart had always wanted to go and we thought he deserved a chance. Frankly, we weren't sure what else to do with him. Though most everyone agreed that he would benefit from another year of high school and therapies, he wasn't having any of that. I tried to imagine how he must feel after soldiering through approximately 2,100 therapy sessions since discharge from Helen Hayes, roughly 1.9 sessions per day! At an open house hosted by a college an hour or so away, the program director told us flat out that kids with TBI were not eligible for inclusion. He had painstakingly crafted a successful program catering to youngsters with manageable learning disabilities like dyslexia and ADD. Why muck it up with brain-injured kids? Finding a school willing to take a chance on Bart would be a tall order. So in a subdued, low-key manner we began to collect letters of recommendation and arrange for transcripts. Bart even wrote an essay to support his applications. With help from the folks in the school guidance department, we managed to get out of couple of college applications to schools in nearby Vermont, a veritable hotbed of higher education for learning-disabled kids.

There was no way he could sit for the SAT, even if he were allowed extended time. The test was simply too long and complex, as well as visually demanding. Taking it would prove a demoralizing failure, an experience he could do without. One Vermont school waived the SAT requirement, another allowed applicants to substitute the college's proprietary entrance exam, a kind of homegrown mini-SAT. Bart could barely scribble with his bum right hand, so they agreed to allow the use of a computer, but with no spell-check or calculator. We appealed those restrictions, pointing out that our school district had always encouraged the use of calculators, even on finals and Regents exams. Likewise, he depended on spell-check to compensate for visual and learning deficits. With the help of that ubiquitous tool he was able to recognize and correct misspellings. The appeals were denied on grounds that other applicants could not avail themselves of those aides, and the school wanted to preserve a "level playing field." Dayle and I were getting a little huffy. With TBI it is never a level playing field, and these readily available accommodations seemed reasonable. Hell, who on earth does secondary-level math without a calculator for crying out loud? But they wouldn't budge.

So he faced the exams bare-knuckled, shorn of the tools he needed to show his best stuff. In a spirit of forlorn hope we drove up to Vermont for the exam—two hours of verbal in the morning, including essays, then a break for lunch, followed by an hour and a half of mathematics in the afternoon. While Dayle and I were angst-ridden, Bart held up remarkably well, so much so that at a festive dinner that evening we toasted him in every language we could think of, saluting him most sincerely, acknowledging that no matter how things went, this day he had done himself proud. (We aren't actually fluent in a lot of languages; we just know lots of ways of saying "cheers.")

On our way out of the Chinese restaurant the proprietor asked eagerly, "Oh, too bad, how did you break your glasses?" Bart was sporting his new thousand-dollar prism glasses, which extended his vision about ten additional degrees to the right. Looking somewhat like thick bifocals, the line between lens segments ran vertical instead of horizontal. Though unusual in appearance, they could hardly be mistaken for broken glasses, unless one knew a way of cracking both lenses in precision matched fashion. Bart had grown progressively self-conscious about his appearance, especially the scar left by the trache at the base of his throat. To conceal it he'd taken to wearing turtlenecks year-round. Casual, thoughtless remarks like this only served to make him more self-conscious, but I guessed he'd just have to learn to deal with them.

It's always amazed me how some people feel perfectly comfortable blurting out the first thing that pops into their head. When the kids were younger, and occasionally even now, perfect strangers would come up in the mall and, pointing at the kids, ask, "Are they yours?" Deeply personal questions may embarrass or humiliate the kids, so, especially when they were younger, we handled them very carefully. A flash of anger or annoyance may send the wrong message. I usually just answered sweetly, "Yes, they are." But for some folks that just whets their appetite, and they persist in probing. "You know what I mean. Are they really yours?" Or, even better, "Are they really brother and sister?" Sometimes, feeling peevish or mischievous, I'd reply, still smiling, "No, they came in a Cracker Jack box," or reply with a question of my own: "You're sure asking a bunch of personal questions. Are you with the police? Mind showing your ID?" There's a limit to how far one must suffer fools. With heroic scars and funny glasses, Bart will doubtless have to test those limits. Eventually he developed a well-rehearsed line that matter-of-factly explained the glasses' special function.

By early June the verdict was in—both colleges turned him down. Though disappointed, I wasn't really surprised. Even for schools catering to the learning disabled, TBI is a bit too much. Angry and hurt, Bart damned the colleges to hell, and then put the whole episode behind him. Not so easy for Dayle and me, who were casting about, scrambling to find some useful program in which to engage him come September. The local community colleges were not really equipped, and besides, the logistics of commuting were daunting.

Dayle called Ralph LaCasio, bringing him up to date and seeking advice. Ralph felt Bart had a fighting chance of gaining admission to the occupational therapy program at Maria College in Albany, at the very least as a part-time or nonmatriculated student. Ralph was a former faculty member and close friend of the head of the OT department, so we hoped his sponsorship of Bart's application would carry considerable weight. We grabbed at that lifeline like folks who know it's their last best chance. It was already mid-June, past the deadline for admission for the fall semester, but we hurriedly got in the application materials, with a boost from the high school guidance office. Ralph assured us that he'd go to bat for Bart with Sandy Jung, then OT department head, briefing her in detail on his condition and progress to date, and generally vouching for his character. By now, Camp Mujigae was in full swing, so with Bart happily working as a junior counselor, I spoke several times with the Maria College admissions office, offering to bring him over for an interview. By odd coincidence, Maria College was located within walking distance of Mujigae. But the dean of admissions and head of the OT department, both of whom needed to interview Bart, were out of town, so we'd have to wait for mid-July to learn if this chance was for real or just pie in the sky. With lots of pie on my face already, I almost didn't dare to hope for such a neat solution to our dilemma.

It really would be neat. Albany would provide Bart with plenty of local support—it is home to Dayle's oldest sister, Cathy, and her family, her first cousin Scott (the anesthesiologist who was so helpful while we were at Westchester Med), and boatloads of Mujigae friends. Maria College is just an hour's drive from New Paltz and down the block from Parsons Child & Family Center, perennial home of Mujigae. It really felt like part of our old stomping grounds. We'd always known about Maria College, but the loose plan had been to have him transfer to Maria's OT program after a couple of years in Vermont. Bart was pretty sure he wanted to pursue therapy as a career, partly because Ralph had assured him that he could, partly because he wanted to help people going through similar battles, and partly because he wasn't sure about what other sorts of careers he could handle. When I expressed reservations to Ralph, with a chuckle he quipped, "Joel, looks like you're right on plan, just skipping the first two years in Vermont." I wasn't so sure Bart could afford to skip those two years, which were to have been devoted to building basic skills, getting cognitive muscles in shape to take on the rigors of an OT curriculum, which, similar to nursing, include chemistry and the dreaded anatomy and physiology. But if Maria College would give him a shot, maybe let him take it slow, then, as they say, "Any port in a storm." But would they give him a shot? And if perchance they did, would he make the grade? It seemed that if there was a more wild-eyed optimist than me, it was Ralph LaCasio, who was downright cocky.

Bart's interviews went surprisingly well. Everyone seemed to understand that if he were admitted, he would be a project. Of course they would be hedging their bets by admitting him as a nonmatriculated student, initially taking remedial courses in math and English. The mission statement of the Sisters of Mercy, who founded and operate the college, states, "In the spirit of the Gospel, our mission is to help people to overcome the obstacles that keep them from living full and dignified lives." Words, as someone said, are the cheapest commodity in the world. Might it be that the Sisters of Mercy didn't just talk their mission, but lived it? While the jury was still out, I called Brother Rick Curry, asking if he would mind putting in a plug for Bart with the college president. He was delighted to oblige. It seemed like their wheels ground slowly, but in a couple of weeks we got a letter in the mail . . . he was in! As one dean told us, "How can we not give him a chance?" It was already early August, with classes starting in about three weeks.

The abrupt transition to college man about town seemed as daunting as the original plunge from the Day Hospital back into high school. There would be no JR or Coach Moore traipsing after him, keeping him on track and on schedule. He'd have to make his own way. Even at a small, friendly, supportive place like Maria College, I feared it would take a small miracle for him to manage. Still, it was worth the old college try.

So we were off tearing around like one-armed wallpaper hangers, trying to arrange living accommodations, bus transit passes, bookstore orders, dorm furnishings, proof of vaccinations, and loads of other minutiae that every college kid needs. It wouldn't do to leave too much to chance. Like any freshman, Bart would have his hands full at first, so why saddle him with unnecessary chores? We made a wallet-sized laminated card with names and phone numbers of family and Mujigae friends who could be called upon in a pinch. On August 25, 2005, a day after Bart's twentieth "arrival day," and almost three years and nine months since the accident, he moved into a college dorm.

As always, I prayed daily for Bart, that he be restored to full honorable manhood, that he come through all these trials a mensch. It seemed my old father was right after all. When seeking practical career advice from my dad at age fourteen, he'd replied that it didn't matter what one did for a living, so long as one is a mensch. At the time it really felt like he'd dodged the question, falling back on Old World soft soap. Yet when the destiny of our entire family was on the line, I found myself praying simply that Bart grow to be a mensch. Compared to that, everything else, even hemianopia, seemed trivial.

Epilogue

Steadily our fellowship has grown as we've come to know other fine people fighting the TBI wars. In daily prayers we ask that each be healed in ways he or she most needs and that their families continue to bear up. We hear by e-mail that Siri is walking freely for ten minutes at a time and has finally joined Pavan here in the United States. In the interim he's visited her in India a couple of times, where while staying with her family, she took therapies and worked heroically to recover use of her left side. Long separation has wrought spiritual and psychological hardships that they have somehow endured. They're very actively exploring emerging technologies, especially stem cell therapy.

Griffy's had a rough time, plagued by seizures for almost three years, resulting in falls and worse. Dotty, who misses the old Griffy terribly, remains steadfast as ever. They've tried a number of alternative therapies as well, and keep an open mind. The last year or so he has been free of seizures and making headway regaining much of his speech and mobility. Griffy still can't interpret the written word, so he asks Dotty to read him the newspapers.

The O'Briens' kids are flourishing. Meredith lives out of state at a residential school for survivors of TBI, making such good progress that she is expected to return to a full, "normal" life. Nick is back in college studying architecture and, though his right hand is still troublesome, is fearlessly getting back to swimming and other activities he loves. As time passes, their disabilities gradually become more invisible. Arnold returned unhurt from his tour in Iraq, where he had been posted to Fallujah during the worst of the fighting.

Rick Curry went on to become Father Rick Curry, SJ. He's moved to Washington, D.C., where he continues working tirelessly on behalf of disabled persons through the Academy for Veterans at Georgetown University.

For his part, Bart struggled through eight months of college, managing with lots of extra tutoring to pass a course or two. It was a tough, lonely, often angry time. Not quite ready for the multifaceted demands of college life, he labored hard in class as well as socially. A wonderfully supportive staff at Maria College gave him every possible boost. The college president stood outside her office every day to greet him, encouraging him to attend classes as well as use the college's other resources. Though he made some good friends among college and dorm staff, he came to feel that, "if the college experience means working like a dog to get Ds and not having any fun," then it probably wasn't for him. Between semesters we put the poor guy through another new alternative therapy, but this one proved a bust. Overall, college was a very mixed bag, but it gave Bart a big lift in confidence—after all, he'd made his own way in an urban environment without too much muss or fuss, a remarkable enough accomplishment.

Dayle tracked down a program, run by Neuropsychologic Rehabilitation Services (NPRS) of Albany, that promised to ramp up Bart's cognitive and emotional skills so that upon completion he might get a job, or return to college with a fighting chance of success. It is one of only a handful of cutting-edge neuro-rehab programs around the country. He's currently enrolled in NPRS and doing brilliantly. In its twenty-seventh year, the program is like Ralph LaCasio on steroids. They know exactly how to exercise all the right muscles—short-term memory, time management, organization, and self-control. Just as important, he's made friends among a peer group of young TBI survivors. Finally, as of old, Super Bowl night means getting together with friends for a blast. He's even dating! While at Maria College the previous semester, he asked Dayle one lonely evening, "Who's ever gonna want to be with me?"

The answer to that forlorn question was Melissa, a student at NPRS. She and Bart made a beautiful, inspiring couple. They had lots in common. Both had grown up in rural Ulster county, played basketball for rival schools, sported riotous senses of humor, suffered severe TBIs while still in their teens, and both were fighting hard to regain their lives. What a joy and relief to see Bart's tender-loving side slowly reemerge. Their relationship lasted a year and a half, and they have remained friends since. The experience left Bart more self-assured and accepting of his disability. Nowadays his Facebook profile includes "TBIer" right next to "die-hard Yankee fan," an acknowledgment absolutely unthinkable even a year earlier. Bart told me not long ago that he probably should always be with a girl who has TBI, "so she'll understand what I go through." By family tradition, at New Year's we each make a wish list to be burned outdoors right at the drop of midnight. This year, at the top of his list was simply, "Find love."

Bart and Melissa may have loved and lost, but their romance was immortalized on national television. *NBC Nightly News* aired a segment on vision restoration therapy, part of a weeklong special called "Mind Matters." The piece followed Bart's struggle over three years, wrapping up with him and Melissa clowning around at his apartment, and then at Melissa's place where he was watching her practice VRT. The news crew filmed at Columbia University Medical Center, our home, and eventually at Bart's place in Schenectady. They spent an entire day at Living Resources, NPRS's sister agency, specializing in life skills and community reintegration, shooting scenes of Bart in classes and interviewing several persons involved in Bart's rehabilitation. During a coffee break, I mentioned that poor Melissa looked about ready to pass out from nerves (emerging from coma with aphasia, she had painstakingly learned to speak all over again—a trial Bart had been spared). Smiling broadly, and gesturing to the ever-present camera crew, Bart quipped, "Yeah she's hurting. But not me—the camera is my friend."

Bart's so much happier these days that most times he's even going easy on me. For three years he rented a small garden apartment in a complex that is home to several other NPRS/Living Resources "trainees." A little distance (eighty miles more or less) has had a salutary effect on our relationship—we're much less likely to get on each other's nerves. Cassidy and Bart have regained a bit of their old closeness. Their relationship is still tentative, still a work in progress, but the happier and more self-confident he becomes, the better she responds. After ten years and counting, he continues making progress on several noteworthy fronts, including short-term memory. Gradually, haltingly, he's made headway accepting changes in his life. He's even beginning to positively embrace the new Bart, who, though strikingly different from the old in some ways, is still hilariously funny, deeply affectionate, and generous to a fault—still a loveable rogue. An unexpected but delightful result of acceptance is that he hardly ever perseverates! You can't imagine what a relief that is for all concerned.

With some help from Living Resources, he managed to find and hold down a part-time job. A couple of years ago, he moved again, this time to a garden apartment, which is not home to any other survivors of TBI, so he's completely mainstreamed, something he sorely desired. He's made new friends and is altogether happier than at any time these last ten years. NPRS and Living Resources have been a boon to Bart. Dayle and I have become adept advocates, following the age-old "squeaky wheel" rule. We're both somewhat shy, so tooting our own horns, even for Bart's sake, does not come naturally. However tiresome, eternal vigilance is the order of the day for TBI families. For his part Bart lives a more normal life than ever, but still needs a little help from Living Resources with grocery shopping, getting to appointments, and organizing his affairs. He sometimes fights bouts of loneliness and social isolation, but with a positive attitude and ironic sense of humor.

Three times we struck out in our search for a remedy for hemianopia. (HBOT, Saint Francis Hospital clinic, and sensory learning therapy each produced net gains in some functional areas, but not in vision per se.) With VRT we managed to tap a little bunt, eventually eking out a 8 or 9 percent vision gain. Evenings, with less sense of urgency, I still surf the Internet for emerging treatments, and I keep in touch with members of the fellowship exploring stem cell therapies. As Bart likes to say, "Time will tell." Finally, after a two-year delay, the family spent Christmas visiting Uncle David in Florida, where Bart enjoyed his boys' night out.

Whether or not he'll ever live a completely independent life is still very much an open question, but you better believe I'm betting on it. While the family was at his side, loyal cheerleaders always, Bart walked—and still walks—every step up the hard rocky way to a new life. Each brave step and misstep give fresh meaning to the cryptic remark of his Korean escort those many years ago, "Here. Here's the strong one."

✦

TBI has been called the invisible disability. Victims often seem perfectly normal while suffering from functional difficulties involving memory, perception, emotional control, general understanding, and executive functioning. Moreover, unlike people with cerebral palsy or developmental disabilities or even AIDS, TBIers are not represented by well-organized, vocal advocacy groups. Most states have a brain injury association, but TBI still suffers from a visibility gap. We need the equivalent of a United Cerebral Palsy. Maybe tens of thousands of vets returning home from Iraq and Afghanistan with brain injuries will help turn an overdue spotlight on TBI.

Appendix A

Some Tips on How to Fight a Really Hard Fight

> "Determine that the thing can and shall be done, and then we shall find the way." —Abraham Lincoln

Without pretending to be an expert, I'd like to offer some tips that may help others facing terrible challenges like TBI. It's plain that there is no foolproof way of fighting, no surefire formula, no ready roadmap to follow in case of catastrophic illness, so you're sure to make mistakes. Don't be too hard on yourself, or on others. Faced with a crushingly powerful adversary, one can only try doing one's best. So, for what they're worth, the following are my suggestions for better fighting.

Live for the day, one day at a time. Resist the seductive tendency to dwell on what might have been or to worry and obsess about the final outcome. The twin sirens of past and future, if indulged, will surely lure you off course. Besides, there's nothing much to be done about either. Be like the marathon runner focused on just the one mile at hand. It's not that you shouldn't make future plans, just don't fret about them or invest too much energy. Remember, today's the day, the Olympic Games.

It's best to forgive, though most of us feel the impulse only waveringly if at all. I've personally struggled with this demon, but when successful, it's been like laying down a heavy burden. What a relief to finally forgive the boys and their parents for moving on with their lives, and wish them only the best. Like most things, forgiving gets easier with practice. As the author of some costly mistakes, and often prey to ugly, hateful feelings, I've forgiven myself and hope for as much from those who've paid the price.

Count your blessings daily. If things are too bleak, or you're so blitzed that nothing springs to mind, keep a log and at bedtime review three good things that happened during the day. When not enough good things are happening, make them happen! Treat a stranger to an act of kindness—that counts as a good thing and is a reminder that you're not helpless, but can still make your mark. The Dalai Lama once said if you want to make someone happy, practice compassion. And if you want to be happy, practice compassion.

Surround yourself with positive people. The worldwide "conspiracy of decency" has members in every community. Seek them out. They'll buck you up, inspire by example, and keep you in psychological and spiritual training for the long haul. Join their ranks. If you don't know enough of them, find resources at support groups for TBI or whatever else ails you or your loved one or other assemblies of people like churches and synagogues, though beware negative types haunting their halls. The idea is to find people who'll help you stay brave and strong so you can be there for the ones really counting on you.

The corollary to the last point is to avoid negative people. This is not as simple as it sounds, since they may include family and other loved ones. "Negative" is a comprehensive category including whiners, naysayers, melancholic and depressive types, cynical and sarcastic wise guys, put-down artists, selfish blowhards, pessimists, and many others. If they make you feel lousy, they will sap your strength. You're in for a long, hard fight; these dour, toxic folks make it harder, often without malice, just by being themselves. If it's too emotionally taxing to drop them completely, then cut way down on exposure time. If you are of a negative bent, follow this suggestion all the same—you need it more than most.

No one is strong enough to successfully wage this kind of struggle solely by triumph of will. Find a wing to nestle under—a safe, calm place, a spiritual haven. Daily prayer, for those inclined, is best. I can't imagine getting by without it. But meditation, positive thinking, "kything," and visualization are good too. For some, inspirational music, poetry, and reading are just the thing.

If your heart is breaking, try singing a different song. The old hymn "How Can I Keep from Singing?" eased me out of some very dark spots. Find a song or two or many that give you a boost and bring you back to a hopeful place; then, if need be, literally force yourself to sing. (In the shower or even in your head is fine.) Keep a CD of "your songs" handy in the car.

Laugh a lot. If you're not naturally inclined, push yourself: rent movies, go visit funny friends. They'll lighten the load for sure.

Take care. Consider vitamins, meditation, and sensible exercise to keep you strong. Moreover there's no disgrace in seeking a doctor's help managing troubled sleep, anxiety, depression, or other miseries.

Think outside the box! Many medical practitioners at the zenith of their careers no longer have an open mind, if they ever did. It's your responsibility to seek alternative therapies, emerging technologies, and to keep abreast of which ones may hold real promise. On the other hand, remember that "not all who rave are divinely inspired." Try to find objective, third-party advisers aside from your primary doctors to help pick the oats from the manure. Not everyone has access to such a team of experts, so when all else fails, use the smell test. (If it smells funny, it's probably rotten.) And remember, do no harm, though that may not always be possible.

Above all, take my brother David's advice: seek daily doses of good and beautiful things at one's fingertips. When you're up to your eyeballs, renew your zest for living, your appreciation of life's sweetness and small pleasures. Make time to play with your dog, to smell the flowers, listen to your favorite music, catch up with a friend, or contemplate nature's beauty. The Hudson Valley is bursting with natural splendors—rivers, mountains, and orchards of plenty. But no matter where you live, whatever your aesthetic preferences, heed the poet's words, "Earth's crammed with heaven, and every common bush afire with God; But only he who sees, takes off his shoes. The rest sit round it and pluck blackberries."

Appendix B

Additional Resources

Books

Cassidy, John W. *Mindstorms: The Complete Guide for Families Living with Traumatic Brain Injury*. Cambridge, MA: Da Capo, 2009.

Woodruff, Bob, and Lee Woodruff. *In an Instant: A Family's Journey of Love and Healing*. New York: Random House, 2007.

Websites

www.bianys.org: New York State Brain Injury Association. Every state has one. Resources for survivors, caregivers, and organizers

www.braininjurynetwork.org: Site by and for survivors and families

www.thebrainproject.org: Virtual Center of Excellence; Sarah Jane Project. Great resource for survivors and families, especially pediatric TBI

www.cdc.gov/traumaticbraininjury/outcomes.html: Government research and clearinghouse of information on TBI

www.dana.org: Overall brain-related resources, research, and summary

www.lapublishing.com: Brain injury books and resource center for TBI and PTSD

www.neuroskills.com: TBI resource guide. Monthly summary of worldwide research

www.realwarriors.net: Resources and programs for servicemen, vets, and families

www.remind.org: Resources and support for injured servicemen, vets, and families

www.woundedwarriorproject.org: Resources and programs for servicemen, vets, and families

About the Author

Joel Goldstein is a transportation and logistics executive at Cambridge Corporate Services in New York City. He is also an adoption advocate and activist, having served for many years on the international adoption board of Albany's Parsons Child & Family Center and of Camp Mujigae, the largest Korean heritage camp in the United States. He was the founding president of the Southern Ulster YMCA, on whose board he continues to serve. Goldstein lives in New Paltz, New York, with his wife, Reiki Master Dayle Groudine. They have two adopted Korean children, Bart and Cassidy. For more information, e-mail the author at NSUnturned@gmail.com or visit www.facebook.com/NSUnturned.